Recent Industrialization Experience of Turkey in a Global Context

Recent Titles in
Contributions in Economics and Economic History

International Agriculture Trade and Market Development Policy in the 1990's
John W. Helmuth and Don F. Hadwiger, editors

Comparative Studies of Local Economic Development: Problems in Policy Implementation
Peter B. Meyer, editor

United States-Japan Trade Telecommunications: Conflict and Compromise
Meheroo Jussawalla, editor

Pacific-Asia and the Future of the World-System
Ravi Arvind Palat, editor

Development versus Stagnation: Technological Continuity and Agricultural Progress in
Pre-Modern China
Gang Deng

Commodity Chains and Global Capitalism
Gary Gereffi and Miguel E. Korzeniewcz, editors

Global Telecommunications Policies: The Challenge of Change
Meheroo Jussawalla, editor

The State and Capitalism in Israel
Amir Ben-Porat

The Economy of Iraq: Oil, Wars, Destruction of Development and Prospects, 1950–2010
Abbas Alnasrawi

The Economy in the Reagan Years: The Economic Consequences of the Reagan
Administrations
Anthony S. Campagna

Prelude to Trade Wars: American Tariff Policy, 1890–1922
Edward S. Kaplan and Thomas W. Ryley

Projecting Capitalization: A History of the Internationalization of the Construction Industry
Marc Linder

Recent Industrialization Experience of Turkey in a Global Context

Edited by
Fikret Şenses

Contributions in Economics and Economic History, Number 155
Dominick Salvatore, Series Adviser

GREENWOOD PRESS
Westport, Connecticut • London

Library of Congress Cataloging-in-Publication Data

Recent industrialization experience of Turkey in a global context /
    edited by Fikret Şenses.
            p.   cm.—(Contributions in economics and economic history,
    ISSN 0084–9235 ; no. 155)
        Includes bibliographical references and index.
        ISBN 0–313–27381–2 (alk. paper)
        1. Turkey—Industries.   2. Industry and state—Turkey.
    I. Şenses, Fikret.   II. Series.
    HC492.R43   1994
    338.09561—dc20   93–30983

British Library Cataloguing in Publication Data is available.

Library of Congress Catalog Card Number: 93–30983
ISBN: 0–313–27381–2
ISSN: 0084–9235

First published in 1994

Greenwood Press, 88 Post Road West, Westport, CT 06881
An imprint of Greenwood Publishing Group, Inc.

Printed in the United States of America

∞™

Copyright Acknowledgment

Table 3.3 from *Asia's Next Giant: South Korea and Late Industrialization* by
Alice H. Amsden. Copyright © 1989 by Oxford University Press, Inc.
Reprinted by permission.

CONTENTS

Illustrations vii

Acknowledgments xiii

Abbreviations xv

1. Introduction
  Fikret Şenses 1

2. The Industrialization Debate
  Frederick I. Nixson 7

3. Upgrading and Diversifying in Late Industrialization
  Alice H. Amsden 25

4. Some Comments on the Role of the Public Sector in
  Industrialization
  John Weiss 39

5. The Stabilization and Structural Adjustment Program
  and the Process of Turkish Industrialization:
  Main Policies and Their Impact
  Fikret Şenses 51

6. The Economic Structure of Power Under Turkish Structural
  Adjustment: Prices, Growth and Accumulation
  A. Erinç Yeldan 75

7.   Liberalization, Transnational Corporations and Foreign Direct
       Investment in Turkey: The Experience of the 1980s
       Ziya Öniş   91

8.   The Public Enterprise Sector in Turkey: Performance and
       Productivity Growth, 1973–1988
       Süleyman Özmucur and Cevat Karataş   111

9.   Subcontracting Practice in the Turkish Textile and
       Metal-Working Industries
       Mehmet Kaytaz   141

10.   Changing Spatial Distribution and Structural Characteristics
       of the Turkish Manufacturing Industry
       Ayda Eraydın   155

11.   International Competitiveness and Industrial Policy:
       The Turkish Experience in the Textile and Truck
       Manufacturing Industries
       Hacer K. Ansal   175

12.   Conclusion and Prospects
       Fikret Şenses   191

Bibliography   197

Index   215

About the Contributors   219

ILLUSTRATIONS

FIGURES

6.1 Capital's Position Toward Wage-Labor and the Rural
     Economy in Turkey, 1980–90   80

6.2 Capital's Position Toward the External Economy
     in Turkey, 1980–90   83

6.3 Capital's Position Toward the State in Turkey,
     1981–90   85

6.4 Structural Schema of Surplus Extraction and Disposition
     During Structural Adjustment in Turkey   87

10.1 The Different Patterns of Change in TFPG Rates Between
     the 1971–82 and 1983–87 Periods   166

10.2 The Growth and Technological Transformation Areas of
     Industry, 1983–87   167

11.1 Exports in the Turkish Automotive Industry, 1980–88   186

TABLES

2.1 Share of Economic Groupings and Developing Regions in
     World Manufacturing Value Added (MVA) at Constant
     1980 Prices, 1970–85 (Selected Years, Percentage)   8

2.2   Share of Income Groups in MVA and Population of
      Developing Countries, 1970–85 (Selected Years, Percentage)   9

2.3   Growth of Manufacturing Value Added, 1970–85
      (Selected Periods), Growth Rate at Constant 1980
      Prices   10

2.4   Share of MVA of All Developing Countries, 1975, 1980
      and 1985 (Excluding People's Republic of China)   11

2.5   Estimated Share of Industrial Output of Developing
      Countries in World Total in 1975 and Projected Shares
      for 1988 and 1989, Percentage   12

2.6   Sectoral Origin of World Market Economy Production:
      Historical and Projected, 1970, 1985 and 2000 (Percentage
      Shares of GDP, at 1980 Prices and Exchange Rates)   14

2.7   Structure of MVA by Broad Economic Categories, Subgroups
      of Developing Countries, 1966–2000 (Selected Years,
      Percentage)   15

2.8   Share of Economic Groupings and Developing Regions in
      World Exports of Manufactured Goods, 1965–86
      (Selected Years)   17

3.1   Relative Rates of Inflation in Selected Countries and
      Regions, 1965–80 and 1980–87   32

3.2   Savings Rates in Selected Countries and Regions,
      1965 and 1987   33

3.3   Comparison of Real Nonagricultural Wage Increases in
      Seven Late-Industrializing Countries, 1970–84   34

3.4   R&D Expenditures, Taiwan and South Korea, 1970–87
      (Selected Years)   36

4.1   Public Enterprises in Manufacturing in Selected Countries
      in the 1970s   42

4.2   Effective Rate of Protection for Manufacturing in
      Selected Countries in the 1970s   45

5.1   Main Economic Indicators in Turkey, 1980–90   56

5.2   Sectoral Distribution of Gross Fixed Investment, 1973–90
      (Selected Years, Percentage Share in Current Price Values)   60

5.3   Composition of Manufacturing Value Added in Large-Scale
      Manufacturing Enterprises, 1963–89 (Selected Years, Percent)   69

5.4   Composition of Employment in Large-Scale Manufacturing
      Enterprises (Comprising Ten or More Workers)   70

5.5   Some Indicators of Growth and Industrialization in Turkey and
      Selected Countries   71

6.1   Production, Accumulation and Distribution in Turkey, 1980–90   77

6.2   Distribution of Fixed Capital Investment, 1983–90
      (Selected Years, Percent)   86

7.1   Foreign Investment Authorizations in Turkey in the Pre-1980 Era,
      1961–79 (In Millions of Dollars)   98

7.2   Sectoral Distribution of Foreign Capital in the Pre-1980 Era,
      End of 1977 (Percent)   99

7.3   Authorized Versus Realized FDI in Turkey, 1980–90 (In Millions
      of Dollars)   100

7.4   Sectoral Distribution of Authorized Foreign Investment in Turkey,
      1980–90 (Percent)   101

7.5   Sectoral Composition of Authorized FDI in Turkish Manufacturing,
      1989 (Percent)   102

7.6   Sectoral Composition of the Stock of Foreign Capital in
      Manufacturing and Services in Turkey, End of 1989 (Percent)   103

7.7   Share of FDI Stock in GDP in Selected LDCs, 1985 (Percent)   104

7.8   Inflows of FDI in Selected Countries, 1988, 1989 (In Millions
      of Dollars)   105

7.9   Distribution of FDI in Turkey According to Type of Investment,
       1980–89 (Percent)   106

8.1   State Economic Enterprises (SEEs) and Their Share in Total
       Value Added, Employment and Investment, 1987   115

8.2   Summary Statistics on Private and Public Manufacturing   118

8.3   Total Factor Productivity Growth Using Value Added   124

8.4   Profitability and Total Factor Productivity in Five Hundred
       Largest Firms   126

8.5   Liberalization and Total Factor Productivity Growth and
       Price-Cost Ratios   128

8.6   Trends in Total Factor Productivity Growth and Profitability,
       1983–88 (Five Hundred Largest Firms in Turkey)   130

8.7   Price-Cost Ratio Regression Results (Turkish Manufacturing
       Industries, 1974–85)   133

8.8   Profitability (Profit/Sales Revenue) Regression Results (Five
       Hundred Largest Firms, 1983–88)   134

8.9   Total Factor Productivity Growth Regression Results (Turkish
       Manufacturing Industries, 1974–85)   135

8.10   Total Factor Productivity Growth Regression Results (Five
       Hundred Largest Firms, 1983–88)   136

9.1   Distribution of Firms in Textiles and Metal-Working by
       Subcontracting Relations, Export Share and Average Employment   144

9.2   Reasons for Offering Subcontracts in Textiles and Metal-Working
       (Percent)   145

9.3   Distribution of Firms by Subcontract Types in Textiles and
       Metal-Working, Export Share and Average Employment   146

9.4   Assistance and Technical Guidance Received by Subcontractors
       in Textiles and Metal-Working (Percent)   149

9.5 Average Labor Productivity, Wage Rate and Employment Growth
     in Textiles and Metal-Working by Subcontracting Relations   151

10.1 Distribution of Employment in Industry by Provinces in Turkey,
     1971–88 (Selected Years, Percent)   160

10.2 Rate of Growth of Employment and TFPG in Turkish
     Manufacturing Industry by Provinces, 1971–87 (Selected Years,
     Percent Annual Increase)   164

10.3 Selected Indicators of Textile Industry in Bursa, 1989   170

11.1 Turkey's Exports of Textiles and Clothing, 1975–87 (Selected
     Years, Millions of US$)   178

11.2 Capacities and Capacity Utilization in the Turkish Cotton
     Spinning and Weaving Sectors, 1977–88 (Selected Years)   179

11.3 Installed "New Technology" in the Turkish Textile Industry,
     1980–88 (Selected Years)   180

11.4 Capacity Utilization in the Truck Industry in the 1980s
     (Selected Years)   184

11.5 Export Price/Ex-Factory Price Comparison in the Turkish
     Automotive Industry, 1984   187

ACKNOWLEDGMENTS

All the chapters in this volume were written upon my invitation. The original idea of compiling a book on this subject arose during my collaboration with Arman Kırım, who was then at the Department of Management at the Middle East Technical University. His resignation from the university and other commitments have unfortunately prevented him from contributing to this undertaking beyond the initial planning stages. I thank him warmly for the initial boost he gave to this project.

My special thanks go to my colleague, Erol Taymaz, also of Middle East Technical University, for his invaluable contributions to the preparation of the final text according to the publisher's technical requirements and for being a constant source of encouragement and moral support.

The secretarial work involved in this project was partially supported by the Middle East Technical University Research Fund.

ABBREVIATIONS

AMA	Automotive Manufacturers Association
BOT	build-operate-transfer
CV	commercial vehicles
EEC	European Economic Community
EOI	export-oriented industrialization
ERP	effective rate of protection
FDI	foreign direct investment
FTC	Foreign Trade Company
GDP	gross domestic product
GNP	gross national product
GVA	gross value added
IMF	International Monetary Fund
ISI	import-substituting industrialization
ISIC	International Standard Industry Classification
ISO	Istanbul Chamber of Industry
LDC	less developed country
LSE	large-scale enterprise
MNC	multinational corporation
MVA	manufacturing value added
NIC	newly industrializing country
OECD	Organization for Economic Cooperation and Development
PSBR	public sector borrowing requirement
RAI	Regulations of Assembly Industry
R&D	research and development
ROA	return on total assets
ROE	return on equity
ROSR	return on sales revenue

SEE	State Economic Enterprise
SITC	Standard International Trade Classification
SME	small and medium-scale manufacturing enterprises
SMIDO	Small and Medium Industry Development Organization
SOE	state-owned enterprise
SPO	State Planning Organization
SSAP	stabilization and structural adjustment program
TFP	total factor productivity
TFPG	total factor productivity growth
TNC	transnational corporation
UN	United Nations
UNIDO	United Nations Industrial Development Organization

Recent Industrialization
Experience of Turkey
in a Global Context

1

INTRODUCTION

Fikret Şenses

Industrialization, which was at the top of the list of social and economic objectives of most developing countries until the mid-1970s, has been relegated very much to the background since then. The severe supply shocks of the 1970s, culminating in the international debt crisis of the early 1980s, have no doubt had a profound effect in the shift of emphasis to short-term issues. Such a shift toward the short term in the design and implementation of economic policies would have been understandable, if not desirable, if it were of a temporary nature. However, there are strong signs that this reorientation is having a lasting impact. The fact that what started as short-term stabilization policies under International Monetary Fund (IMF) auspices to cope with short-term instability were often linked with structural adjustment programs in collaboration with the World Bank played a crucial role in generating this outcome. As a result, preoccupation with domestic inflation and balance of payments difficulties was accompanied by steps such as trade and financial liberalization and privatization, with a strong bearing on industrialization and medium and long-term development.

Turkey provides an ideal setting for tracing the slide of industrialization on the list of social and economic objectives of developing countries. The start of Turkish industrialization in earnest can be traced back to the 1930s, when a highly interventionist state initiated an all-out industrialization strategy under heavy protection. Although the private sector started to exert itself increasingly after the early 1950s, the state remained an active partner in the industrialization process. The main engine of industrialization was import substitution, which the government aimed to extend into intermediate and capital goods in the wake of the world economic crisis of the 1970s. In the face of galloping inflation and a severe balance of payments crisis, Turkey introduced a major stabilization and structural adjustment program (SSAP) in January 1980. The nature of policies introduced under this program and their major impact have been extensively documented.[1] There is, however, a conspicuous absence of a major attempt to examine the interaction of Turkey's SSAP with the process of industrialization. This book is an attempt to redress this imbalance. The primary objective of the book is to examine the main macroeconomic and microeconomic issues surrounding Turkish industrialization in the global context, with particular emphasis on the 1980–90 period.

The rapid transformation in industrial trade strategy from archetypal import substitution under heavy state direction to the outward orientation in the 1980s has had a profound effect on the process of industrialization in Turkey. It is believed that the recent industrialization experience of Turkey will be of interest for other semi-industrialized countries.

The chapters in this volume fall into three main groups. The first three chapters (2–4) address the crucial issues surrounding industrialization in a global context and are intended to provide background for the subsequent chapters addressed more specifically to the Turkish case. In a world of growing interdependence among all groups of countries, developed and developing alike, such a global focus is necessary. Indeed, it is not a coincidence that some of the chapters on Turkey also find it necessary to discuss the Turkish case in international perspective. The second group of chapters (5–8) focuses on broad macroeconomic issues of Turkish industrialization. Finally, the third group of chapters (9–11) examines the Turkish industrialization experience more specifically on the basis of the spatial distribution of industry and in terms of individual sectors.

The chapter by Frederick Nixson starts with a statistical overview of the industrialization experience of developing countries and then focuses on some key issues in the industrialization debate. The statistical overview reveals the unduly low share of less developed countries (LDCs) in world exports of manufactured goods and manufacturing value added and their heavy concentration on a small number of newly industrializing countries (NICs). Nixson recognizes industrialization as a necessary condition for development and draws a number of lessons from the industrialization experience. Among these, the most prominent are the complementarity between import–substituting and export-oriented industrialization, the strategic role of the state in the industrialization process and the importance of a stable domestic macroeconomic environment and changes in the global economy. He also emphasizes the crucial importance of exports and new technology and calls for a more pragmatic approach toward foreign direct investment to boost indigenous technological capabilities and capital formation. Nixson highlights the main points of alternative paradigms in their assessment of postwar industrialization experience, and is critical of the dependency/neo-Marxist theorists in their neglect of the key role of the state in the industrialization process.

Alice Amsden focuses on the failure of late industrializing countries in the 1980s to generate a significant shift in their industrial structures toward higher skill- and technology-intensive products and seeks to identify the institutional framework that would facilitate such a transformation. Drawing mainly on the East Asian industrialization experience and more specifically on Taiwan, she challenges the market-based paradigms as propagated also by the Bretton Woods institutions. While recognizing the merits of the flexible specialization model in Taiwan based on small-scale industries and a high degree of interdependence among a network of firms of different sizes, she argues that small-scale industries cannot be relied on as the agent of high technology industrialization. She demonstrates that large enterprises have played a prominent role in the development of small-scale enterprises and indigenous diversified business groups. Amsden argues that government guidance and support rather than the market were the central element in the efforts of East Asian economies to upgrade and diversify their industrial structures. As opposed to the concept of restructuring proposed by the Bretton Woods institutions, which emphasize privatization, liberalization or deregulation, she calls for efforts to reorganize dying or threatened industries through planning and coordination by government, business,and labor. Finally, she emphasizes the need for a development strategy based on industrialization, growth and social equity.

The chapter by John Weiss surveys arguments on the role of the public sector in the industrialization process and shows how thinking on the subject has shifted in the last thirty years from optimism to disillusionment. He draws a distinction between an active interventionist role and a minimalist approach. State activity is discussed first in terms of direct production by public industrial enterprises, and second in terms of government planning and controls to influence resource allocation. He finds no evidence to suggest that the level of technical efficiency in public enterprises is lower than their counterparts in the private sector. Weiss calls for an extension of the performance criteria of public enterprises beyond financial indicators to incorporate government intervention in such key spheres as price setting and employment policy as well as indicators of technical and economic efficiency. He accepts the difficulties of setting detailed targets at the subsector and enterprise levels, but argues that both short-term and longer-term macro planning should remain of importance to most developing countries. He also draws attention to the successful stimulation of industrial activity in some countries through selective government intervention and without a consistent planning framework. The overall conclusion is that state intervention can play an important role in the industrialization process, particularly in countries with a weak private sector.

The main objective of the chapter by Fikret Şenses is to assess the performance of the manufacturing sector in the 1980s against the background of the new set of economic policies introduced under SSAP. After a brief review of the main components of import-substituting industrialization before 1980 and their main impact, the chapter focuses on the interaction of SSAP with the process of industrialization. Şenses discusses the evolution of key factor prices such as the exchange rate, interest rates and wages in conjunction with changes in import and export policies as an integral part of liberalization attempts. This is followed by a detailed discussion of the impact of the new policy framework on such key indicators of manufacturing sector performance as investment, exports, employment, output and productivity. Şenses argues that industrialization was neglected under SSAP, as evidenced by the withdrawal of the state from the industrialization process and the lack of manufacturing investment. He shows that despite the rapid growth of manufactured exports, the overall performance of the manufacturing sector fell short of expectations, most notably in employment, investment and productivity, with no sign of structural change toward more capital- and skill-intensive activities.

The chapter by Ziya Öniş discusses the main issues surrounding foreign direct investment (FDI) as a component of Turkey's post-1980 adjustment process. Öniş compares and contrasts the restrictive pre-1980 FDI environment with the liberal post-1980 environment. He identifies the main contours of Turkey's FDI experience during the 1980s and relates this to the changing pattern of transnational investment at the global level. He documents the acceleration in FDI flows to Turkey in the 1980s (particularly during the 1988–90 period) and shows that, in line with global trends, there was a sharp increase in FDI in services, most notably in banking and tourism. According to Öniş, apart from the drastic change in the domestic policy environment, the global environment—including country- or location-specific forces such as large domestic markets as well as proximity to major international markets—have also influenced the pattern and magnitude of inflows of FDI to Turkey. He therefore rejects the view that a neoliberal stance on its own will necessarily result in large inflows of FDI. Finally, he warns that inflows of FDI to Turkey will also depend on Turkey's ability to maintain a stable domestic political and macroeconomic environment.

The interaction between some key features of the industrialization experience and the broader shifts in the economic structure of power and income distribution are the main subject of the chapter by Erinç Yeldan. In his attempt to provide a systematic explanation for the dramatic swings in surplus transfer under SSAP, he divides the post-1980 period into three phases on the basis of their distinct patterns of surplus creation. According to Yeldan, suppression of wage income, resource transfers from the rural to the urban sectors through price scissors, the system of incentives for the encouragement of investment and exports and the incidence of tax evasion on corporate incomes have emerged as the major instruments of surplus transfer, with a different degree of effectiveness in each phase. He identifies the capitalist classes as the main beneficiary of these sizable transfers of surplus and argues that as the economic surplus was redistributed toward groups with consumerist tendencies (most notably rentiers) with low saving and investment propensities, traded sectors, particularly manufacturing, were starved of productive investment.

The performance of public enterprises in Turkey, with special emphasis on their profitability and productivity, is the main subject of the chapter by Süleyman Özmucur and Cevat Karataş. The authors provide a detailed account of the macroeconomic role and main impact of public enterprises in Turkey, and examine their role in value added, employment, investment and savings in historical perspective. In their focus on evaluating the relative efficiency of public enterprises, they employ various estimates of profitability and total factor productivity (TFP) based on regression models. Separate estimates are given for the private and public sectors and for individual manufacturing branches, covering different subperiods in both the pre-1980 and post-1980 periods. Alternative profitability measures employed by Özmucur and Karataş yield conflicting results, but on the whole point to slight differences between the private and public sectors. They find that the average TFP growth during the 1973–79 and 1979–85 periods was -9.0 and 7.6 percent for the public manufacturing sector and -4.6 and -2.5 percent for the private manufacturing sector, respectively. Finally, Özmucur and Karataş identify the growth of value added as an important determinant of TFP growth.

The chapter by Mehmet Kaytaz examines the extent and nature of subcontracting in the Turkish textile and metal-working industries. The basic question studied is whether the subcontracting relationship promotes the development of small and medium-sized enterprises. Basing his findings on a survey conducted in the Istanbul and Kocaeli region in late 1989, Kaytaz shows that in small and medium-sized industries, subcontracting is practiced widely while large-scale enterprises offer more subcontracts in textiles than in metal-working. In both sectors, insufficient capacity emerges as the chief reason for offering subcontracts. Kaytaz argues that in metal-working subcontracting is more developmental than in textiles, as subcontracts are more specialization oriented. It seems that export-oriented growth has led to an increase in the volume of subcontracts, as evidenced by export activities having a higher proportion of firms offering subcontracts. Likewise, the decline in the rejection rate in the 1980s, especially in establishments receiving subcontracts from foreign joint ventures or from firms producing for export markets, can be linked to the transition to an export orientation during this period. Kaytaz draws attention to the absence of explicit policies of encouragement for subcontracting until recently, and argues that through comprehensive policies aimed at large and small-scale enterprises, subcontracting may lead to a faster rate of industrialization.

Ayda Eraydın documents and evaluates the changing spatial distribution of the Turkish manufacturing industry against the background of the debate on the changing character of industrial activity in the global context à la Fordist and post-Fordist (flexible) production systems. Her findings confirm the heavy concentration of industrial activity in Turkey, with the İstanbul region alone accounting for 52.4 percent of the total number of industrial firms and 45 percent of total employment in 1988. Her results on TFP growth for individual provinces for the 1971–82 and 1983–87 periods indicate generally higher rates for the latter period. Eraydın employs technical change and growth performance by spatial units to identify the future growth nodes of industrial activity. Using the textile industry in one of the future growth nodes (Bursa) as a case study, Eraydın presents evidence about the changes in the structure of production and the emergence of new organizations of work in response to export-oriented policies.

Hacer Ansal aims to identify factors affecting international competitiveness in the manufacturing sector by drawing on the experience of textile and truck manufacturing industries, based on nine case-study firms. The structure, technological efforts and development of both industries are examined against the background of industrial policies implemented during the pre-1980 and post-1980 periods. Ansal found that, unlike truck manufacturing, the textile industry was not confronted with a structural constraint in achieving international competitiveness in terms of economies of scale. She shows that there was considerable new technology investment in the textile industry after the mid-1980s, which was accompanied by efforts to increase productivity, improved product quality, diversification of the product mix, and a rapid increase in exports. In contrast, the weak and fragmented truck industry did not benefit from such a transformation and failed to attain international competitiveness. In disagreement with the neoclassical prescription of neutral policy regimes, Ansal concludes that the attainment of international competitiveness requires *selective* government intervention and industry-specific policy measures.

NOTE

1. See, for example, Şenses (1983), Celasun and Rodrik (1989), Nas and Odekon (1988), and Arıcanlı and Rodrik (1990).

2

THE INDUSTRIALIZATION DEBATE

Frederick I. Nixson

Industrial growth no longer seems a preserve of the North, much less Eurocentric. The relationship based on the existence of a metropolitan industrialized core with a lesser developed periphery is now irreversibly changed. The family of industrialized countries has grown to include the so-called newly industrializing countries. While many inequalities persist in terms of income, capital stock, skills and financial resources, no country in the world forgoes its right to industrialization. (UNIDO, 1988b: v)

INTRODUCTION

The experience of industrialization in less developed countries has rarely matched expectations. Nevertheless, it is the contention of this chapter that industrialization remains a necessary (although not a sufficient) condition for the sustained growth and structural transformation of the less developed economy, a process that we shall refer to as "economic development."[1]

Chenery, Robinson and Syrquin (1986: 350) also argue that in general industrialization is necessary, on both theoretical and empirical grounds, for continued growth, and that a period in which the share of the manufacturing sector rises substantially is "a virtually universal feature of the structural transformation."[2]

UNIDO (1979: 71) has noted that "for the newly emerging countries of the post-war period, industrialization was seen as synonymous with development, and development implied catching up with the advanced countries, using basically the same means."

The manufacturing sector was thus seen as an "engine of growth," characterized by dynamic increasing returns to scale (the positive relationship between the growth of output and the growth of productivity), which were the consequences of "learning-by-doing" and technological improvements. Overall, it was argued that the growth of the manufacturing sector would

Table 2.1
Share of Economic Groupings and Developing Regions in World
Manufacturing Value Added (MVA) at Constant 1980 Prices, 1970–85
(Selected Years, Percentage)

Year	Developing Countries[a]	CPEs[b]	DMEs[c]	Developing Regions				
				Africa	West Asia	South and East Asia	Latin America	Europe
1970	10.4	16.0	73.6	0.8	0.7	2.3	6.1	0.5
1975	12.0	19.5	68.5	0.9	0.9	2.8	6.8	0.6
1980	13.0	20.2	66.8	0.9	1.0	3.4	7.0	0.7
1985	12.8	21.2	66.0	0.9	1.2	3.9	6.1	0.7

Source: UNIDO, 1988a, Table 1, p. 21.
[a] The People's Republic of China is excluded from the data. Its estimated share of global MVA was 3.9 per cent in 1981 and 5.6 per cent in 1985.
[b] Centrally Planned Economies
[c] Developed Market Economies

raise productivity not just in the sector itself, through an extension of the division of labor, but also in the other major sectors. . . . Further productivity gains and technical progress arising in manufacturing [would] be passed on to other sectors through their purchases of capital and intermediate goods. (Weiss, 1988: 113)

In recent years, two issues in particular have dominated the general debate concerning industrialization strategies and experiences. The question of strategy has largely focused on the choice between the so-called "inward-looking" strategy of import-substituting industrialization (ISI) and the so-called "outward-looking" strategy of export-oriented industrialization (EOI). Although some might argue that this strategy debate is at an end, given the apparently superior economic performance of those countries following the strategy of EOI, recent work has indicated that the issues are less straightforward than the proponents of either strategy have so far been prepared to recognize. Those issues are discussed below under the heading The Experience of Industrialization."

The second question this chapter attempts to address concerns the interpretation of the experience of industrialization in the post–World War II period. The debate here has been not only between the neoclassical and structuralist/dependency schools of thought, but perhaps more vigorously between neo-Marxist and dependency theorists on the one hand and an emerging "classical" Marxist perspective on the other. While recognizing the risks of overgeneralization, the neo-Marxist and dependency perspectives basically assert that either development

Table 2.2
Share of Income Groups in MVA and Population of Developing Countries,
1970-85 (Selected Years, Percentage)

	MVA at constant 1980 prices				Population			
	1970	1975	1980	1985	1970	1975	1980	1985
Low income	19.6	18.0	18.1	20.4	68.4	68.2	67.9	67.7
Middle income	18.7	20.4	20.7	23.5	15.6	15.8	15.9	16.1
High income	61.7	61.6	61.2	56.1	16.0	16.0	16.2	16.2
Developing countries	100.0	100.0	100.0	100.0	100.0	100.0	100.0	100.0

Source: UNIDO, 1988a, Table 3, p. 23.

cannot occur while LDCs remain a part of the global capitalist economy, or that the development that does occur is "dependent," "disorganic," or "perverse." (Leeson & Nixson, 1988: 66–67).

The classical Marxist perspective, on the other hand, points to the more positive achievements of ISI in laying the foundations of a modern, industrial economy, emphasizes the progressive nature of capitalist development in the LDCs (especially with respect to the development of the forces of production) and ascribes a high degree of autonomy to the process of capitalist development in the periphery. We return to these issues below, in our Conclusions section.

THIRD WORLD INDUSTRIALIZATION: A STATISTICAL OVERVIEW

In this section, we attempt to highlight certain aspects of recent Third World industrialization, using UNIDO (1988a) data.

Table 2.1 illustrates the share of various economic groupings and regions in global manufacturing value added (MVA). Precise figures vary according to source, time period selected and price indices used, but there is general agreement as to the trends that are observed. Developing countries (column 1) have experienced a relatively limited increase in their share of global MVA (the projection for 1988 was 13.8 percent—see UNIDO, 1988b), and the fall in the share of the developed market (capitalist) economies was largely a result of the rise in the share of the centrally planned economies. The United Nations (1990, chapter 8) predicts that by the year 2000, the share of the LDCs will have risen to 16 percent and the share of the developed capitalist economies will have fallen further to 59 percent. (The prediction of a rise in the share of Eastern Europe and

Table 2.3
Growth of Manufacturing Value Added, 1970–85 (Selected Periods), Growth Rate at Constant 1980 Prices

Region or Area	MVA Current Prices 1985	1970 1985	1970 1973	1973 1975	1975 1980	1980 1985
Centrally Planned Economies						
Total MVA	NA	5.6	7.5	8.8	5.1	4.0
Per capita MVA	NA	4.8	6.6	7.9	4.2	3.1
Developed Market	2007692	2.6	6.4	-3.3	3.9	3.0
Economies	2554	1.8	5.3	-4.2	3.1	2.3
Developing Countries	354665	5.1	8.2	5.0	5.9	2.8
	144	2.6	5.6	2.4	3.4	0.5
Low income	82435	5.6	5.8	4.1	6.2	5.2
	50	3.1	3.3	1.7	3.7	2.8
Middle income	83641	6.7	9.5	7.4	6.3	5.3
	213	3.9	6.6	4.6	3.6	2.6
High income	188589	4.4	8.5	4.4	5.7	1.1
	469	1.8	5.8	1.8	3.1	-1.2
Africa	30610	4.8	6.5	3.3	5.0	3.3
	59	1.8	3.7	0.4	1.9	0.3
Latin America	143357	3.5	7.9	3.8	4.9	0.3
	370	1.1	5.2	1.3	2.4	-1.9
West Asia	39400	7.0	9.2	6.7	5.8	6.9
	373	3.9	6.0	3.6	2.7	3.8
South and East Asia	125886	7.7	9.5	7.0	8.3	6.2
	89	5.4	7.0	4.6	5.9	3.9
Developing Europe	15411	5.9	7.4	8.7	7.4	2.4
	655	5.0	6.4	7.7	6.4	1.7
Least developed	5262	1.7	2.2	4.9	0.3	2.6
countries	15	-0.9	-0.4	2.2	-2.2	-0.0

Source: UNIDO, 1988a, Table 4, pp. 24-38.
Note: Total MVA in millions of dollars, per capita MVA in dollars
NA = Not available.

the USSR to 25 percent of global MVA was obviously made prior to the onset of the radical economic and political changes which have swept those countries since

Table 2.4
Share of MVA of All Developing Countries, 1975, 1980 and 1985 (Excluding People's Republic of China)

	1975		1980		1985
1. Brazil	17.3	Brazil	18.3	Brazil	16.0
2. Argentina	14.1	Mexico	11.6	Mexico	10.7
3. Mexico	11.0	Argentina	10.4	India	7.5
4. India	7.0	India	6.5	Argentina	7.4
5. Turkey	4.3	Rep. Korea	5.0	Rep. Korea	6.4
6. Rep. Korea	3.5	Taiwan Prov.	4.6	Taiwan Prov.	5.4
7. Taiwan Prov.	3.2	Turkey	3.4	Turkey	4.3
8. Iran	2.8	Venezuela	2.6	Iran	2.9
9. Venezuela	2.7	Philippines	2.3	Indonesia	2.9
10. Philippines	2.3	Iran	2.3	Cuba	2.7
11. Colombia	2.3	Indonesia	2.3	Saudi Arabia	2.5
12. Cuba	2.0	Colombia	2.1	Venezuela	2.4
13. Peru	1.9	Saudi Arabia	2.1	Thailand	2.0
14. Saudi Arabia	1.8	Thailand	1.8	Colombia	1.9
15. Puerto Rico	1.5	Hong Kong	1.6	Philippines	1.9
Sub-total	77.7		76.9		76.9

Source: UNIDO data base.

late 1989).

Table 2.2 shows the shares of different income groups in the MVA of the LDCs. Between 1970 and 1985, there was a slight increase in the share of the low-income group of countries, but it hardly began to offset the huge disparity between their share of LDC MVA and their share of LDC population.

Table 2.3 presents data on rates of growth of total and per capita MVA, with LDCs classified both according to income levels and region. The slowdown in growth in the early 1980s is apparent (what Singh, 1984, has referred to as the "interrupted industrial revolution of the Third World"), but it is also noticeable that West, South and East Asia maintained reasonably high rates of growth of per capita MVA during this period.

The unevenness of the experience of industrialization in the Third World is highlighted by the data given in Table 2.4. The top 15 LDCs (excluding China) accounted for 77.7 percent of LDC MVA in 1975, 76.9 percent in 1980 and 76.9 percent in 1985. During this period, the big Latin American economies (Brazil, Mexico and Argentina) and India were dominant, but their share of LDC MVA fell consistently, from 49.4 percent of the total in 1975 to 41.6 percent in 1985. At the same time, there was a significant rise in the share of two highly

Table 2.5

Estimated Share of Industrial Output of Developing Countries in World Total in 1975 and Projected Shares for 1988 and 1989, Percentage

Industry	Share of developing countries in world total Projected			Average annual growth rates			
				Developed countries		Developing countries	
	1975	1988	1989	1975-85	1985-89	1975-85	1985-89
3 Manufacturing	11.2	13.8	14.1	3.0	3.8	4.6	26.7
311 Food products	16.1	19.9	20.3	2.4	3.0	4.9	4.1
313 Beverages	15.2	19.1	19.4	2.0	3.8	4.4	5.5
314 Tobacco products	33.4	39.4	40.5	0.5	0.8	2.9	22.3
321 Textiles	20.9	24.1	24.8	1.2	2.4	2.3	5.5
322 Wearing apparel	13.2	17.4	18.0	1.2	1.8	3.4	5.6
323 Leather and fur products	14.9	17.2	17.7	0.4	1.6	1.3	4.5
324 Footwear	15.5	20.0	20.5	0.7	0.1	2.5	4.2
331 Wood and wood products	11.1	11.7	12.1	1.5	4.4	3.2	2.3
332 Furniture and fixtures	7.4	7.9	7.9	2.0	4.5	2.9	4.1
341 Paper and paper products	8.8	11.4	11.7	3.5	4.7	5.7	7.5
342 Printing and publishing	9.3	8.0	8.0	3.2	5.0	2.0	3.7
351 Industrial chemicals	8.9	13.5	14.0	3.7	3.8	8.0	6.8
352 Other chemical products	16.1	19.1	19.5	4.0	4.6	6.0	5.5
353 Petroleum refineries	24.4	37.3	37.9	0.1	1.5	4.8	6.0
354 Miscellaneous petroleum and coal products	7.8	13.6	14.4	1.4	- 0.6	7.3	2.3

successful, export-oriented industrializers (South Korea and Taiwan), from 6.7 percent in 1975 to 11.8 percent in 1985.

Table 2.5 gives details of the distribution of industrial branches between developed and less developed countries. It can be seen that the latter were important producers of tobacco products, refined petroleum products, textiles, nonmetallic mineral products, footwear, processed food products, beverages and other chemical products. In terms of projected growth rates, however, electrical machinery, professional and scientific equipment, nonelectrical machinery, iron and steel and plastic products are identified as rapidly growing industries, especially in East and Southeast Asia.

Table 2.5 Continued

355 Rubber products	14.1	17.6	18.1	2.6	3.1	4.1	7.1
356 Plastic products	12.0	14.5	14.8	5.8	6.5	7.5	8.7
361 Pottery, china and earthenware	11.4	13.4	13.6	1.8	2.7	3.0	5.1
362 Glass and glass products	13.0	14.0	14.5	2.8	3.3	2.9	6.4
369 Other non-metal mineral products	14.0	20.5	21.1	1.4	2.9	4.9	7.0
371 Iron and steel	8.1	14.9	15.5	0.6	1.3	5.1	9.0
372 Non-ferrous metals	8.6	11.4	11.7	2.4	3.3	4.9	5.7
381 Metal products	8.4	12.3	12.6	2.2	3.0	4.8	8.4
382 Non-electrical machinery	4.4	4.7	4.8	4.4	4.4	3.3	9.8
383 Electrical machinery	6.7	10.8	11.2	6.3	5.6	8.3	16.1
384 Transport equipment	7.2	8.3	8.5	2.9	3.9	3.6	6.9
385 Professional and scientific equipment	2.6	4.9	5.0	4.2	4.5	8.7	11.5
390 Other manufacturing industries	12.8	17.6	17.9	3.5	4.3	6.6	7.0

Source: UNIDO, 1988b, Table 2, page 6.
Note: All calculations are based on constant 1980-United States dollar figures.
Figures are derived from 125 sample countries - 34 "developed" and 91 "developing" (Consolidated Industrial Statistics).
China and other centrally planned Asian economies are not included in the sample.

Economic growth is always associated with structural change, and indeed growth could not be sustained without changes in the structure of the economy, taken to mean changes in the composition of demand, the product mix, the sectoral composition of employment and required patterns of human and material capital, as well as changes in external trade and capital flow structures (UNIDO, 1988b: 103; for a general survey of the literature on structural change, see Nixson, 1990).

Intersectoral change refers to changes in the proportions of total output and/or employment accounted for by the three main economic sectors—agriculture, industry (with manufacturing as a subdivision) and services. Table 2.6 presents data on sectoral shares of gross domestic product (GDP) for 1970 and 1985, with projections to the year 2000. The share of the agricultural sector falls consistently for all country groupings but remains the largest sector in the least developed

Table 2.6
Sectoral Origin of World Market Economy Production: Historical and Projected, 1970, 1985 and 2000 (Percentage Shares of GDP, at 1980 Prices and Exchange Rates)

Country Group	Agriculture			Industry						Services		
				Total			Manufactures					
	1970	1985	2000	1970	1985	2000	1970	1985	2000	1970	1985	2000
Developed Market	4.4	3.6	3.1	40.6	36.9	34.8	25.7	25.3	24.0	55.0	59.5	62.1
Developing Countries	20.7	16.9	13.8	41.3	36.1	39.8	15.1	18.8	23.0	38.0	47.0	46.4
Petroleum exporters	15.0	13.6	12.5	61.0	44.6	45.0	5.6	9.4	9.8	24.0	41.8	42.5
Major manufactures exporters	26.6	17.3	11.5	31.0	36.0	43.0	21.8	25.8	32.0	42.4	46.8	45.4
Other manufacturers oriented	16.6	15.2	13.8	32.6	32.3	34.8	21.8	21.5	23.4	50.8	52.5	54.1
Primary commodities exporters	26.3	23.8	19.1	30.7	24.9	34.2	11.4	10.9	20.6	43.0	36.1	46.7
Least developed	57.3	48.4	41.3	14.4	15.5	18.3	8.7	8.3	9.6	28.3	36.1	40.4

Source: United Nations, 1990, Table 8.1, p. 194.

countries. The manufacturing sector experiences a relative decline in the developed market economies but expands in all other country groupings, to a very limited extent, however, in the case of the least developed countries. By the year 2000, the services sector dominates in all but the Least Developed and Petroleum Exporters groupings.

Intrasectoral change, within the manufacturing sector itself, is also of significance. Table 2.7 presents data on changes in the structure of MVA for different country categories and for different time periods, with projections to the year 2000. The share of the consumer goods industries declines in all country categories, but remains the largest sector except in the Major Exporters of Manufactures category. The share of capital goods in total MVA rises in all categories, but is especially pronounced in the case of Major Exporters of Manufactures. In the Asian NICs in particular, rapid growth of the capital goods sector is predicted by the United Nations (1990: 184) and structural change has proceeded most rapidly in these countries:

Table 2.7
Structure of MVA by Broad Economic Categories, Subgroups of Developing Countries, 1966–2000 (Selected Years, Percentage)

Country group and branch	1966–1970	1976–1980	1981–1985	2000
Major exporters of manufactures				
Consumer goods	59[a]	46	43	32
Capital goods	26	34	35	42
Intermediate goods	15	20	22	26
Other countries with relatively large manufacturing sectors				
Consumer goods	58	50	50	47
Capital goods	23	27	26	27
Intermediate goods	19	23	24	26
Oil exporters[b]				
Consumer goods	50	46	46	40
Capital goods	15	19	18	18
Intermediate goods	35	35	36	42
Least developed countries				
Consumer goods	76	69	68	63
Capital goods	11	14	13	15
Intermediate goods	14	16	19	22

Source: United Nations, 1990, Table 8.4, p. 197.
[a] Shares may not add to 100 percent because of rounding
[b] Excluding high-income oil exporters for lack of comprehensive data

Post export-led development strategies and increasing sources of technology available to the Asian newly industrialized economies resulted in technological capability in these countries sufficient to compete with developed countries in a wide range of products. Although their specific patterns vary, they are gaining competitiveness in segments of mature technology—advanced industries such as petrochemicals, segments of micro-chemicals, automobiles, general purpose machinery, electrical machinery, home electronics, and precision tools and equipment. They are also in the process of entering the lower spectrum of high-tech capital intensive industries: semi-conductors, small computers, automated office equipment, optic fibers, telecommunications, and pharmaceuticals. Reflecting the shift in comparative advantage, the shares of technology intensive products in their exports have increased rapidly. (United Nations, 1990: 186)

Various methods for the identification and measurement of structural change within the manufacturing sector have been utilized. Industries can be classified as light or heavy, identified by end use of output (consumer nondurables, industrial intermediates, capital goods), and classified with respect to the income elasticity of demand for their products (early, middle and late industries). (For a more detailed discussion, see Ballance, 1987: chapter 4.) Many useful insights can be gained from such exercises, but generalizations regarding changes in industrial structure across countries have only limited applicability. UNIDO (1983: 66) has itself warned that "simplistic interpretations" may ignore "a whole network of other determinants of structural change such as the extent of state involvement, the production technologies employed and the degree to which they can be transferred internationally, and the structure of firms."

EXPORTS OF MANUFACTURED GOODS

Changes in the structure of output are reflected in changes in a country's exports. Between 1965 and 1988, the share of manufactured goods in total LDC exports increased from 16 to 64 percent (United Nations, 1990: 12–13). In 1988, manufactures accounted for 72.6 percent of global exports (including fuels), but for the LDCs the equivalent figure was 45.4 percent, although for South and East Asia, manufactured goods accounted for 72.0 percent of total exports (all data from United Nations, 1990: 39–40).

The developed market economies still dominate global trade in manufactured goods, accounting for 79.2 percent of world exports of manufactured goods in 1986 (see Table 2.8). The equivalent share of the LDCs was 11.7 percent in the same year (having fallen from 12.2 percent in 1980). What is most striking in Table 2.8, however, is the increase in the share of South and East Asia from 3.0 percent in 1965 to 8.4 percent of world exports of manufactured goods in 1986.

The growth of manufactured exports from the newly industrializing countries has indeed been impressive. Six NICs (Brazil, Mexico, Hong Kong, Singapore, Taiwan and South Korea) enjoyed a rate of growth of manufactured exports (measured in current dollars) of 29.5 percent per annum between 1965 and 1973, and 17.8 percent per annum between 1973 and 1985 (for the four Asian NICs only—the so-called G-4) (OECD, 1988: 10).

In 1989, there was a marked deceleration in the growth of manufactured exports from South and Southeast Asia, with currency appreciation, domestic inflation and rising real wages in the major exporters of manufactured goods (the four Asian NICs) reducing the international competitiveness of their manufactured exports. The "new" exporters of manufactures in that region (Indonesia, Malaysia, Thailand and the Philippines), however, continued to expand the value of their manufactured exports (UNCTAD, 1990a: 5).

The NICs have thus made remarkable economic progress, but they face an uncertain future and they cannot afford to relax their export promotion efforts. In the traditional export sectors (textiles and clothing, for example), the Asian NICs in particular are facing increasing competition from a number of low-wage

Table 2.8
Share of Economic Groupings and Developing Regions in World Exports of Manufactured Goods, 1965–86 (Selected Years)

	1965	1970	1980	1986
Developed Market Economies	79.5	81.0	79.3	79.2
Eastern Europe and the USSR	12.1	10.5	7.5	7.4
China	0.6	0.4	0.8	1.3
Developing Countries	7.5	7.9	12.2	11.7
North Africa	0.3	0.3	0.3	0.2
Sub-Saharan Africa	1.3	1.2	0.7	0.2
Western Asia	0.4	0.5	1.3	0.4
South and East Asia	3.0	3.4	6.7	8.4
Latin America and the Caribbean	2.0	2.0	2.6	1.9
Mediterranean	0.7	0.6	0.7	0.9

Source: United Nations, 1990, Table 2.8, pp. 41–42.
Note: Percentage share of manufactures (SITC 5-9) in total commodity trade (SITC 0-9) measured in current US dollars

competitors (China, Thailand, the Philippines, Sri Lanka). In some "up-market" sectors where the NICs have made significant export efforts, problems of overcapacity and declining prices have emerged (in shipbuilding and steel-making, for example).

The major thrust of the NICs' response to these problems has been to move toward higher value added production, both in traditional areas (such as textiles and clothing) and in new markets, especially in high technology (OECD, 1988: 71). Greater emphasis is being placed on research and development (R&D), and the NIC governments have introduced support policies, including increased financial commitments, to strengthen research efforts and enhance technological capabilities. They are also aware of the need to develop a more highly educated work force and a skilled professional elite, and efforts have been made to expand higher education. Korea, for example, has rapidly expanded its output of engineering graduates, and has recently announced plans to raise its R&D expenditure to 5 percent of gross national product (GNP) by the year 2001 (as reported in the *Korea Times*, 27 October 1990).

With respect to priority sectors, their main focus appears to be on advanced electronics (computer peripherals, integrated circuits, minicomputers and microcomputers) and automobiles. The basic technologies needed for these activities have generally been developed in the advanced capitalist economies, and these developments have necessitated a focus on the acquisition and generation of new technologies by the NICs, and a wide variety of nonequity forms of foreign investment now exist (for example, licensing, franchising, management contracts, marketing contracts, joint ventures, turnkey plant sales, coproduction or production-sharing agreements, etc. See Helleiner, 1988.

THE EXPERIENCE OF INDUSTRIALIZATION

The dominant strategy of industrialization in LDCs in the post–World War II period has been import-substituting industrialization. This strategy has been subjected to a great deal of criticism from a number of theoretical perspectives (for a fuller summary, see Colman & Nixson, 1986: chapter 9), of which the neoclassical and structuralist/dependency critiques are the most important.

The neoclassical critique focuses on the alleged misallocation of scarce resources that arises from excessive, irrational and misguided government intervention in product and factor markets. Prices are distorted in product markets through the imposition of tariffs (and various quantitative restrictions), which create a divergence between domestic and international prices. The prices of labor and capital do not reflect their true scarcity values because of, *inter alia*, minimum wage legislation, inappropriate social security provisions and the existence of other imperfections in labor markets on the one hand, and maximum limits on interest rates and overvalued exchange rates on the other. "Getting prices right" (especially the interest rate and the exchange rate) becomes the key to neoclassical policy prescriptions (World Bank, 1987 contains a full statement of the neoclassical position; see also Kitchen & Weiss, 1987).

There is a great deal in the neoclassical critique that is of immediate relevance to policy makers. Structures of tariff protection (especially when effective rates are considered) are often excessive and irrational; import-substituting regimes are often characterized by excessive bureaucracy with the attendant inefficiency, delay and corruption; rent-seeking activities are encouraged; the agricultural sector is either neglected or effectively discriminated against; and exchange rates are typically overvalued, thus further discriminating against exports. While it is overly simplistic to argue that getting prices right is all that we need to concern ourselves with, there is nevertheless increasing agreement that prices do, indeed, matter, and that a large divergence between, for example, the official and black (or parallel) market rate of exchange cannot, in the longer run, be conducive to sustained, equitable development.

Structuralist/dependency critics of ISI focus on a different set of issues. They criticize the exacerbation of structural/sectoral imbalances brought about by the ISI strategy; they are critical of its distributional implications, its apparently excessive reliance on foreign capital and technology and its transfer of inappropriate products and consumption aspirations to low-income economies (not import substitution, but import replication, in large part related to the distribution of income within the import-substituting economy). At the level of political economy, various structuralist/dependency writers have focused on issues relating to the class structure, arguing that those who enjoy economic and political power in LDCs constitute a "comprador" bourgeoisie, allied to and dependent on the interests of foreign capital.

What is commonly assumed to be an alternative industrialization strategy is that based on the export of manufactured goods—export-oriented industrialization.[3] This strategy, which in large part, derives its intellectual rationale from the neoclassical critique of ISI, emphasizes the virtues of free trade and development according to comparative advantage, the benefits of international competition (through its impact on price, quality, reliability, etc.) and the advantages of an open, liberal economic environment in general. The outstanding examples of successful EOI are the so-called NICs, whose experience has already been referred to above.

ISI and EOI are no longer seen as necessarily mutually exclusive strategies such that the complementarities between the two strategies require emphasis. Singer and Alizadeh (1988), among others, have emphasized the importance of ISI in establishing an industrial base that may well be a necessary precondition for the subsequent pursuit of an EOI strategy. Teitel and Thoumi (1986: 485–86) argue that in Latin America ISI has led to the development of technological capacity, economies of scale, linkages and infrastructural facilities, and that "ISI policies followed by these countries do not seem to have resulted in permanent inefficiencies in many manufacturing industries." The experience of South Korea clearly demonstrates that ISI does not cease to be important once policies of EOI are being pursued. The South Korean government has effectively intervened on a highly selective basis to import substitute in key industrial sectors (intermediate goods and heavy industries), partly in order to lower the import content of manufactured exports. In such circumstances, it is indeed difficult to characterize the strategy as either ISI or EOI.

An additional point is related to the external economic environment. The emergence of the G-4 countries in the late 1960s and early 1970s was in part due to the adoption by these countries of highly effective export promotion policies at a time of rapidly expanding world trade in manufactured goods. The less favorable global economic environment of the 1980s and the continued uncertain prospects in the 1990s raise the question as to the possibility of future successful EOI (Singer & Alizadeh, 1988), notwithstanding the emergence of second-tier NICs. In this context, the questions raised in Cline's (1982) seminal article on the generalizability of the G-4 model of EOI remain relevant. (For a critique, however, see Bhagwati, 1990.)

THE LESSONS OF EXPERIENCE

A number of useful lessons can be drawn from the study of the post–World War II experience of industrialization in LDCs. At the general level, three points deserve emphasis:

1. The state plays a strategic role in the development process in general and the industrialization process in particular, irrespective of the strategy of industrialization that is pursued. Amsden's (1989) work on South Korea highlights the key role that the state has played, including its ownership and/or control of commercial banks (thus ensuring the allocation of credit in line with government-determined development objectives), the imposition of price controls and the use of subsidies deliberately to distort relative prices ("getting prices wrong") in order to stimulate economic activity. Amsden (1989: 18) concludes that "without a strong central authority, a necessary although not sufficient condition, little industrialization may be expected in "backward" countries," and that the state always intervenes in the market mechanism to ensure that the allocation of scarce resources is consistent with government policies.[4] (See also White & Wade, 1988.)

2. ISI and EOI are complementary to one another and a balance needs to be struck between them. Singer and Alizadeh (1988: 72) argue that for any one country at any particular point in time, that balance will largely be a matter of political judgment, rather than firm economic analysis, reflecting in large part the present state and future of the global economy. They continue:

   What is suggested is a systematic combination of IS and EO, with a different emphasis on IS and EO at different periods and for different sectors. In the nature of things in developing countries, the sequence from IS to EO will be more frequent than the reverse, both in time and for given sectors. But EO itself will also lead to new opportunities for IS, to reduce the import content of exports and increase linkages from the export sector to the rest of the economy, preventing dualism and a disarticulated industrial structure.

3. The macroeconomic environment within which industrialization is pursued requires greater attention. "Monetary, price and balance of trade and payments implications" (Singer & Alizadeh, 1988: 69–70) must be taken

into account, and the macromanagement of the economy cannot be treated separately from sectoral development strategies.

The more specific lessons that can be drawn from the experience of LDCs follow in part from the general comments made above and have particular significance in terms of their implications for policy prescription:

1. All strategies of industrialization are import-intensive and thus require access to adequate supplies of foreign exchange for their successful implementation. Foreign exchange can only be acquired in three ways: it can be earned by exporting; it can be borrowed (from either private commercial banks or bilateral or multilateral aid institutions); or it can be made available as aid, either in the form of grants or concessional loans.[5] Both common sense and real-world experience lead to the conclusion that it is neither possible nor desirable for countries to depend too heavily or for too long on the latter two sources. It is an inescapable fact, therefore, that countries must *earn* the major part of their foreign exchange requirements, and thus the promotion and diversification of exports to convertible currency markets becomes crucially important.

2. The role of foreign direct investment in the industrialization process is currently undergoing a reevaluation, with a more pragmatic, less political approach being adopted by many LDCs (United Nations Center on Transnational Corporations, 1988: 10). Transnational corporations (TNCs) are at the forefront of technological development (information technology, biotechnology, new materials, etc.) and they are a major channel through which technology is transferred to LDCs. The service sector (especially banking and financial services in general) has become increasingly transnational in the 1980s, and some foreign participation in the further development of this sector in LDCs might be desirable. Additionally, TNCs are increasingly seen as providing access to the markets of the developed capitalist economies, and their participation in export promotion strategies may thus be vitally important. None of this should be taken to mean that conflicts of interest between TNCs and host countries have been eliminated, nor that effective and properly enforced foreign investment laws and codes of conduct (both national and international) are not important. FDI should be seen as essentially a complement to domestic capital formation, and the transfer of technology should be seen as a process that accelerates the development of indigenous technological capabilities.[6] The United Nations Center on Transnational Corporations report (1988: 11) concludes:

In an era of large international capital flows and rapid technological change, developing countries will increasingly look to TNCs for economic stimulation. For their part, TNCs will frequently be in a position to provide significant long-term benefits to many developing countries. An important component in the next generation of development policies is that this mutuality of interest continues to grow.

3. Greater attention needs to be given to both inter- and intrasectoral balances—In the former, between the industrial and agricultural sectors, for example, and in the latter, between the light and heavy (or consumer and intermediate/capital goods) subsectors.

CONCLUDING COMMENTS

In this final section, we return to the issues raised above concerning the conflicting interpretations of the industrialization experience.

Dependency and neo-Marxist writers tend to approach the issue of industrialization from a global perspective, locating their analysis of the actualities of, and possibilities for, LDC industrialization within a world systems framework and emphasizing the constraints on development imposed by the subservient position of the LDC within the global economic system. In other words, they move from the general to the specific and place greatest weight on external factors.

Classical Marxism, on the other hand, tends to move from the specific to the general. It focuses on issues of class formation and class conflict within the nation- state as the most important, dynamic elements in the development process, and thus asserts the primacy of internal factors. However, as Bernstein (1982: 231–32) has argued, we need "to transcend the more or less static dichotomy of "internal" and "external" factors," and the "global dimension" in the study of development should not be seen as unidirectional.

Development (that is, growth and structural change) continues to occur in the developed capitalist economies and has profound implications for Third World development prospects. Developments in the Third World in turn impact on the developed capitalist economies. The NICs are not merely a reflection of the changing economic interests of the developed capitalist economies and rivalry between their capitals. We need to look in detail at the dynamics of the development process within national economies (notwithstanding the ambiguity of that concept), whilst not neglecting their position within the global capitalist economy and the tensions and conflicts that arise between the imperatives of national development on the one hand and the constraints imposed upon those efforts by the global economy on the other hand. (Nixson, 1991: 84)

Many of the radical critics of the experience of Third World industrialization often (implicitly) make two highly misleading assumptions. First, they seem to assume that all significant industrialization in the Third World is export oriented, thus ignoring or undervaluing the very real achievements of ISI. Second, they also seem to assume that all export-oriented industrialization is of the global processing variety, that is, restricted to the assembly or processing of parts, components, and such for immediate reexport (as analyzed in Helleiner's seminal 1973 article). (This is the implication of the discussion in Peet, 1991: chapter 9, for example.) It should not be necessary to point out that countries such as South Korea, Taiwan, India, Brazil, Mexico and Turkey have gone beyond that stage and are increasingly important exporters of both an ever-widening range of manufactured goods and industrial technology itself.

Of course, not all economies have the capacity for autonomous development and some, owing to their geographical size, strategic location, resource endowments and other factors, might never develop it. Nevertheless, to force all the NICs in the mold of dependency theory is to twist the facts to the needs of theory and to refuse to acknowledge the very real processes of capitalist accumulation and development that are occurring in at least some of these countries. The key role of the state and the emergence and consolidation of national capital are the factors given least weight by most dependency/neo-Marxist theorists, yet it is these very forces that are transforming the semi-industrial economies of the Third World. The fact that this process of growth and change is not leading to some idealized process of development (conceived of, essentially, as progress) will come as a surprise only to those whose collective heads have been buried in the sands of dependency theory for the past twenty-five years.

NOTES

1. This is a concept of development based on what we have referred to elsewhere (Nixson, 1984, 1987; Leeson & Nixson, 1988) as the "historical analytic," in contrast to the more usual "policy prescriptive" definition of economic development.

2. Many countries have achieved high rates of economic growth through the exploitation of minerals and other natural resources, and indeed Reynolds (1983) has argued that historically, industrialization has not been a precondition for increases in per capita incomes. He distinguishes between extensive growth (a period when increased productive capacity is fully absorbed by population with no rising trend in per capita income) and intensive growth (when the capacity to produce rises appreciably faster than population, thus resulting in a sustained rise in per capita incomes. The time at which extensive growth becomes intensive growth is labeled "the turning point," and it is characterized typically by an acceleration of agricultural (or occasionally mineral) output and a rising trade ratio. The rising income from exports broadens the domestic market for manufactured goods, but the initial supply response comes largely from small-scale rural industries and handicraft workshops. Reynolds argues that there is usually a lag of several decades before factory industry becomes prominent and that factories were almost entirely absent at the turning point for those countries that reached their turning points before 1900. Conversely, in the period 1900–50, Reynolds identifies considerable industrial development in countries such as Egypt, Turkey, India and China, which were still in their extensive growth phase.

3. It is important to point out that there is no single model of EOI. The NICs have little in common with one another, apart from their experience of rapid industrialization (OECD, 1988). They differ with respect to the size of their economies, their resource endowments,

the role of the public sector, the role of direct foreign investment and in their historical backgrounds and socioeconomic, sociopolitical and sociocultural characteristics. The point to be emphasized is that each example of EOI is in some sense unique to the economy implementing it.

4. Where Korea differs from other LDCs in its use of subsidies is that the state has exercised discipline over subsidy recipients. In exchange for subsidies, the state has imposed performance standards on private firms (production and export targets, for example) and has penalized those firms that have not achieved those targets. Subsidies have thus been given on the basis of reciprocity (Amsden, 1989: 13). The subsidy "epitomizes the struggle to industrialize after the Second World War." Singer and Alizadeh (1988: 68) also conclude that "it is becoming increasingly clear that it is not the extent and the duration of state intervention which determines the success or failure of ISI and EOI. It is rather the economic-political situation the state faces both internally and externally, its political commitments and its administrative capacity which matter."

5. Countertrade, barter deals and other arrangements do not directly provide a country with convertible foreign currencies. They may, of course, make available commodities that would otherwise have been purchased with foreign currency.

6. The acquisition and generation of new technology is the *sine qua non* for future industrialization. As UNCTAD (1990b: 63) has noted: "At the heart of the development process and of the transfer and development of technology are human skills."

3

UPGRADING AND DIVERSIFYING IN LATE INDUSTRIALIZATION

Alice H. Amsden

INTRODUCTION

In the 1980s, many industries in Turkey and other late-industrializing countries failed to graduate to higher skill or technology-intensive production, either by diversifying into new markets or by moving into higher-quality segments in existing markets. This failure raises the question of what the "dynamic" of dynamic comparative advantage is. What are the institutions that support a country's climb up the ladder of comparative advantage, enabling it to progress from simple to more complex manufacturing activity?

There are two operational aspects to the concept of dynamic comparative advantage: (1) what products countries should produce as they develop, given their changing resource endowments; and (2) which organizations may be relied upon to accomplish such industrial transformation. The first aspect of dynamic comparative advantage has received the most attention, because it has been construed by economists as a problem of "getting the prices right." Yet the practical question of what specific products countries midway between developed and developing can (and not only should) produce competitively warrants more systematic study and intelligence-gathering than it receives within a market-price analytical framework.

The second aspect of dynamic comparative advantage—the institutions responsible for accomplishing industrial change through upgrading or diversifying the existing industrial structure—has received altogether too little attention, and is the subject of this chapter. The problems of diversifying and upgrading have become critical in late-industrializing countries in the 1990s. As Oktar Türel points out, the Turkish manufacturing industry became more, not less, dependent on unskilled, labor-intensive production between 1976 and 1987. Average labor productivity tended to decrease rather than increase over time. One of the most important questions facing the Turkish economy in the 1990s is how to raise productivity by rearing higher value added industries (Türel, 1993).

The economic development literature is now full of references to learning, whether it be learning in order to produce (production capability), learning to expand capacity or execute new projects (investment capability) or learning to innovate (R&D capability). Little, however, is written specifically on learning how to invest in diversification or graduation into a higher-quality market niche. These aspects of learning deserve special treatment, because they often involve different skills from those a company requires to create new or additional capacity in its primary market segment.

At the national level, the true dynamic of comparative advantage is not just a choice of what to produce but also a process—de facto an industrial policy—to achieve sequentially more skill- and technology-intensive production. In any country the process of industrial transformation is affected not merely by market forces but also by how business and government are organized and managed, and by how they interact with each other and with labor.

By and large, development economists have given a simple answer to the question of how countries climb up the ladder of comparative advantage. Most suggest that this process happens automatically so long as countries get the prices right and allow market forces to guide the choice of products to manufacture. In, for example, Bela Balassa's stages theory of comparative advantage (1981b), less skilled and capital-intensive production presumably acts as the entry point to more complex industrial activity, providing the capital and managerial know-how necessary to move from lower to higher manufacturing stages. Taiwan is now taken as evidence of this free market approach, because over half of manufacturing output in Taiwan is accounted for by small-scale firms (with no more than 300 workers). It is presumed that small-scale firms in Taiwan have grown organically and have acted as the agents of industrial change, cropping up in new industries in response to changes in market prices.

In fact, the process of diversifying and upgrading has proven not to be automatic, not even in the case of Taiwan, as argued shortly.

The process of industrialization, as Albert Hirschman (1958) pointed out in the 1950s, is rife with stumbling blocks, bottlenecks, externalities, and market failures. Hirschman argued that imbalances in the industrial structure would provide entrepreneurs with signals about potential new investment opportunities. Unfulfilled linkages would indicate where investment capital might most profitably be placed. The manufacturing sectors to be promoted by the government were those with the greatest linkages. While Hirschman's conception of industrialization has largely been proven correct, the imbalance signals he wrote about have not been strong enough to guide the industrialization process in such countries as Turkey, Taiwan, Brazil, and South Korea. These late-industrializers have had to develop without the competitive asset of new pioneering technology, the driving force behind industrialization in eighteenth-century Britain and nineteenth-century United States.

Instead, the process of late industrialization has been characterized by borrowing technology and the conscious mobilization of institutions—often big businesses and state bureaucracies—deliberately to push industrialization ahead (Amsden, 1989).

One of the most important institutions to emerge in conjunction with highly interventionist states in late industrialization is the diversified business group. This form of big business has acted as the agent of diversification in a wide range of countries. As stated in the summary proceedings of an international business historians' conference:

In developing countries such as South Korea, Taiwan, the Philippines, Thailand, India, Brazil, Argentina [and, one might add, Turkey], industrial groups which resemble Japan's former zaibatsu have sprung up since the Second World War. (Yasuoka, 1984: xi)

These groups have internalized the learning process to the point where diversifying into new industries appears to represent an important economy of scope. Conglomerates in developing countries, unlike those in, say, the United States, have tended to be tightly managed at the top because they have grown rapidly under one owner without diluting their equity. They have borrowed capital and technology abroad. With central coordination and rapid expansion into the bottom end of many markets, they have become especially good at diversifying themselves. Big business groups have internalized many of the technological complementarities and managerial linkages that Hirschman described.

Nevertheless, with the emergence in the 1980s of a global ideology of liberalization and deregulation, big business and big government have fallen into disrepute. The favored agent of the World Bank and IMF to execute industrial change has become the small-scale firm. The small-scale firm has allegedly dispensed with the need for governments to choose what products to manufacture and what large-scale enterprises to spoon-feed. The Taiwan model, with its emphasis on small firms and exports, has become doubly attractive because most other late-industrializing countries have had to expand their exports in order to repay their foreign debts, and Taiwan's economy is one of the most export oriented in the world with exports amounting to over 50 percent of GNP.

In Turkey's case, one explanation for its flagging productivity and regressing industrial complexity is its small-scale firm structure. The average firm size in Turkey fell from 115 in 1976 to 87 in 1985 (Türel, 1993). Fast-growing Taiwan, whose experience with small scale firms appears to be opposite to that of Turkey, is therefore of more than academic interest.

This chapter will restrict discussion to the small-scale firm as an agent of industrial change in the context of Taiwan, where it supposedly operates best. The general lessons are the following: In the case of many small firms in Taiwan, their growth was not organic, as the free market model presumes; instead, they appear to have been cradled by large firms—either state enterprises, multinationals, or private big business groups. Small firms have tended to become predominant in Taiwan not because a preponderance of small firms is the natural order of the universe, but because of the presence of an exceptionally domineering state. The Taiwan state appears to have prevented big business from growing larger. It also created conditions conducive to high personal savings, which allowed large numbers of small enterprises to flourish. The Taiwan model does not provide evidence for the view that industry is capable of pulling itself up the ladder of comparative advantage merely by the free play of market forces. As for the capability of small firms to move up-market into higher-quality market niches, the available evidence from Taiwan is not especially encouraging. There is evidence that the private sector is not investing much in R&D. Where upgrading is occurring, foreign investors appear to be playing a major role. Apparently, upgrading does not happen without state intervention, either.

THE SMALL FIRM AS AGENT OF INDUSTRIALIZATION: EVIDENCE FROM TAIWAN[1]

Big Business in the Wings

In the free market conception, industrialization is a process of moving from labor-intensive to capital- and skill-intensive production. Assuming economies of scale are weak in labor-intensive industries but become stronger as manufacturing activity grows more complex, then one would expect firm size to change as well in the course of industrialization. On average, small firms would be expected to dominate in the early stages of growth, giving way later on to larger firms. In fact, exactly the opposite pattern has characterized Taiwan.

In the early 1970s Taiwan had more manufacturing output in large firms (500 or more workers) than any other developing country, including Korea, for which data are readily available. Only since the early 1970s have small firms gradually gained a majority share of manufacturing activity. This raises two questions. Why did Taiwan start out with large-scale industry, and why did the share of large firms in manufacturing output decline over time?

Taiwan, and other developing countries that successfully transformed their economies from raw material- to manufacturing-based, began industrializing with large-scale enterprises because industries associated with the rudiments of infrastructure development—such as cement, oil refining, simple chemicals and heavy machinery—all require relatively large capital investments. Moreover, in the 1960s, before people in developing countries began buying rather than making their own clothing, cotton spinning and weaving, and not apparel, was the leading sector, and cotton spinning tends to be undertaken in relatively large-size firms.

Whether it is practically possible to industrialize without developing rudimentary import-substitution industries, on the basis of small-scale firms oriented exclusively toward export markets, will be discussed shortly, when attention is turned to the question of why small-scale firms have become the dominant mode in Taiwan's industrial structure. The answer is that small exporters often rely for key inputs on domestic, large-scale import-substituting industries. Historically, the incipient agent of late industrialization was the large-size enterprise, even in Taiwan. The city–states of Hong Kong and Singapore may be exceptions, but they never had to escape from the problems of a primary product-based economy, which is the usual meaning of the term industrialization.

Three types of large-size enterprise predominated in Taiwan: state companies, by far the most important type, accounting for as much as 56 percent of manufacturing output in the early 1950s; foreign enterprises, although the government prevented them from operating in the "commanding heights"; and indigenous diversified business groups, which still account for about 30 percent of turnover (Chou, 1988). Each type of large-scale enterprise contributed in a certain way to the growth of smaller firms.

In the case of state enterprises, they were an important source of high-level personnel. Initially, the cream of Taiwan's educational system preferred employment in the public sector. Along the lines of the National Universities of Tokyo and Seoul, Taiwan National University was founded to serve the needs of the state bureaucracy. According to one anthropologist (Silin, 1976), eventually there was a migration of managers from the public sector to large Taiwanese firms. In turn, experienced personnel left large Taiwanese firms to found their own small companies.

In the case of multinational firms, some were strongly pressured by the government to transfer technological capability. Multinationals that were not oriented toward the export market were only licensed selectively by the government to operate in Taiwan. The Singer Sewing Machine Company was allowed to locate in Taiwan, provided it gave technological assistance to a large number of local parts suppliers. The technological capability of Taiwan's metal-working sector can to a significant degree be traced back to the Singer company. The capability of small plastic manufacturers is partly attributable to technical assistance from the United Distillers Company. In the case of electronics, the sector began in Taiwan with as much as 65 percent of its output in foreign hands (Schive, 1978).

Finally, big local companies in Taiwan have served as an important source of financing for small firms. Taiwan's financial system continues to be tightly repressed. Writing in mid-1985, Hang-Sheng Cheng writes: "Taiwan retains a system dominated by bureaucratic government banks, which continue to ration credit at below-market-clearing interest rates under behind-the-scenes direction of the central bank" (1986: 143).

Small and medium-sized firms have been discriminated against under this financial system. According to Shea and Kuo (1984), the share of large firms borrowing from domestic banks averaged more than three times that of small and medium-sized firms from 1965 to 1972, and as much as 1.5 times from 1972 to 1982.

Discrimination by the formal banking sector has meant that for start-up capital in particular, small business has had to rely on personal savings, friends, relatives, and other nonbank sources, including windfall gains from urban real estate sales. On the other hand, for trade credit, equipment and working capital loans, big business appears to have been an important source of financing for small business. According to Biggs (1988), the financial dependence of small business is highly significant and supported by various government measures.

The reasons for discrimination against small and medium-sized business by the formal banking system are related to risk and transaction-cost minimization, not rent seeking. Biggs (1988: 9) writes:

In simple fact, banks have functioned as little more than a chain of pawn shops: three-quarters or more of what they lend must be secured by collateral, generally in fixed assets. And, as bank officials are held personally responsible (in terms of salary and promotion) for every penny of "the state's money" by government auditors, they have taken few risks; their main object being to avoid errors and to advance through the bureaucracy.

If, moreover, government-controlled banks have been unwilling to lend to small borrowers for reasons related to risk and transaction costs rather than rent seeking, there is nothing to indicate that a liberalized banking system, dominated by privately owned banks, would behave any differently. Privately owned banks would also want to lend to borrowers with ample fixed assets to minimize the uncertainties of default and the costs of handling a large number of small loans. In fact, bank reform and privatization in Korea have not seen an end to government intervention, which now has an object of insuring that a certain percentage of loans is allocated to small and medium-sized firms. The price mechanism has not been relied upon to insure such a flow of funds (Amsden & Euh, 1990).

In sum, the linkages between big and small business in Taiwan include transfers of personnel, technical assistance and capital. To the extent that the formal banking sector (private or public) is reluctant to lend to small and medium-sized enterprises for reasons related to transaction costs and risk aversion, the presence of big business, in its capacity as financial intermediary, may be regarded as a boon to firms at the bottom end of the size distribution.

The trinity of big business in Taiwan—state corporations, multinationals and local diversified enterprises—grew in conjunction with government guidance and support. For example, although real interest rates in Taiwan have been relatively high by the standards of late industrialization—due to negligible inflation—big private enterprises have paid lower effective real interest rates by on-lending to smaller firms at a premium. The dynamic of dynamic comparative advantage in Taiwan, as in other late-industrializing countries, has at its core a symbiotic relationship between big business and the state.

Nevertheless, the linkages between small and large firms in Taiwan appear to be evolving differently from those elsewhere. Subcontracting is not taking the form of a large prime contractor dominating concentric layers of satellite firms, as in Korea and Japan. Instead, the division of labor tends to be finer than elsewhere. For various reasons, subcontracting takes the form of networks rather than hierarchies, as outlined by Piore and Sabel (1984) in their writings on flexible specialization. Even big companies in Taiwan concentrate on manufacturing a limited number of production stages, with little vertical integration.

Large firms, producing under conditions of increasing returns, however, still appear to be indispensable in providing small firms with a large number of inputs that would otherwise have to be imported. The dynamic of dynamic comparative advantage in Taiwan has become flexible specialization, with small (and large) firms producing customized products in minuscule lots with short lead times. Raw material and work-in-process inventories are pared to minimize overhead. A large number of small orders with short lead times may not be satisfied cost-effectively through imports. Big firms supply small firms with vital inputs, promptly and in small quantities. The new dynamic driving industrialization in Taiwan has become one of interdependence among firms of different sizes, and not domination by small firms exclusively.

The Government in the Wings

Traditional market theory predicts the dominance of small firms in the early stages of industrialization. Large enterprises are expected to be specialized. Yet the work of Alfred Chandler (1990) points to altogether different stylized facts in economic history: Since the late 1880s, industrialization has been spearheaded in most countries not by a large number of small firms, but rather by the modern industrial enterprise, which is composed of large-scale plants, is managed hierarchically, and is multidivisional. Taiwan's firm size distribution, therefore, is unusual by world standards and does not represent some natural order. The government appears both to have inhibited the growth of large firms and to have provided conditions conducive to the survival of small ones.

The evidence on government limitations to the growth of large firms is sketchy, however. The motive is there: The entrepreneurial class in Taiwan is distinct ethnically from the Chinese mainlanders who have dominated the government. Therefore, the Taiwan government is unlikely to have wanted a managerial class concentrated enough to challenge its authority. But more evidence must be gathered on the government's industrial licensing policy, which determines the firm size distribution in developing countries. Such evidence must

Table 3.1
**Relative Rates of Inflation in Selected Countries and Regions,
1965–80 and 1980–87**

	Average Annual Rate of Inflation (percent)	
	1965-80	1980-87
Taiwan	7.8[a]	0.2[a]
	8.2[b]	3.1[b]
S. Korea	15.2[a]	3.7[a]
	14.7[b]	6.1[b]
Turkey	20.7[c]	37.4[c]
Sub-Saharan Africa[d]	12.3[c]	15.2[c]
Africa		
South America[d]	29.3[c]	109.1[c]
East Asia[d]	8.8[c]	5.4[c]
South Asia[d]	8.4[c]	7.8[c]

Sources: Taiwan: Council for Economic Planning and Development, 1988.
S.Korea: Economic Planning Board, 1984 and 1989.
Other: World Bank, 1989.
[a] Wholesale Price Index
[b] Consumer Price Index
[c] GDP Implicit Deflator
[d] Low-and Middle-Income Countries Weighted Averages

come from company histories, which are now just beginning to be written in Taiwan. The history of Formosa Plastics, Taiwan's largest conglomerate, does suggest that the government was instrumental both in helping this group to reach its present size, and in preventing it from growing even larger. It seems that the government frustrated Formosa Plastic's diversification plans in order to protect the interests of incumbent companies, both public (in petrochemicals) and private (in cement) (see Takao, 1989a and his references to the company history of Kuo Tai).

Without question, the Taiwan government provided suitable conditions for the proliferation of small enterprises: fast growth coupled with low inflation, which may be hypothesized to encourage personal savings, and low wage increases, which allowed small firms to compete in world markets on the basis of low costs. These conditions have also tended to characterize the other late-industrializing countries that have been outstanding exporters to world markets: Singapore and,

Table 3.2
Savings Rates in Selected Countries and Regions, 1965 and 1987

	Gross Domestic Savings as Percent of Gross Domestic Product	
	1965	1987
Taiwan	20	41
S. Korea	8	38
Turkey	13	23
Sub-Saharan Africa[a]	14	13
South America[a]	21	20
East Asia[a]	23	35
South Asia[a]	15	19

Source: Taiwan: Council for Economic Planning and Development, 1988.
[a] Low-and Middle-Income Countries, weighted average

more recently, Thailand and Chile (both of which, however, are largely agroindustry exporters). In all cases, a highly authoritarian state buttressed small firms' competitiveness by keeping down the growth rate of prices and wages. At one point, Singapore adopted a policy to raise wages in order to drive industry into higher value added markets. After a while that policy was reversed, but the point is that the government had the power to influence wage rates to a significant degree.

Tables 3.1, 3.2 and 3.3 provide comparative data on inflation, savings and wage rates in Taiwan. What is striking is a high rate of national savings and a low rate of inflation. Many factors have contributed to low inflation in Taiwan, including the government's commitment to stability before growth. The Guomindang regime has feared the type of rampant inflation that cost it its power in prewar China. Taiwan, unlike Korea and Japan, has religiously avoided budget deficits and monetary laxness. In addition, to the extent that inflation reflects conflict among the social classes for a larger income share, such conflict has been kept under tight government rein in Taiwan. Both labor and business have been disciplined by the state. Although real wages in 1970–84 rose faster in Taiwan than in Brazil, Argentina, Mexico, India and Turkey, output and productivity also rose faster. Output and productivity were growing fast in both Korea and Taiwan in the same period, but real wage increases in Korea have far outdistanced those in Taiwan. The Korean government has also been authoritarian, but less effective than the Taiwan government in repressing social unrest.

Table 3.3
Comparison of Real Nonagricultural Wage Increases in Seven Late-Industrializing Countries, 1970–1984

Year[a]	Korea[b]	Brazil[c]	Argentina	Mexico	Turkey	India[d]	Taiwan
1970	100	100	100	100	100	100	--
1971	102	110	105	103	100	100	--
1972	104	114	99	104	99	--	100
1973	119	119	107	104	98	106	107
1974	130	119	126	107	96	97	98
1975	131	127	124	114	116	110	110
1976	154	129	80	123	122	120	126
1977	187	134	76	125	146	116	138
1978	219	142	77	122	147	124	151
1979	238	134	87	121	155	130	163
1980	227	130	100	116	124		166
1981	225	118	91	119	130		171
1982	241	115	79	117	129		180
1983	261	97	97	86	130		188
1984	276	84	112	83	111		191

Source: Amsden, 1989.
[a] Base = 100 deflated by consumer price index
[b] Real earnings in manufacturing sector
[c] Average wages for skilled workers in construction. Data are from the Central Bank.
[d] Rupees per hour for industrial workers

High rates of saving and low rates of increase in prices and wages are central features of the Taiwan model. They may not, however, be easily transferred to a country like Turkey, which is in search of a new growth dynamic amidst considerable political and social tensions.

The Multinationals in the Wings

To increase competitiveness, the Taiwan government tried for many years to arrange mergers among small-scale enterprises, in the belief that the size of the average firm was suboptimal. (The 1981 industrial census indicated that the average firm size in Taiwan was only 8.6 employees, compared with a 1985 estimate for Turkey of 87). Now the government is emphasizing a new strategy:

converting small-scale producers of labor-intensive manufactures into high-tech manufacturers—call the process upgrading.

The question is: Is the small-scale firm capable of acting as the agent of high-tech industrialization? The encouraging fact about Taiwan—as well as South Korea and Singapore—is the existence of a highly educated population and a large number of citizens working abroad at high-level jobs. When émigrés return, they bring technological capability with them and are responsible for many high-tech start-up companies. The discouraging fact about Taiwan is that little investment is being undertaken in domestic R&D.

The micro-level case study is the best methodology to assess the extent to which small-scale enterprises in Taiwan have succeeded in moving to a higher-quality market niche, through an improvement in product and process. Enough case studies to judge what is happening are just beginning to emerge. Whatever these say, however, the macro data are discouraging insofar as Taiwan appears to be relying on inward direct foreign investment as opposed to its own efforts for upgrading, which may be a strategy other late-industrializing countries cannot, and should not, follow.

Whereas Taiwan is relying on foreign investors for upgrading, Korea is attempting to build its own technological capability, centered on a core of big business groups. This may be inferred from the following data. First, Korea is spending far more on R&D than Taiwan. As Table 3.4 indicates, the ratio of R&D to either GNP or sales (which are larger than GNP) shows Korea's higher level of R&D investments. Korea has also relied more than Taiwan on disembodied foreign technical assistance (as opposed to foreign direct investment) to prepare itself to stand on its own feet. The number of cases of foreign technology imports between 1962 and 1988 was 5,443 in Korea compared with 3,000 in Taiwan. Increasing independence on Korea's part is indicated by the declining ratio over time of foreign technology payments as a percentage of R&D expenditure (Korea Industrial Research Institute, 1989). Comparable data are unavailable for Taiwan.

Second, Taiwan is recording far higher levels of inward direct foreign investment than Korea. Between 1982 and 1989, approved inward foreign investment totaled $6,331 million in Taiwan and only $5,186 million in Korea, although Taiwan's economy is not quite 70 percent as large as Korea's.[2]

Each strategy has its strengths and weaknesses. The Taiwan strategy is likely to have earlier payoffs, and Taiwan's faster GNP growth rate in the last two years of the 1980s may be indicative of this. Korea's strategy may pay off more handsomely in the long term, as indicated by its higher growth rate of productivity. In recent years, the productivity growth rate has been consistently higher in Korea than Taiwan (see, for example, Balassa & Williamson, 1987; Dollar & Sokaloff, in press). Nevertheless, Taiwan's strategy is discouraging because, if the aggregate data truly reflect a lack of attention to R&D, they suggest that even in a developing country with a high level of education and saving, the small firm cannot be counted on to transform itself into an

Table 3.4
R&D Expenditures, Taiwan and South Korea, 1970–87 (Selected Years)

	1970	1975	1980	1981	1982	1983	1984	1985	1986	1987
A. Percent of GNP										
Taiwan	--	--	0.72	0.94	0.91	0.94	0.99	1.08	1.04	1.16
S. Korea	0.38	0.42	0.58	0.65	0.90	1.05	1.26	1.59	1.82	1.93
B. Percent of Sales										
Taiwan									0.48	0.41
									0.54[a]	0.43[a]
S.Korea									1.35	1.52
									1.83[a]	1.89[a]

Source: Taiwan: Council for Economic Planning and Development, 1989, and National
Science Council Taiwan, 1989.
Korea: Korea Industrial Research Institute, 1989.
[a] Manufacturing

entrepreneurial, high-tech concern.

Mid-Tech

How much investment is undertaken in R&D is only one part of the problem
of upgrading that faces late-industrializing countries. Another part concerns what
to do about industries that are no longer competitive, given rising domestic wages
or competition from lower-wage countries. No matter how much investment in
R&D a country undertakes, the new value added of such investment can typically
not overcome the problem of restructuring old industries—labor-intensive ones or,
a step beyond, capital-intensive industries that utilize large amounts of labor. Part
of the dynamic of dynamic comparative advantage of late-industrializing countries
that are midway between developed and underdeveloped is creating institutions to
restructure dying industries.

When the World Bank or IMF discusses restructuring, typically it emphasizes
reforming the public sector (privatization), phasing out state subsidies to business
(liberalization), and reducing the rules governing private firms' behavior
(deregulation). Yet the attempts of indebted countries to develop labor-intensive
manufactures for export have made restructuring of an altogether different type
more relevant: It is restructuring to exit from or rejuvenate labor-intensive or mid-
level industries that have become increasingly uncompetitive. This type of

restructuring has become of great importance in such countries as Japan, Korea and Taiwan. One may hypothesize that the more export-oriented a country is, the more the central issue of restructuring becomes the reorganization of dying or threatened industries. Certainly, this type of restructuring, as opposed to privatization, liberalization, and deregulation, is in practical terms emerging in the 1990s as the key industrial policy issue in debt-ridden countries like Turkey, although its importance tends to be overlooked in the market model.

The lesson from Japan is that restructuring is difficult to accomplish. To succeed at all, it requires planning and coordinating by government, business and labor. Ronald Dore (1986) discusses the case of the Japanese textile industry. What Dore succeeds brilliantly in conveying is how imperfect the process of restructuring actually was, as well as how important planning and coordinating were in making the Japanese textile industry a success story, in terms of minimizing the social costs of capacity reduction and of specializing in a higher quality niche (synthetic fibers).

Japan also testifies to the economic importance of creating institutions that are responsible for revitalizing a wide range of industries—the "mid-tech"—which includes all but the most labor-intensive and high-tech manufacturing sectors. In 1985, at a time when Japan's investments in R&D were approximating those of the United Sates, Japan's trade surplus in industries with high levels of R&D was $28 billion, compared with $5.7 billion for the United States. Japan's trade surplus in medium–R&D intensity industries was much greater, at $81.5 billion, compared with a trade deficit of $59.7 billion for the United States (UNCTAD, 1987).

Rediscovering the Past

The dynamic that determines a country's ascent up the ladder of comparative advantage reflects resource endowment, history, relations between the social classes, institutional wear and tear and other fundamental features of a country's character. Therefore, one country can never be expected to emulate faithfully the industrial policies of another country. Nevertheless, the nature of the dynamic driving diversification and upgrading in late industrialization has been examined in far less detail than market-related reforms such as liberalization, privatization and deregulation. A better understanding of the dynamic in the fastest growing late-industrializing countries may help other late industrializers to create equivalent institutions that serve their own ends.

One unassailable conclusion from the East Asian experience is highly relevant no matter what the country: The march up the ladder of comparative advantage in East Asia has not been left to chance, even in Taiwan. It has been carefully, if not perfectly, planned. There is a debate in Japan, Korea and Taiwan about who took the initiative to create new industries—business or government. Detailed case studies will probably reveal that in some industries, the credit (or blame) falls to one party, and in other industries, to the other. But apart from the issue of who saw the light bulb flash first, business and government collaborated in pushing industrialization ahead. The price mechanism was not relied on either to trigger industrialization or to maintain its tempo.

The ideological posturing about privatization, liberalization and deregulation in Turkey and other late-industrializing countries in the 1980s will probably also turn out to have weaknesses and strengths. But certainly growth and social equity in the 1980s were largely ignored as policy questions, or were only considered tangentially. Market pricing was the central concern. Hopefully the 1990s will witness a shift, and a return to growth and social equity as the key issues. At such time, late-industrializing countries might fruitfully rediscover the development literature of the 1950s, such as the work of Albert Hirschman mentioned above. Models that were in vogue in the 1950s, such as models of balanced or unbalanced growth may no longer be relevant. But what remains highly relevant is the preoccupation of development economists at the time with the dynamic driving industrialization ahead.

NOTES

1. For more information, see Amsden (1991).

2. Korea: The Bank of Korea, Monthly Bulletin, February 1990; Taiwan: Ministry of Economic Affairs, *Statistics on Overseas Chinese and Foreign Investment, Technical Cooperation, Outward Investment and Outward Technical Cooperation*, September 1989.

4

SOME COMMENTS ON THE ROLE OF THE PUBLIC SECTOR IN INDUSTRIALIZATION

John Weiss

INTRODUCTION

Thinking on the appropriate role for the public sector in industrial development has shifted considerably in the last thirty years. As Little (1982:54) puts it, in the early 1960s, "almost all LDC governments accepted the idea that they should play a large role in the economy, sometimes by extensive public ownership, but more usually by direct intervention in the private sector." This chapter discusses the state's role in industrialization, first as a producer, through investment in industrial enterprises, and second as an allocator of resources through planning and associated controls.

In the early 1960s, thinking on the state sector in the radical literature is brought out clearly in Sachs (1964). There, two distinct patterns of public sector involvement are contrasted, which, although they are named after particular countries, are meant to refer to a general pattern or trend rather than the actual experience of the countries concerned. On the one hand there is a broadly capitalist path, labeled the Japanese pattern, where

- the public sector is concerned chiefly with providing infrastructure
- public enterprises may be used to start up new industrial activities, but when profits are achieved these enterprises are sold off to the private sector
- the state encourages and promotes the domestic private sector and has an open–door policy toward foreign capital
- there is little direct economic planning.

This is in contrast with the socialist orientation of what is termed the Indian pattern, where

- the public sector has a key role in developing strategic industries, with a view to increasing the state's control over industry

● comprehensive economic planning is provided.

A surprising point from today's perspective is the confident assertion that not only is the Indian pattern more progressive socially, but that under similar conditions it should achieve a higher rate of economic growth (Sachs,1964: 81). This confidence illustrates the expectation in the early development literature that industrialization in many countries would have to be state led, given the weakness of the indigenous capitalist class. Currently, however, there is widespread disillusionment with the public sector as both a producer and allocator of resources. A recent World Development Report summarizes the consensus view on public enterprises when it states,

The performance of SOEs [state–owned enterprises] varies widely with and between countries, but their record has frequently been poor, particularly in developing countries. They have frequently failed to play the strategic role in industrialization that governments had hoped for. (World Bank, 1987: 66)

Authors writing from a variety of perspectives have concurred in the view that state enterprises in developing countries are often an economically inefficient use of government funds, whose main role is as a vehicle for the politics of patronage and patrimonialism (Sandbrook, 1988).

Similarly, there is general disillusionment with the effectiveness of planning and controls, with the recent abandonment of central planning in Eastern Europe and some socialist developing economies demonstrating the limitations of attempts to control resource allocation tightly in a macro planning system.

What Sachs labeled the Japanese pattern, of a minimalist or caretaker state, is now widely recommended as the most economically effective form of state involvement. This chapter acknowledges the validity of much of the available evidence, but argues that it is to concede far too much to conclude from the experience of the last thirty years that the state has no important role to play in future industrialization as either a producer or allocator of resources.

PUBLIC SECTOR INDUSTRIAL ACTIVITY

Generalization across the public sectors of different developing countries is difficult, since the scale of public sector industrial involvement varies considerably, as do the motives for locating industrial enterprises in the public sector. In some instances these may be explicitly political, where the enterprises arise from the confiscation or nationalization of private assets; in others the motives may be what can be termed developmental, with the state investing to supply goods whose capital intensity or risky nature make them unattractive to private investors. In other cases, natural resource-based industries, or those subject to significant economies of scale, may be in the public sector to avoid generation of monopoly profits in the private sector. However, from crosscountry comparisons there is a tendency for public enterprises to be in capital–intensive manufacturing branches, such as petroleum refining, chemicals, steel and transport equipment, probably reflecting the developmental motive for investment (Short, 1984: 125).

Table 4.1, taken from a combination of World Bank and IMF sources, gives an indication of the weight of public enterprises in manufacturing in the 1970s for a sample of developing countries. The table also gives the growth performance in total manufacturing output for the sample countries.

The crux of the case for public enterprise inefficiency is that the public sector is incapable of playing a genuine entrepreneurial role. Political and bureaucratic intervention, it is argued, limit the scope for strict commercial decision taking, and critically, since public enterprise rarely suffer from threat of takeover, the discipline of the market does not force state managers to maximize profits either in the short or long run. To this argument of nonmaximizing behavior is added a hypothesis on "crowding out," so that a large public sector, financed by taxation or borrowing from the private sector, competes with the latter for resources. Higher public sector industrial investment can thus be at the expense of private investment.

Much of the evidence of poor performance is based on financial results. For example, Short (1984) assembles comprehensive data on financial deficits in public enterprises for a large sample of countries. However, it is well known that financial indicators do not necessarily reflect economic efficiency in a real world in which taxes, subsidies, externalities, monopolies and other market disequilibria create a divergence between market prices and economic costs and benefits (Little & Mirrlees, 1974). Furthermore, poor financial performance in the public sector does not inevitably reflect managerial failings. Price setting or other aspects of operations, such as employment policy, may be controlled by governments in the interests of such objectives as price stability or job creation. Also, where the state has invested heavily in industries that are relatively unprofitable internationally, such as steel, fertilizers and transport equipment, this will bring down the average profitability of public industrial enterprises.

Nonetheless, financially unprofitable state enterprises must be a cause for concern, even if in economic terms their returns are positive. They can only continue as viable enterprises in the long run with either an improvement in their internal operations or a shift in government price policy that allows the enterprises wider economic impact to be reflected in their financial position. Financial losses are not only a drain on government revenue, but also a reason for a reduction in managerial autonomy, as governments may intervene more in the affairs of enterprises that rely on treasury financial support. Initial political interventions leading to financial losses that generated further interventions have been termed a vicious circle of reductions in managerial autonomy (Ayub & Hegstad, 1987: 88).

Table 4.1
Public Enterprises in Manufacturing in Selected Countries in the 1970s

	Share of Public Enterprise in Manufacturing[a] (%)		Total Manufacturing Expansion 1973–81 (Average Annual Growth %)[b]
Congo	15.7	(1976)	1.7
Ethiopia	60.9	(1979–80)	3.6
Ghana	32.9	(1970)	−0.5
Ivory Coast	25.2	(1979)	8.7
Kenya	13.1	(1970–73)	6.8
Senegal	19.0	(1974)	0.9
Sierra Leone	14.2	(1979)	0.2
Somalia	59.1	(1974–77)	2.9
Tanzania	37.9	(1974–77)	−2.8
Bangladesh	70.6	(1978)	7.9
Burma	56.2	(1980)	5.5
India	15.7	(1978)	5.1
S.Korea	14.9	(1974–77)	13.4
Pakistan	7.8	(1974–75)	6.5
Singapore	14.2	(1972)	10.0
Sri Lanka	33.5	(1974)	3.6
Thailand	5.2	(1970–73)	10.9
Bolivia	5.9	(1973–75)	4.7
Argentina	5.0	(1975)	−0.8
Mexico	30.0	(1975)	6.9
Brazil	19.4	(1975)	6.2
Panama	4.0	(1977)	2.7
Turkey	29.0	(1980)	3.4
Syria	58.0	(1977)	5.9
Tunisia	59.0	(1978–79)	10.9
Egypt	65.0	(1979)	8.2
Zambia	51.0	(1975)	−0.7

Source: Short, 1984, Table 2; World Bank, 1983, Figure 5.5; UNIDO, 1984, Table 1.
[a] Share of either manufacturing output or value added
[b] Annual growth of manufacturing value–added at 1975 prices

Strict comparisons between performance of public and private industrial enterprises must extend beyond financial indicators to look at measures of economic or technical efficiency, defined as the maximum output for a given set of inputs. For productivity comparisons to be valid, however, the public and private firms must be similar in their product quality, type of technology and level of output. Few existing empirical studies conduct this precise comparison, and a careful survey of the available evidence concludes that

There is no evidence of a statistically satisfactory kind to suggest that public enterprises in LDCs have a lower level of technical efficiency than private firms operating at the same scale of operations. . . . The comparative performance of public and private firms in LDCs is a relatively unexplained area once one moves away from simple profitability studies. There is some scattered evidence that productivity may be lower in the public sector, but public enterprises can be found at the top and the bottom of the range. (Millward, 1988: 157–58)

At the macroeconomic level, evidence on the link between size of the public sector and economic performance is again unclear. Several cross-sectional studies relating the share of the public enterprise output in GDP in the 1970s with growth of GDP have failed to reveal a statistically significant relationship (Cook & Kirkpatrick, 1988: 9–10). In another cross-country study, Landau (1986) found government consumption expenditure to be negatively associated with economic growth, although government investment had a weak positive effect, which he suggests reduces to zero once the repercussions of taxation and crowding out are incorporated. However, the significance of the crowding out hypothesis itself has been difficult to establish empirically (Blejer & Khan 1984).

These studies do not focus specifically on industry, and to test the role of the public enterprise in industrial development for this chapter, cross-sectional regressions have been run for 27 countries using the data from Table 4.1. However, there is no statistically significant relation between the share of public enterprise in manufacturing (given by its share in output or value added) and growth of the sector during 1973–81.

This lack of statistical relation between the level of public enterprise activity and industrial growth suggests the hypothesis that public sector inefficiency may be found in particular market environments, and that economies with inefficient public enterprise may also have inefficient private sectors. The argument that it is market environment, not ownership, that is the key to economic performance has been the most convincing rebuttal of the case for privatization in developing countries (Killick & Commander, 1988). This perspective helps make sense of the fact that, in a few of the economically more successful developing countries, public enterprises appear to have played an important role in industrialization. Korea, Brazil and Taiwan are economies where this role has been documented.

In Korea in the 1960s and 1970s, public enterprises dominated the more concentrated manufacturing branches such as petroleum refining, tobacco manufacture, fertilizers and railway equipment. Jones (1975) argues that at this time many public enterprises were operating at levels of efficiency comparable with those of private producers, and concludes that "by world standards for public enterprise the Korean sector does extremely well" (p. 205).

Trebat comes to similar conclusions regarding Brazil up to the late 1970s stating that

in my view it is not plausible to argue that Brazil's rate of economic growth over the last three or four decades could have been significantly higher had the government elected not to use public enterprise in many basic industries and instead waited for the appearance on the scene of private entrepreneurs. (1983: 238–39)

In Brazil, public industrial investment was concentrated in the capital-intensive basic industries of mining, steel and petrochemicals, with public enterprises in these branches generating positive and relatively high rates of profit from the mid–1960s to the late 1970s. In particular, the state petroleum company, PETROBRAS, adopted an aggressive entrepreneurial role creating subsidiaries in petrochemicals and fertilizers, in the face of reluctance by private domestic capital to move into these activities (Trebat, 1983: 51). Also, the process of technological learning and adaptation in the Brazilian steel public enterprise USIMINAS has been documented extensively, and has been cited as a successful example of the development of a domestic technological capability (Dahlman, 1984).

Finally, in Taiwan, despite the right-wing political regime, public enterprises have played a major role in manufacturing. Public investment was again concentrated in heavy industry, particularly petroleum and petrochemicals, steel, fertilizers, shipbuilding and heavy machinery. In 1980, seven of the 10 largest industrial concerns were public enterprises. For state industrial enterprises, profits were positive during the 1960s and 1970s, but probably well below those of the private sector. However, the active role of the state in direct investment has been interpreted as one of its most effective means of direct intervention to influence resource allocation (Wade, 1988: 47–48).

If one accepts the view that it is market environment, not ownership, that matters, the question of what creates an efficient market environment must still be answered. A common interpretation stresses the role of foreign trade, with competition from producers abroad in either domestic or export markets stimulating domestic enterprises to lower costs and improve quality. Much emphasis has been given to the effect of controls and taxes on trade, in stifling foreign competition and creating trade distortions, in the sense of deviations of relative domestic prices from those prevailing on the world market (World Bank, 1983). However, there is no direct correlation between public industrial ownership and degree of trade distortion for industrial goods, so that an interpretation of import-substitution industrialization as inevitably involving a heavy public sector involvement is quite misleading. Using the effective rate of protection on

Table 4.2

Effective Rate of Protection for Manufacturing in Selected Countries in the 1970s

	ERP (%)		ERP (%)
Ethiopia	125	Bangladesh	144
Kenya	92	India	100
Tanzania	116	Pakistan	181
Ghana	105	Sri Lanka	118
Ivory Coast	62	Egypt	42
Senegal	70	Turkey	75
Nigeria	40	Argentina[a]	38–97
S.Korea	32	Brazil	46
Thailand[a]	37–70	Bolivia	54

Source: Agarwala (1983), Table 1.

[a] Two estimates for different years.

manufacturing (ERP) as a measure of trade distortion, Table 4.2 reports estimates of ERP for a sample of countries in the 1970s. There is a significant negative relation between level of ERP and industrial growth for countries in the sample.[1] However, the level of public ownership is not correlated with the level of trade distortion, which supports the earlier result that the level of public ownership in industry does not explain industrial performance.

Competition can arise from internal as well as external pressures. The key feature of competition can be seen as capital mobility, in response to perceived rates of profit, rather than the absolute number or size of firms in a market (Jenkins, 1987: 45–46). This emphasis on capital mobility allows markets dominated by a few firms to be classed as competitive even though the abstract conditions of perfect competition, with large numbers of buyers and sellers who are price takers, plainly do not exist. For domestic competition to create pressure for improved public enterprise efficiency requires that capital is sufficiently mobile for public enterprise to both diversify into new activities and to feel the threat of the potential entry of other producers into its established markets. Behavior of this type requires both nonmonopoly positions for public enterprise and a significant degree of autonomy from ministerial or civil service control. There is some evidence to support the view that managerial autonomy improves performance; for example, for the 1970s the success of Brazilian state enterprise, subject only to loose controls, has been contrasted with the poor performance of state enterprises in Ghana, where political intervention was much more common (Ayub & Hegstad, 1987: 99).

STATE CONTROL OVER RESOURCE ALLOCATION

Industrialization in the majority of developing countries has been associated with an interventionist state—with governments trying to determine resource allocation through various direct controls on prices, investment and foreign trade, often combined with some form of macroeconomic planning. These interventions have been heavily criticized for distorting relative prices and curbing private sector initiatives, while macro planning is seen as largely an irrelevance, with relatively sophisticated plans built on weak data bases. Little (1982:57), for example, comments caustically that

They [macro planners] were armed with their Harrod/Domar equations and with linear programming, and they demanded input-output tables which albeit full of holes, were sometimes supplied. With these aids they concocted supposedly consistent plans of mainly empty boxes.

The critique of the interventionist state rests on both pragmatic and theoretical arguments. At the pragmatic level, the state is seen as overstretched, with a bureaucracy of limited technical skills, attempting to control economies where many key variables are either given externally (particularly prices for exports and imports), or derived from decisions of large numbers of private producers (particularly subsistence farmers) that are difficult to influence with conventional economic instruments. In this view, key decisions on directly productive activities should be left to individual enterprise managers (either private or public), who will inevitably be better informed than state bureaucrats.

This view is backed by theoretical arguments on the optimality of decisions taken by atomistic enterprises. Here, the underlying model is that of perfect competition, where under the set of familiar assumptions, economic efficiency can be achieved. The argument is not that this model is an accurate reflection of the real world, but that in practice most markets work reasonably well, in the sense that supply and demand respond fairly promptly to price changes, and price movements tend toward an equilibrium position (Little, 1982: 25). So-called market failures, whether arising from externalities, monopolies or other real-world conditions, are acknowledged, but the superior solution to the problems they pose is seen as a set of taxes and subsidies, rather than more direct interventions. The advantage of the tax-subsidy solution is that, in theory, by-product distortions can be minimized (Corden, 1974). Nonetheless, once real world "second–best" conditions are allowed for, the case for markets over direct controls becomes an empirical one. The superiority of tax-subsidy interventions operating through the price system must be demonstrated, not simply asserted (Cody, Kitchen & Weiss, 1990).

Given this set of arguments, what is left of the case for an active government industrial policy? What must be conceded initially is that macro planning as an exercise in both forecasting and control has generally proved very disappointing in both capitalist and socialist contexts. In capitalist developing economies, even those with a significant public sector, plans have generally had relatively little influence over enterprise decisions, with most comparisons of targets and actuals revealing major discrepancies. Further, in the 1980s, in many countries the focus of economic policy shifted toward short-run issues of macro balance, leading to a new emphasis on planning. Instead of the familiar parameters, such as capital-output ratios, savings rates and input-output coefficients, planners must now focus on short-run movement of such variables as the real exchange rate, tax revenue or the money supply, that have a key role in the new open-economy macroeconomics (Dornbusch, 1980).

In socialist developing economies, the role and perception of planning have also shifted in the last ten years or so. The difficulties of operating a tight centralized system with industrial enterprises given physical output targets and directions to supply to particular users, have been recognized in developing economies as well as in Eastern Europe. The potential role of market allocation in socialist economies, particularly where central planning can be seen as premature given the low level of development of the productive forces of the economy, is stressed increasingly (Fitzgerald, 1988). China has introduced greater use of the market in a context still determined by central plan priorities—a so-called "guided market system" (White & Wade, 1988). Other socialist developing economies have moved considerably further. Mozambique, for example, is a case of a nominally socialist government abandoning central planning totally by giving industrial enterprises freedom to set their own production targets and prices, subject only to nominal ex-post government approval (Ottoway, 1988).

Some form of macro planning, both short and longer term, should remain of importance to most developing countries, both to identify macroeconomic imbalances and to set the overall framework within which enterprise decisions are made. However, the basic difficulty, and often the undesirability, of attempting to set and implement very detailed targets at the subsector and enterprise level must be acknowledged.

Nonetheless, if the record of macro planning in the developing world is poor, there is evidence that selective and well thought-out government interventions, not based on a consistent planning framework, in some contexts have been highly effective in stimulating industrial activity. Most of the evidence on this comes from Japan in the 1950s and 1960s (Weiss, 1986), and South Korea and Taiwan in the 1960s and 1970s (Luedde-Neurath, 1988; Wade, 1988). The essential point is that in these cases a committed nationalist bureaucracy, operating with considerable autonomy from interest groups, intervened in a variety of ways to create a resource allocation that differed from what would have resulted from individual enterprise decisions expressed through the market. The competitive environment necessary for enterprise efficiency was maintained through a combination of internal competition between domestic enterprises, particularly important in Japan, and the pressures of foreign trade competition in export markets.

Selective government interventions included:

1. Promotion, via credit allocation or tariff protection of what were seen as key industries, on the basis of their productivity potential or income elasticity of demand

2. Attempts to avoid the costs of "excessive competition" by restricting entry of new firms to particular industries and by encouraging mergers and rationalizations

3. Screening of imports of foreign technology and restricting activities of foreign investors to protect their domestic competitors

4. Public investment in priority areas, where private capital was unwilling to enter

A key feature of this experience was that direct controls, whether the use of import or investment licensing, credit allocation or export targets, were generally backed by a set of complementary price policies. For example, real exchange rates were set at levels that did not discourage exports, and priority activities received selective tariff incentives as infant industries. Further, although the policies used were clearly interventionist, the worst excesses of distortions found elsewhere were not present in these economies.

CONCLUSIONS

A strong and effective government can be seen as an essential requirement for long-run economic development. However, this conclusion can be interpreted in different ways as far as the scale and form of public sector involvement in industry are concerned. The position argued here is that public industrial enterprise must not be seen as inevitably inefficient, since there is evidence that under certain market environments they can achieve levels of efficiency broadly comparable with those of the private sector.

However, the case for public investment is stronger than this. The assumption of the early development economists that state industrial investment will have a key role in many economies, due to the weakness of the private sector, retains validity in the 1990s. Industrialization as a historical process requires entrepreneurial groups. A private, indigenous capitalist class exists in developing countries, and has grown considerably stronger in the last thirty years. However, in many economies it is rarely able or willing to invest, on its own, in capital-intensive, high-risk industries. Some form of partnership with either the state or foreign investors will be necessary to bring private capital to these industries.

However, if the economy or the industry is not attractive to foreign capital, the state will have to be the main partner for the private sector. In addition, at any point in time there will be some branches of industry in need of restructuring. In the past in many countries enterprises in these branches have been taken into the public sector rather than face closures and severe job losses. State guidance of industrial restructuring will remain an important part of industrial policy, and may continue to require public ownership, as well as interventions, to promote resource reallocation.

In terms of government interventions to influence resource allocation, it has been argued here that not all such interventions have had negative results. It is naive to suggest that the experience of Korea and Taiwan with selective interventions provides a simple interventionist model for others to copy. However it is important to stress that decisions on such issues as the structure of industry, the distribution of protection and the role of foreign investment and technology have a long-run dimension that should be a primary concern of governments. The available evidence does not support the view that this concern should be abandoned as a result of an intellectual enthusiasm for noninterventionism.

Finally, the political economy of public sector activities must not be forgotten. Public enterprise must not be seen in isolation from class and interest groups in an economy. Economies with a heavy public enterprise involvement and tight controls over the private sector (Sachs's Indian pattern) have been described as intermediate regimes (Kalecki, 1976). This is a political regime based on an alliance of state functionaries and lower income groups such as small domestic capitalists and peasants. Large domestic and foreign capitalists have only a minor influence in the alliance. However, such regimes can be seen as transitory, since if the state sector generates conditions for private accumulation, a large-scale domestic capitalist sector can emerge. Under these circumstances it may become difficult to keep public enterprise managers in their role as state entrepreneurs in the face of higher income opportunities outside the state sector, and there may be pressure for the sale of state industrial assets to transfer their profitability to the private sector. Successful state-led industrialization can thus create conditions for the emergence of Sachs's Japanese pattern. On the other hand, economic failure of intermediate regimes also threatens the alliance on which they are based. Economic failure can lead to the emergence of other alliances dominated by either large domestic and foreign capitalists or by workers and peasants. Either outcome will change the nature of the regime, the former shifting it to the right toward the Japanese pattern, and the latter to the left toward a form of socialism.

Public enterprise will continue to operate under differing political regimes. The distinction between the Japanese and the Indian patterns is a useful reminder that it can play different roles under different circumstances. Although the economic superiority of the former pattern is now widely argued, one should not forget the potentially important developmental role for state economic activity both in terms of direct investment and various interventions. The case for private sector, market–based development is not as persuasive as some discussions might imply.

NOTE

1. Cross–sectional regression analysis for the 18 countries gives the relation:

$$g = 9.5518 - 0.0483 * ERP$$
$$(2.02)$$
$$R^2 = 0.20$$

t ratio is in brackets and is significant at the 5 percent level. g is average annual real growth of manufacturing, 1973–81 from Table 4.1. ERP is effective rate of protection on manufacturing from Table 4.2.

5

The Stabilization and Structural Adjustment Program and the Process of Turkish Industrialization: Main Policies and Their Impact

Fikret Şenses

INTRODUCTION

The stabilization and structural adjustment program (SSAP) introduced in Turkey in January 1980 has represented a radical transformation of economic policies with far-reaching effects throughout the economy. The overriding objective of the program, which was implemented under IMF-World Bank auspices, was to change the system of incentives away from archetypal import substitution under state direction toward export orientation with an overall emphasis on market-oriented policies.

This chapter examines the interaction of this program with the process of Turkish industrialization. For a fuller understanding of the policy transformation since 1980, the first section provides a brief sketch of trade and industrialization policies before 1980 and the ensuing pattern of industrial growth, with emphasis on the 1970s. The second section outlines the main features of SSAP, such as trade and financial liberalization that have a special bearing on the industrialization process. The third section assesses the impact of the changes in the economic policy framework on the structure and pattern of industrialization, with special reference to such key issues as exports, investment and employment. Finally, section four presents a summary and draws conclusions for the chapter.

TRADE AND INDUSTRIALIZATION POLICIES BEFORE 1980 AND THEIR IMPACT—AN OVERVIEW

As a reflection of their strong commitment to rapid growth and industrialization, successive Turkish governments until 1980 took a strongly interventionist stance in devising trade and industrialization policies. The form of interventionism initially involved providing substantial incentives to create an indigenous entrepreneurial class in the 1920s, which was followed by the state itself taking over this role in the early 1930s through the creation of a number of state enterprises in a variety of manufacturing activities. State involvement in the industrialization process continued after the emergence of private industrial activity under multiparty democracy which was introduced in 1946. If anything, the introduction of comprehensive central planning in 1960 increased the degree of state intervention, as the State Planning Organization, apart from its direct control over key decisions of State Economic Enterprises, was in a position to guide the course of private sector activity.

The increased liberalism of political life under a new Constitution in 1961 led Turkish governments to embrace a populist approach to broaden their political base among the various claimants to political power, headed by trade unions and agricultural producers. This reinforced the broad consensus of various societal forces over industrialization which, by generating rapid growth, was expected to meet popular demands for employment and higher standards of living. It was therefore no coincidence that the series of coalition governments that came to power in Turkey in the 1970s were also adamant in their commitment to growth and industrialization.

Except for the 1950–53 and 1970–73 periods, during which there were short-lived attempts at foreign trade liberalization, trade and industrialization policies until 1980 were characterized by import-substituting industrialization under heavy protection. The ISI process in Turkey bore a close resemblance to that in other developing countries in terms of its pattern as well as its major impact. Overvalued exchange rates, quantitative restrictions and direct prohibitions of imports, bilateral trade, a strict system of exchange control, high tariffs and guarantee deposits on imports, together with a variety of tax and credit incentives for manufacturing investment, were used as the main tools of trade and industrialization policy. Other forms of state intervention, such as the maintenance of negative real rates of interest, the tendency to control the prices of SEEs to assist other sectors and the use of these enterprises as the "employer of last resort," were instrumental in reinforcing this pattern.

ISI after the early 1960s envisaged the deepening of the industrial base through vertical integration and extension of the industrialization process beyond light consumer goods. This involved a shift toward the production of consumer durables in the early 1960s and intermediate and capital goods thereafter. A notable feature of the industrialization process was the increase in public sector activity, particularly in such relatively capital-intensive branches as petrochemicals, basic metals, fertilizers and paper. This increase, in itself, which in itself acted as an effective instrument of structural change within this sector. The rapid increase in manufacturing investment in the 1970s was facilitated by the availability of sizable foreign exchange resources arising from the favorable response of exports and emigrant workers' remittances to the 1970 devaluation and, more significantly, by heavy short-term borrowing from the buoyant international financial markets.

The rapid growth in manufacturing output under this pattern of industrialization, which averaged 7.5 percent per annum during 1965–80, was responsible in establishing a large and diversified industrial base. This was accompanied by a rise in the share of manufacturing in GDP from 14.1 percent in 1963 to 19.1 percent in 1979 and considerable change in the structure of manufacturing value added and employment away from consumer goods toward intermediate and capital goods. As a reflection of this impressive growth performance, Turkey ranked fifth in 1984 among developing countries (behind China, Brazil, Mexico, India and South Korea) in terms of the size of manufacturing value added. The growth in manufacturing production relied on the creation of new capacities in both the private and public sectors and was based largely on the expansion of domestic demand. (For more details, see Şenses, 1989b.)

Despite this impressive growth performance, a number of problems became increasingly apparent in the second half of the 1970s, which in the final analysis rendered this pattern of industrialization nonsustainable. These problems can be briefly sketched under three main headings. First, extensive protection over a long period of time was instrumental in the creation of substantial rents[1] and the emergence of a highly inefficient industrial structure. The effective rate of protection for the manufacturing sector as a whole was estimated at 314 percent in 1968, with a great deal of variation among various manufacturing activities. (See Şenses, 1990b for details.) Despite the implementation of various export promotion schemes, after 1963, industrial trade strategy remained heavily biased against exports. As a result, exports, which were dominated by a handful of agricultural commodities, in 1978 accounted for only 4.5 percent of GNP, which was far below cross-country norms. Second, relative factor prices were highly distorted, thanks to the maintenance over long periods of time of overvalued exchange rates and severely negative real rates of interest under deep financial repression.[2] Real wages, on the other hand, exhibited a strong upward trend as a reflection of populist policies yielding to the demands of a growing and increasingly militant labor movement. These, together with the shift of the pattern of import substitution toward intermediate and capital goods, were instrumental in increasing the incremental capital output ratio, in the manufacturing sector from 1.6 during 1963–67 to 2.4 in 1968–72 and to 4.7 in 1973–77 (see Şenses, 1990a: 10). As a result, there was little growth in employment in this sector, which increased from 0.4 million in 1963 to only 1.0 million in 1980.

Third, pushing the pace of industrialization too far beyond the available resources and the persistence of populist policies in the face of severe external shocks led to the emergence of macroeconomic instability of massive proportions in the late 1970s. The short-term credits obtained from international financial markets resulted in the deterioration of external debt indicators and the complete loss of international creditworthiness. In the face of constrained import capacity, growing dependence of production and new investment in the manufacturing sector on imports led to the emergence of severe balance of payments difficulties, culminating in the suspension of transfers abroad by the Central Bank in February 1977. Growing public sector deficits and import shortages, on the other hand, were largely responsible for the acceleration of inflation from an average annual rate of 17.9 percent during 1974–77 to a massive 69.0 percent during 1978–80.[3] As capacity utilization rates declined sharply in the face of import shortages, there was a sharp deterioration in investment and growth performance in the manufacturing sector. The rate of growth of manufacturing investment declined from an average annual rate of 7.5 percent during 1963–77 to -10.2 percent during 1977–80. Similarly, the rate of growth of manufacturing output, which averaged 14.2 percent per annum during 1973–77, averaged -0.6 percent during 1978–80.

SSAP AND THE NEW POLICY ENVIRONMENT FOR INDUSTRIALIZATION

SSAP was introduced in January 1980 against the background of a great deal of domestic political instability, initially as a short-term stabilization program under IMF auspices to cope with galloping inflation and severe balance of payments difficulties. Under the guidance of the World Bank it was soon transformed to incorporate measures for structural adjustment, which over time increased in prominence. In fact, the main phases of economic policies under SSAP were to a large extent determined by the degree of influence of these two institutions in shaping domestic economic policies as well as developments in the domestic political environment.

It is possible to divide the 1980s into two broad phases, roughly separated by the general elections in November 1987. As the opposition to SSAP in the Parliament and from different sections of the population (most notably the trade unions) was gaining momentum, the military took over in September 1980 to deal with domestic political instability, but kept the SSAP intact. This ensured that SSAP was implemented without any significant opposition in its crucial early years. Although the military regime formally ended in November 1983, the restrictions imposed during this period meant that there was no significant organized challenge to SSAP during the first phase. It was not surprising, therefore, that the main policies of SSAP were implemented during this phase by a strong team of technocrats and were guided by a three-year stand-by agreement with the IMF (1980–83) and five successive Structural Adjustment Loans (1980–84), followed by three Sectoral Adjustment Loans from the World Bank. (Conway, 1992: 139) The special relations with the two institutions were reflected by the inflow of substantial resources under these agreements and Turkey's willingness to comply with their provisions with extremely "low slippage" (see Kirkpatrick & Öniş, 1991).

The second phase represented a sharp contrast to the first, as the liberalization of political life elevated distributional issues to the foreground. This meant SSAP was strongly challenged by sections of the population that lost out heavily during the first phase, and the government yielded to these pressures. Without the straitjacket imposed by IMF and World Bank conditionality, these pressures, in the face of growth-oriented policies that had commenced a few years earlier, led to a substantial rise in public sector deficits, inflation and domestic and external indebtedness (Table 5.1). Parallel to these developments, the second phase was also characterized by a number of policy reversals, most notably in exchange rate, wages and interest rates.

Against this background, SSAP was primarily aimed at reducing the role of the state in the industrialization process and policy realignment in both domestic factor markets and the foreign trade regime.

Shifts in Relative Prices and Foreign Trade Liberalization

A key element of SSAP was the move toward a more flexible interest rate and exchange rate policy. In July 1980, interest rates were deregulated. Although in Turkey's oligopolistic banking sector this deregulation initially resulted in the agreement of the largest commercial banks on a common interest rate policy, the overall result was a big increase in both lending and borrowing rates. In 1981, real interest rates became positive for the first time since the early 1970s. Despite deregulation, the Central Bank in practice has found it necessary to keep a close eye on interest rate determination by commercial banks. In February 1988 commercial banks were authorized to set interest rates freely, but subject to the maximum rates determined by the Central Bank. The overall trend toward high real rates of interest was accompanied by the granting of subsidized rates to a variety of activities. It has been estimated, for example, that about one-half of total lending by the banking system was at varied preferential rates with state economic enterprises, agriculture, craft businesses, small businesses, and investors with investment promotion certificates as well as exporters among the main beneficiaries. (See Şenses, 1990a for details.)

Exchange rate policy exhibited similar trends toward increased flexibility under strong guidance by the Central Bank and an overall tendency for depreciation of the lira in real terms. The sharp devaluation in January 1980 by 48.6 percent was followed in May 1981 by the adoption of a policy of daily adjustments to the exchange rate on the basis of trends in international financial markets and the differential inflation rate between Turkey and its main trading partners. In practice, the policy was based on continual real effective depreciation of the lira, with the rate of depreciation varying from one year to another according to the targets set

Table 5.1
Main Economic Indicators in Turkey, 1980–90

	GNP Growth (1)[a]	Manufac-turing Growth (2)	Exports (3)	Imports (4)	Inflation Rate[b] (5)	PSBR[c] GNP (6)
1980	-1.1	-6.4	2.9	7.9	107.2	-10.5
1981	4.1	9.5	4.7	8.9	36.8	-4.5
1982	4.5	5.4	5.7	8.8	27.0	-4.3
1983	3.3	8.7	5.7	9.2	30.5	-6.0
1984	5.9	10.2	7.1	10.8	50.3	-6.5
1985	5.1	5.5	8.0	11.6	43.2	-4.6
1986	8.1	9.6	7.5	11.2	29.6	-4.7
1987	7.5	9.9	10.2	14.3	32.0	-7.8
1988	3.6	1.8	11.7	14.3	68.3	-6.2
1989	1.9	3.2	11.6	15.8	69.6	-7.2
1990	9.2	10.0	13.0	22.3	52.3	-10.2

Source: Central Bank of Turkey, Annual Report, Various issues; OECD, Economic Surveys, Turkey, various issues.
[a] Percent for all columns except cols. 3–4, which are in billion dollars
[b] Based on wholesale prices, 1981=100, 1981 weights for 1980–89 and 1987=100, 1987 weights for 1990
[c] Public sector borrowing requirement

by the Central Bank. During the period from the end of 1979 to the end of 1988, the real effective rate of depreciation of the lira was estimated at 55 percent, corresponding to an average annual rate of depreciation of 6.1 percent (Aşıkoğlu, 1992: 106).

SSAP was implemented against the background of a highly restrictive environment for organized labor. The military takeover in September 1980 saw the banning of all trade union activity, the suspension of free collective bargaining and strike activity, the imprisonment of a large number of trade union leaders and the introduction of new labor legislation aimed at curbing the power of trade unions in wage determination. During military rule, wages were determined by the High Arbitration Council, which granted wage increases on the basis of projected inflation rates that somehow consistently turned out to be a gross underestimate of the actual rate. Even after the return to free collective bargaining in 1984, workers demands for higher wages were strongly discouraged by a highly bureaucratized process of collective bargaining and strike procedure. The available data on wages, which admittedly are surrounded by a number of conceptual and statistical difficulties, indicate a sharp fall in real wages during the 1980–88 period. The index of real wages and real labor costs declined from 100.0 in 1980 to 89.3 and 65.8 respectively in 1988 (Şenses, 1992).

It seems that policy makers who had been primarily concerned with attaining external equilibrium in the first place became increasingly concerned with the possible inflationary effects of rapid exchange rate depreciation and high real rates of interest, and showed a tendency to reverse their earlier policies. As a part of the government's antiinflationary stance, real rates of interest were allowed to turn negative, falling to -7.6 percent in 1988 and -5.2 percent in 1990. The formation of a foreign exchange market in August 1988 with the participation of the Central Bank and commercial banks notwithstanding, there was continued government intervention into the exchange rate determination process (Aşıkoğlu, 1992: 106). Exchange rate appreciation, which started in the final quarter of 1988 continued until 1991, represented a cumulative average annual real rate of appreciation of more than 20 percent during 1989–90. (OECD, 1992: 29). Similarly, there was a sharp increase in real wages in 1989 and 1990, rising by 31.3 percent and 16.4 percent in the private sector and by 38.7 percent and 25.9 percent in the public sector (OECD, 1992: 25). The primary factor behind the rise in real wages was trade union pressure as shaped by changes in the political climate. It seems that wage increases in 1989 and 1990 were defensive in nature and served the purpose of bringing real wages back to 1980 levels.[4]

One of the chief objectives of SSAP was to change the system of incentives toward exports through decisive moves in the direction of trade liberalization. Liberalization attempts represented a gradual process, entailing a move from quantitative restrictions to price measures. Certain significant measures such as the abolition of quotas in 1981 notwithstanding, the major steps in this direction were taken after December 1983. The substantial relaxation of exchange control and the lifting of the ban on the importation of all items (with only several exceptions) on that date were followed by a reduction in the number of items subject to approval before importation. As a result of the substantial steps taken toward trade liberalization, imports in 1990 were subject only to price measures (Togan, 1992). The removal of quantitative restrictions on imports was accompanied by successive tariff revisions after 1984, with generally lower rates imposed in the major tariff revisions in 1984 and 1989. Apart from the substantial depreciation of the lira, efforts to shift the system of incentives toward exports also involved the provision of export incentives through tax rebates, export credits at preferential rates of interest and duty free imports. The total subsidy rate implicit in these incentives as a whole was estimated at 23.4 percent in 1983 (see Şenses, 1990a). Institutional reform, with the task of improving administrative efficiency and informing exporters about external market opportunities, was accompanied by the strong encouragement given for the consolidation of exporting firms. These so-called foreign trade companies, which were designed to "exploit economies of scale, especially in marketing" and "serve as key intermediary to small scale exporters" accounted for about one-half of total exports by the second half of the 1980s (Öniş, 1991: 31). Even a cursory examination of information available on export incentives indicates that they emphasized manufacturing branches with above-average domestic resource costs (see Şenses, 1989b). There was a general escalation of tax rebates from labor- and resource-intensive activities to capital-intensive intermediate goods and skill-intensive capital goods (Celasun, 1991: 19).

Export promotion schemes, while providing substantial incentives for exporters, were also responsible for the creation of new distortions. The extent of state intervention through export incentive schemes was so large that it probably led to much time and effort devoted to obtaining export incentives. Exporters responded to these incentives with such zest that some resorted to illegal activities by overstating their export receipts to take advantage of the generous tax rebate scheme. The so-called fictitious exports were estimated to account for 12.6 percent of total exports to OECD countries during 1981–85 (see Şenses, 1990b).

In compliance with the GATT regulations, tax rebate rates were gradually lowered after the mid-1980s, leading to their eventual abolition at the beginning of 1989. After 1989, export incentives became less generous, with the provision of credits at preferential rates of interest and subsidies for key inputs such as energy acting as the main incentives for exporters. As expected, the changes in the system of export incentives and the considerable overvaluation of the lira during 1988–90 led to a fall in the effective exchange rate for exports during this period. Exporters were therefore hard pressed to maintain their price competitiveness in international markets and began digging into their profit margins (OECD, 1992: 29–31).[5]

Empirical studies on the extent and structure of protection in the manufacturing sector have revealed that, although protection was still high by the standards of countries with liberal foreign trade policies, there was a substantial reduction in the level of both nominal and effective rates of protection as well as their variation among different manufacturing branches (Togan, 1992). Parallel to the reduction in rates of protection was an overall decline in the bias against exports during the 1980s as a whole.

In addition to the shift of trade incentives toward export orientation, there was a sharp increase in the number of investment certificates, which increased from a total of 4,802 during 1968–80 to around 25,000 during 1981–90. The share of manufacturing (in investments benefiting from the incentives granted through these certificates) declined from 90.1 percent in 1979 to 26.0 percent in 1983 and 40.3 percent in 1987 and 1988 (Güvemli, 1992: 5). Although the share of manufacturing increased further to 48.3 percent in 1989 and as high as 68.9 percent in 1990, the sectoral distribution of investment certificates within manufacturing represented a move away from intermediate and investment goods toward export-oriented consumer goods such as textiles and clothing, which on average accounted for 45.3 percent of the total during 1988–90.

Overall Neglect of Industrialization

There has been a clear neglect of industrialization under SSAP, as evidenced also from the declared objective of the government to withdraw from direct manufacturing activity. This withdrawal was based primarily on the sharp reduction in public investment in the manufacturing sector as an integral part of the broader privatization objective. The government was fully committed to privatization, envisaging the gradual transfer of State Economic Enterprises into private ownership. The progress in this sphere in the first phase was not, however, as rapid as initially envisaged, not least because public opinion at large was opposed to such a move. Although more decisive moves in this direction came later in the second phase, some major steps were taken in the first phase, which in the final analysis were instrumental in laying the foundations for a strong proprivatization constituency.

The deregulation of SEE prices right at the outset was the first major step in this direction. Through their increased autonomy in setting their prices, the SEEs were able to improve their financial position without resorting to funds from the Central Bank and central budget. The fact that SEEs were operating in highly monopolistic and oligopolistic markets enabled them to pass increased costs on to prices without facing the need to increase their productivity and efficiency. The second major step in the same direction was the cutback of the public investment program in 1981–82, reflecting World Bank influence through Structural Adjustment Loans. Although investment in certain intermediate goods such as petrochemicals, paper, and iron and steel, which had reached fairly advanced stages by then, were completed as planned, projects in engineering industries that were at a preliminary stage were axed (Türel, 1993). This situation was further aggravated in subsequent years as public investments increasingly shifted to such activities as transport, energy and communications, with investment in manufacturing relegated very much to the background. The share of manufacturing in total fixed investment by the public sector declined from 23.8 percent in 1973 and 20.7 percent in 1978 to 18.7 percent in 1984 and only 4.5 percent in 1990 (Table 5.2). This was reflected in the severe decline in the share of public sector manufacturing investment in total fixed investment, falling from 12 percent at the end of the 1970s to 7.3 percent in 1985, 5.7 percent in 1986, and 3.3 percent in 1987.[6]

The poor record of public sector investment in the manufacturing sector can be linked to the sharp increase in public sector deficits after the mid-1980s, which saw public sector borrowing requirement (PSBR) as a percentage of GNP rise from 4.7 percent in 1986 to 10.5 percent in 1990 (Table 5.1). Parallel to the increased external indebtedness of SEEs and the increased reliance on bond

Table 5.2
Sectoral Distribution of Gross Fixed Investment, 1973–90
(Selected Years, Percentage Share in Current Price Values)

	1973	1978	1980	1984	1987	1990
Gross Fixed Investment						
Public Sector						
Agriculture	9.3	10.4	7.0	8.8	9.1	9.5
Manufacturing	23.8	20.7	28.9	18.7	6.3	4.5
Energy	13.1	18.6	24.4	25.9	24.3	21.4
Education	7.2	4.8	3.6	3.3	4.6	7.0
Transportation	26.4	23.9	18.2	22.5	32.7	34.1
Other	20.2	21.6	17.9	20.8	23.0	23.5
Total	100.0	100.0	100.0	100.0	100.0	100.0
	(46.9)	(50.6)	(56.0)	(60.0)	(53.6)	(43.5)
Private Sector						
Agriculture	14.3	11.5	8.2	13.3	6.6	4.8
Manufacturing	33.9	29.9	24.6	27.6	26.3	27.5
Transportation	12.6	22.6	12.1	20.1	12.4	12.7
Tourism	1.9	1.0	0.6	1.2	3.8	6.2
Housing	33.0	31.5	49.3	30.8	43.7	41.1
Other	4.3	3.5	5.2	7.0	7.2	7.7
Total	100.0	100.0	100.0	100.0	100.0	100.0
	(53.1)	(49.4)	(44.0)	(40.0)	(46.4)	(56.5)

Source: State Planning Organization, *Main Economic Indicators (1973–81)*, Ankara, April 1981, and Central Bank, *Annual Report*, various issues for other years.

financing of these deficits from the private sector at high interest rates after 1988, there was a big rise in the debt service burden of the public sector in general. A major contributor to the PSBR was the sharp increase in SEE deficits, which as a percentage of GNP rose from 3.4 percent in 1986 to 5.3 percent in 1990 (OECD, 1992: 38).

Apart from increased wage payments after 1988, there were at least three other factors that contributed to the worsening financial position of the SEEs. The first was related to increased government intervention in the late 1980s, which was especially strong around local and general elections and involved most notably the timing, if not the magnitude, of price increases and employment levels of these enterprises. Not only were price hikes delayed before elections, there was also a reversal of the policy of freezing SEE employment. For example, while the index of SEE employment (1979 = 100) rose to 127.9 in 1989, most of the increase during this period took place before 1984, reflecting the big increase in the number of workers in 1984 after the 1983 general elections. The index rose only slightly during 1984–89, rising from 100 in 1984 to only 102.4 in 1989. With the onset of early general elections in 1991, however, the upper limits for new employment creation in these enterprises were exceeded by a big margin, both before and after the election.[7]

The second factor was related to the neglect of productivity and efficiency issues surrounding these enterprises despite their urgent need for restructuring in the face of their aging capital stock. Although public enterprise reform, which had come on to the agenda on several occasions in the pre-1980 period, resurfaced in the early 1980s, not much progress was made in this sphere.

Finally, the third factor contributing to the deterioration of the financial position of SEEs can be traced to the new policy environment facing these enterprises, especially after the mid-1980s. SEEs in Turkey, unlike their counterparts in other OECD countries, have a strong presence in the manufacturing sector. Manufacturing SEEs specialize heavily in the production of intermediate goods and to a lesser extent in consumer goods, and operate in monopolistic and oligopolistic markets facing little competition from the private sector (OECD, 1992: 88). Although the SEEs retained some of their privileges, such as their external debt being guaranteed by the government, by the end of 1984 they lost all their tax, tariff and credit preferences[8] and were required to borrow at market interest rates. In accordance with the government's aim to subject these enterprises to increased competition, state monopolies in tea and tobacco were abolished in 1985 (Şenses, 1991: 217). Furthermore, as they were faced with increased import competition, the effective rate of protection for SEEs in the manufacturing sector (excluding food, beverages and tobacco) declined from 85 percent in 1983 to 55 percent in 1989 (OECD, 1992: 92). The falling market shares and capital utilization rates in the face of increased external competition led to higher costs, especially in industries with "scale sensitive costs like chemicals, basic metals and capital goods" (OECD, 1992: 95). With early calls for reform and restructuring not going any further than sheer rhetoric, the deterioration of the financial position of these enterprises and the burden it imposed on public finances provided the main rationale for shifting public opinion in favor of privatization.

The fact that no significant steps were taken toward privatization until the late 1980s was due less to a lack of commitment by the government than to political shrewdness to contain possible opposition early in the program. Instead, the introduction of ingenious devices such as the sale of revenue-sharing certificates of certain public infrastructural facilities to the public during 1984–86 can be seen as part of the government's preparatory work in establishing a proprivatization constituency in a country with a deep-seated tradition of state involvement in economic life. The first major case of privatization, involving the sale of a part of public sector shares in a telecommunications company, took place in February

1988, shortly after the government received a fresh mandate from the public following the November 1987 elections. By the end of 1990, privatization in the manufacturing sector was confined to several cases involving mainly minority government holdings in private firms and subsidiaries, despite the increased determination of the government to carry out a major privatization drive. The major constraints facing the government in this respect were the underdeveloped state of the capital market and the mounting challenge of main opposition parties, especially after the sale of public sector enterprises to foreigners came on the agenda in 1988.

The withdrawal of the state from the industrialization process with an overall emphasis on privatization was evident also from the wholehearted support extended to foreign direct investment. In sharp contrast to policies before 1980, FDI policy became increasingly more liberal under SSAP, especially after 1984. The reorganization of the bureaucratic mechanism in 1984 to expedite the decision-making process was followed in 1985 by the decision to establish two free trade zones, which commenced operations in 1987. This culminated in 1986 with the decision (in accordance with OECD norms) to eliminate all discriminatory clauses against FDI (including profit transfers abroad) and to allow 100 percent foreign ownership for all FDI in all sectors (see Erdilek, 1988; Öniş, 1991:30; Öniş, this volume).

Finally, the drastic reduction in the effectiveness of the State Planning Organization, which had been a strong guiding force and inspiration for accelerating the industrialization process, was also indicative of the overall neglect of industrialization under SSAP.

THE IMPACT OF SSAP ON THE MANUFACTURING SECTOR

The assessment in this section covers mainly the period from the introduction of the program in 1980 until 1989, the last year for which detailed statistics on the manufacturing sector are available. This assessment is therefore confined to only the initial response of the manufacturing sector, as the full effect of SSAP is yet to emerge. As discussed above, key components of the program, such as trade liberalization, gained momentum only after 1984, while there was only slow progress on the privatization front by the end of the 1980s. Apart from policy reversals in key factor prices during its implementation, another difficulty is related to the fact that the stabilization and structural components of the program were intermingled. Subject to these qualifications, this section will examine the impact of SSAP on exports, investment, output, productivity, employment and the extent of structural change.

Exports

By far the most satisfactory record of the program was in the field of exports. As total exports rose from $2.9 billion in 1980 to $13.0 billion in 1990, the share of manufactured goods in total exports increased sharply from 28.8 percent to 72.1 percent. As a result, the share of exports in GNP rose from only 4.0 percent during 1977–80 to 15.1 percent during 1984–88 with a parallel rise in the share of Turkish exports in world exports from 0.15 percent in 1980 to 0.43 percent in 1988 (TÜSİAD, 1989: 28). It was remarkable that this impressive export performance was realized against the background of slow growth in international trade and with only a minimal contribution from FDI (see Şenses, 1989a). Disaggregation of manufactured exports by factor content and major category has revealed a heavy concentration on labor-intensive and natural resource–based products, which in 1987 accounted for more than 75 percent of the total, with textiles, clothing and iron and steel alone accounting for more than half of the total in 1990.

The bulk of manufactured exports were directed to traditional markets in Western Europe, with the European Community alone representing 49.8 percent of the total in 1987. In the crucial early years of the export boom during 1980–85, however, Middle Eastern countries accounted for nearly half of the total increase in manufactured exports. It has been shown that manufactured exports to the Middle East were relatively more capital intensive. This was in sharp contrast to exports to Western Europe, the bulk of which were labor intensive (Şenses, 1989a).

The factors contributing to this spectacular performance in exports have been examined in detail.[9] A major factor behind this performance was the reactivation of the excess capacity in industries established under ISI for export growth, which saw capital utilization rates in the manufacturing sector increase gradually from 51.1 percent in 1980 to 72.4 percent in 1984, 75.0 percent in 1987, and 78.0 percent in 1990. Among other contributing factors, the most frequently cited are the role of domestic demand restraint through restrictive monetary and fiscal policies during the 1980–82 period in facilitating an exportable surplus, the increase in OPEC income during the same period and the Iran-Iraq war in providing convenient external market opportunities. The most crucial factors in this performance were, however, heavy currency depreciation in real terms and the provision of direct export incentives. The slowdown in incentives provided from these two sources in the late 1980s was associated with a relatively poor performance in exports (Table 5.1), confirming the responsiveness of exports to these policy instruments.

Investment

The transition to an export-oriented industrial trade strategy under SSAP was characterized by a notable lack of investment in the manufacturing sector. The average annual rate of growth in manufacturing investment declined from 9.4 percent during 1964–76 to only 4.0 percent during 1981–86 as opposed to 40.4 percent in tourism and 27.2 percent in energy sectors in the latter period (Rittenberg, 1991:155) which led to a fall in the share of manufacturing in total investment from 26.0 percent in 1979 to only 13.9 percent in 1989.[10]

Parallel to the shift of public investment away from manufacturing toward transportation, communications and energy, there was a move in private investment toward such sectors as tourism and housing. The share of manufacturing in total private investment declined from 29.9 percent in 1978 to 27.5 percent in 1990 (Table 5.2). Within manufacturing, sectors such as leather products, nonmetallic products, and transport equipment constituted the main preferred sectors, while private investors seem to have shied away from such sectors as food, wood, rubber and plastics, chemicals, iron and steel, nonferrous metals and machinery and professional equipment (Türel, 1993). A recent survey among exporters indicates that only half of those interviewed had undertaken investment in export activities. The bulk of such investments (77.4 percent) was, however, for the "renovation, modernization and extension" of existing plants (Şenses, 1990c: 71).

The record of foreign direct investment also fell below expectations. There was a considerable increase in FDI flows in the 1980s, especially during 1989–90, with the cumulative authorized FDI rising from a total of only $228.5 million in 1979 to $2.9 billion in 1990. Manufacturing has lost its relative importance also in the composition of FDI, with services (especially sectors like banking) being the main beneficiary. There was, however, no significant change in the distribution of FDI among different manufacturing activities, with chemicals, transport equipment, and food and beverages representing the main sectors (see Erdilek, 1988: 151–52 and Öniş, this volume).

The poor performance of manufacturing investment is generally attributed to three factors: (1) heavy real currency depreciation, (2) high real rates of interest, and 3) macroeconomic instability, increasing in its intensity in the late 1980s. It is our contention that manufacturing investment received a major blow from a series of policy changes under SSAP right at the outset and was unable to recover from it. One of the strongest adverse effects on the investment climate in the manufacturing sector was channelled through rapid real currency depreciation early in the program. This was instrumental in pushing up domestic prices of imported machinery, equipment and raw materials, with obvious connotations for investment and production. The investment climate deteriorated further as a result of sharp increases in the prices of key inputs produced by the SEEs following price decontrol and a sharp increase in the real rate of interest following financial liberalization. Given the very high debt-equity ratios of manufacturing enterprises, such a sharp increase in real rates of interest caused bankruptcies in some enterprises while in others it, by cutting into profit margins, reduced an important source of investment finance. It was therefore not surprising that of all the policies introduced under the SSAP, high interest rates were the major source of complaint by the business community. The cutback in the public sector investment program, domestic demand restraint during 1980–82 and the uncertainty generated by the military takeover were among other aspects of the initial investment shock responsible for the poor investment performance.

The adverse impact of financial liberalization on manufacturing investment could be observed also from the allocation and terms of credit to this sector. As credits were diverted to short-term uses and to other sectors such as housing, industry was starved of investable funds. The share of manufacturing in total credits by the Central Bank, for example, fell from 29.4 percent in 1982 to 18 percent in 1988, while its share in total credits by commercial banks fell from 34.8 percent in 1981 to 21.2 percent in 1988. Given the underdeveloped state of the domestic capital market and its dominance by government securities, investors had to resort increasingly to commercial banks to meet their financial requirements. The oligopolistic structure of the banking sector allowing commercial banks to operate with very high spreads meant unduly high real lending rates. The increased resort to financial markets to finance the growing public sector deficit in the second half of the 1980s aggravated this situation by exerting an upward pressure on interest rates. The government's commitment to attaining external balance by maintaining the real rate of exchange made it imperative (to avoid capital flight) to preserve its high interest rate policy.

The failure to get inflation under control meant big nominal changes in interest rates and the exchange rate, which, together with substantial changes in such other aspects of the policy environment as customs duties, increased the uncertainty of potential investors, given also the basically unstable political environment. The availability of alternative profitable sectors in services (most notably in trade) as well as the proliferation of new financial instruments with higher real rates of return in the short term were among other factors with an adverse impact on manufacturing investment. It seems that an investment climate characterized by lack of "innovative entrepreneurship and modern management" and investors' preference for "short run financial investment in stocks, bonds, and other instruments, or deposits with financial institutions, with quick returns at the neglect of long-term real investment in plant and equipment" was not conducive to growth in manufacturing investment (see Şenses, 1990a and 1989b).

Productivity, Employment and Structure of Production

Real output in the manufacturing sector increased by an average annual rate of 8.4 percent during 1981–87 and 5.2 percent during 1988–91, which does not compare favorably with the rates of growth of 10.1 percent and 8.4 percent attained during the 1963–70 and 1971–78 periods, respectively. In the face of slow growth in investment, growth in the 1980s was achieved mainly through the reactivation of excess capacity, with the major impetus for higher rates of capacity utilization coming from exports.

Estimates of productivity growth in the manufacturing sector are surrounded by the familiar statistical and methodological problems and are not directly comparable. Despite their shortcomings, it is possible to piece together a number of general observations from these estimates.[11] First, productivity performance under SSAP was rather unimpressive, with no significant improvement over the pre-1980 period. Average annual rate of growth of labor productivity increased from 4.5 percent during 1963–70 and 4.3 percent during 1971–78 to 5.8 percent during 1981–87, before falling to only 2.8 percent during 1988–91 (OECD, 1993: 49). Estimates based on total factor productivity growth (TFPG), on the other hand, indicate a slight increase from an average annual rate of growth of 1.4 percent during 1965–76 to 1.7 percent during 1981–88 (Uygur, 1990). Second, there was a reversal in the relative performance of the private and public sectors, with the average annual rate of TFPG rising from 1.1 percent during 1965–76 to 2.2 percent during 1981–88 in the private sector, while declining from 2.6 percent to 1.0 percent in the public sector during the same period (Uygur, 1990). Third, the increase in the rate of capacity utilization emerged as an important factor behind productivity growth in the 1980s. In the absence of a concerted attempt to increase capital deepening and technical change, two-thirds of the increase in manufacturing value added per worker during 1980–87, for example, was attributed to the increase in capacity utilization (Türel, 1993).

These aggregate trends in productivity should not, however, conceal the fact that there was considerable variation by branch of activity as well as an overall increase in quality consciousness and responsiveness to consumer demand. Although it is hard to substantiate it, this was visible as much in export-oriented sectors such as textiles as in inward-looking sectors such as the automotive sector, with their emphasis on quality improvement and the development of new and differentiated products.[12] This new outlook was apparent even in the public sector, with SEEs exposed to increased competitive pressures outperforming those in sheltered manufacturing activities in terms of productivity growth.[13]

Employment

It is often put forward that the transition to an export-oriented industrialization strategy will accelerate employment growth in the manufacturing sector. The alleged favorable employment effects would arise basically from the encouragement of labor-intensive activities through the correction of relative factor price distortions and the shift of the structure of industrial production toward sectors with higher labor intensity. The record of the manufacturing sector under alternative trade and industrialization strategies does not support these expectations. The average annual rate of employment growth during 1981–91 was only 2.4 percent as opposed to 5.4 and 3.9 percent during 1963–70 and 1971–78, respectively. It seems, however, that the link between export orientation and employment growth was stronger in major export-oriented sectors (each accounting for more than 10 percent of total manufactured exports during 1984–86). Employment in large enterprises (with 10 or more workers) in these sectors (textiles, clothing and iron and steel) increased from 175.5 thousand in 1980 to 280.0 thousand in 1989. This represented a much more rapid rate of growth than total employment in large manufacturing enterprises, which increased from 787.0 thousand to 1021.4 thousand during the same period.

It is difficult to attribute this record entirely to export orientation under SSAP, which was also characterized by strong stabilization elements, especially early in the program, and with fluctuations in such key prices as wages, interest rates, and the exchange rate. The failure to generate rapid employment growth, despite significant moves in the desired direction in relative factor prices and sector preferences within manufacturing, can be attributed to weak investment performance in this sector and to a lesser extent to the emphasis of export incentives on sectors with relatively high capital intensity. (See Şenses, 1990a for details.)

Structure of Production

A major characteristic of the economy is the importance of the agricultural sector, which in 1990 accounted for 17.8 percent of GNP and 48.5 percent of total civilian employment. The sectoral composition of output and employment, however, has indicated continual structural change away from agriculture toward industry and services. One notable aspect of this structural change was the increase in the share of the manufacturing sector in total employment from 9.6 percent in 1970 to 10.1 percent in 1980 and 13.8 percent in 1990, as its share in GNP rose from 11.8 to 18.7 and 21.8 percent during the same period. While its share in total employment seems to have increased more rapidly in the 1980s,[14] there was a remarkable slowdown in the pace of structural change toward this sector in terms of aggregate production.

The slowdown in the pace of structural change under SSAP was evident also in terms of the composition of manufacturing production. In sharp contrast with the 1963–80 period, there was only a slight fall in the share of consumer goods, with only slight changes also in intermediate and investment goods (Table 5.3). As a result, nearly half of total manufacturing production in 1989 consisted of consumer goods. The heavy concentration of manufacturing production on light consumer goods and intermediate goods with a high degree of natural resource content continued in the 1980s, with no visible trend toward skill-intensive branches. It seems that the fall in public manufacturing investment has slowed down the pace of structural change toward the manufacturing sector, as a whole as well as structural change toward intermediate and capital goods within this sector, for which the state has traditionally been the main vehicle.

The lack of structural change within the manufacturing sector could be observed also in terms of employment, with hardly any change in the share of different activities during the 1980–89 period, which again constituted a sharp contrast with the pre-1980 period. The biggest change was in textiles and clothing, the most important export-oriented activity, whose share in total manufacturing employment increased by more than five percentage points during this period (Table 5.4).

Although the absence of more recent data prevents us from getting a more complete picture, data on size of establishments also confirm the lack of structural change. The share of small establishments (with fewer than 10 workers) in total manufacturing employment remained constant at 21.7 percent during the 1980–85 period. Certain manufacturing activities were heavily concentrated in these small establishments, which in 1985 accounted for 88.9 and 69.3 percent of total employment in furniture and clothing and 66.4 and 39.4 percent of total value added in wood and furniture and metal products, respectively (Şenses, 1989b). More recent data available for large-scale enterprises (with 10 or more workers) for the 1980–89 period indicate that the average size of enterprises, after falling from 90 in 1980 to 87 in 1985, increased to 108 in 1989.[15] Despite this increase, the manufacturing sector was still dominated by small enterprises, with only 18.6 percent of large enterprises in 1989 employing 200 or more workers.[16]

Despite the significant fall in its share in employment and value added from 36.5 and 40.4 percent in 1980 to 24.9 and 35.0 percent in 1989, respectively, the public sector continued to play a major role in the manufacturing sector. Although it is difficult to make meaningful and up-to-date international comparisons, the limited data available show that Turkey, in terms of the share of public sector in total manufacturing production, maintains an intermediate position among a selected group of developing countries.[17] In 1985, petroleum and coal, tobacco and beverages were the branches in which the public sector share was particularly high, accounting for more than two-thirds of total value added in each of these activities.

Table 5.3
Composition of Manufacturing Value Added in Large-Scale Manufacturing Enterprises, 1963–89 (Selected Years, Percent)

	1963	1970	1980	1985	1989
Consumption Goods	52.0	40.7	33.6	35.6	31.7
Food Beverages Tobacco	29.0	26.1	18.3	20.9	16.7
Textiles and Clothing	23.0	14.6	15.3	14.7	15.0
Intermediate Goods	32.6	44.9	48.5	45.8	51.2
Wood and Furniture	1.7	1.1	1.3	1.3	1.0
Paper and Printing	5.3	4.5	2.8	3.6	3.1
Chemicals & Petroleum					
Coal,Rubber & Plastics	13.2	23.5	27.7	25.8	29.0
Non-metallic Mineral Prod.	5.6	5.2	6.8	6.5	7.3
Basic Metals	6.8	10.6	9.9	8.6	10.8
Investment Goods	15.4	14.4	17.9	18.6	17.1
Metal Prods,and Machinery					
and Equipment	14.8	12.8	17.6	18.0	16.8
Other Manufacturing Prods.	0.6	1.6	0.3	0.6	0.3
Total	100.0	100.0	100.0	100.0	100.0

Sources: Şenses, 1989b for 1963–85 and State Institute of Statistics, 1992.
[a] comprising ten or more workers

The foregoing discussion shows that agriculture still accounts for a large portion of both GDP and employment, which was larger than the average for the middle-income countries. The share of manufacturing in GDP, on the other hand, is very close to the average for middle-income countries (Table 5.5). Even in the case of exports, which registered rapid structural change toward manufactured exports, international comparisons reveal that the share of machinery and equipment was lower and the share of textiles and clothing was higher than in all country groups, including low-income countries. While gross investment increased at a lower pace than in all country groups except the middle-income countries, the rate of growth of exports surpassed the rate for all country groups by a considerable margin (Table 5.5).

Table 5.4
Composition of Employment in Large-Scale Manufacturing Enterprises
(Comprising Ten or More Workers)

	1963	1970	1980	1985	1989
Consumption Goods	59.3	51.2	47.0	45.7	47.7
Food beverages Tobacco	25.9	24.0	23.6	20.6	19.1
Textiles and Clothing	33.4	27.2	23.4	25.1	28.6
Intermediate Goods	24.2	28.0	32.1	32.0	31.6
Wood and Furniture	2.2	2.3	2.1	2.2	2.0
Paper and Printing	4.2	4.3	3.6	3.9	3.5
Chemicals and Petroleum	7.0	8.1	9.5	9.6	9.7
Non-metallic Mineral Prod.	6.6	7.2	7.5	7.6	8.0
Basic Metals	4.2	6.1	9.4	8.7	8.4
Investment Goods	16.5	20.8	20.9	22.3	20.7
Metal Products, Machinery					
and Equipment	15.8	19.2	20.3	21.4	20.2
Other Manufactured					
Products	0.7	1.6	0.6	0.9	0.5
Total	100.0	100.0	100.0	100.0	100.0
Total (000 employees)	299.0	504.1	787.0	927.6	1021.4

Sources: Şenses, 1989b: 40 for 1963–85 and State Institute of Statistics, 1992.

CONCLUSION

Although there were some policy reversals toward the end of the 1980s when the political regime became more liberal and the role of the external agents became weaker, the policy framework for industrialization has been radically transformed in the post-1980 period. This transformation was most visible in key spheres such as price decontrol, the realignment of key factor prices and trade liberalization. Although a certain degree of government intervention in all of these areas still exists, there was a great deal of progress in asserting the role of price mechanism and shifting the structure of incentives toward export orientation. In addition, there was a big increase in infrastructural investments (most notably in transport, energy and communications), with a strong bearing on the

Table 5.5
Some Indicators of Growth and Industrialization in Turkey and Selected Countries

	Low Income	Lower Middle Income	Upper Middle Income	High[a] Income	Turkey
Manufacturing Production					
Share in GDP (1990 per cent)	27	23[b]	25	23[c]	24
Per capita[d]	82	519[e]	904	-	328
Growth[f]	11.1	3.5	3.5	3.3	7.2
Structure of Exports(1990)					
Primary Goods	47	62	45	19	32
Machinery & Transport Equip.	9	11	20	42	7
Textiles and Clothing	21	9	9	5	37
Growth of Manuf. Exports	5.4	7.2	1.9	4.3	9.1
Growth of Gross Investment	7.4	-0.4	0.2	4.2	3.8
Structure of Labor Force (1980)					
Agriculture	72	55	29	7[g]	58
Industry	13	16	31	35[g]	17
GDP					
Share of Agriculture	31	17	9	..	18
Share of Industry	36	31	40	..	33

Source: World Bank, 1987, 1991 and 1992.
[a] OECD members, unless otherwise stated
[b] 1989
[c] 1985 data for industrial market economies
[d] Manufacturing value added/mid-year population in dollars
[e] Middle Income Countries as a whole
[f] All growth rates refer to annual average (percentage) rate of growth during 1980–90
[g] Industrial market economies

industrialization process. As the export pessimism that had characterized the pre-1980 period was removed and valuable experience was gained in export markets, there was a big boom in manufactured exports, which was reinforced by efforts to improve quality of products and increase price competitiveness. With little new investment in the manufacturing sector, this boom was achieved mainly through the reactivation of excess capacities that were conveniently available at the beginning of SSAP in January 1980. This process was also responsible for much of the growth of manufacturing output and productivity during the 1980s.

Given the much slower pace of structural change toward the manufacturing sector and toward skill-intensive manufacturing branches in the 1980s as compared with the ISI period, the real challenge facing policy makers is to increase investment in this sector with a view toward diversifying and upgrading its product mix. With the public sector withdrawing from the industrialization process and strongly committed to privatization, there is little hope of increasing public manufacturing investment under SSAP. Even if there is a revival of interest in industrialization, large and growing public sector deficits are unlikely to permit such a turnaround. It seems that the commitment to maintain real rates of exchange to attain external balance and positive real rates of interest as part of the process of financial liberalization are having, apart from their likely adverse effect on domestic inflation from the supply side, a strong adverse effect also on private investment in this sector. Increased uncertainty of potential investors arising from macroeconomic and political instability seems to aggravate this situation. The ability of policy makers to overcome these obstacles and trade-offs in their short- and medium-term policy management will determine whether the experiment with market-based export orientation will take root and succeed in elevating the industrialization objective back to its pre-1980 levels.

NOTES

1. One estimate of the extent of rents arising from the system of import licenses put the figure as high as 15 percent of GNP in 1968 (see Barkey 1990: 24).

2. As the appreciation of the lira against the dollar in real terms during 1973-80 reached approximately 30 percent, the real rate of interest on six-month deposits in the late 1970s was -30 percent (Şenses, 1990a: 9).

3. For a detailed discussion of the extent and main impact of the economic crisis during 1978–80, see Şenses (1991).

4. With an early general election clearly in sight, real wages continued to increase sharply in the 1991 wage rounds, taking them even beyond their levels in 1980. It has been estimated that in the course of several months in 1991, real labor costs in the public and private sectors rose substantially by 56.6 and 50.6 percent, respectively (see Şenses, 1992).

5. Many managers of foreign trade companies interviewed by Krueger and Aktan (1992: 167), while noting the difficulties they were confronted with as a result of the appreciation of the lira after 1989, were confident that the government would correct this situation.

6. The share of the public sector in total manufacturing investment declined from 56.8 percent in 1979 to 28.9 percent in 1986 and 11.2 percent in 1990.

7. For a detailed survey of employment issues in the manufacturing sector see Şenses (1992).

8. Central Bank credits directed to SEEs, for example, declined from 50 percent in 1980 to 13 percent in 1985 (see Waterbury, 1992: 60).

9. See Barlow and Şenses (1992) for an overview of the main hypotheses that have been put forward to explain the upsurge in Turkish exports in the 1980s.

10. Further liberalization of the import regime, the appreciation of lira, the fall in real rates of interest, and the sharp increase in real wages together prompted a big increase in private manufacturing investment in 1990. This process, which involved a big increase in imports of investment goods, proved temporary, with private investment again declining in the following year. (See OECD, 1992: 13 for details.)

11. See Celasun (1991) for a review of the findings of various studies on TFPG.

12. See Kırım (1990a) and Ansal, this volume for details.

13. See OECD, 1992: 92 on this point.

14. If the year 1978 is taken as the basis of comparison to avoid the crisis years, this distinction becomes less sharp, as manufacturing accounted for 12.3 percent of total employment in 1978.

15. Although the average size of establishments in the public sector in 1989 was still more than seven times as high as in the private sector, this increase was due to the rise in the private sector from 60 to 84 during the 1980–89 period.

16. Large enterprises here comprise the sum of public enterprises and private enterprises with 25 or more workers.

17. See Şenses (1989a) on this point.

6

THE ECONOMIC STRUCTURE OF POWER UNDER TURKISH STRUCTURAL ADJUSTMENT: PRICES, GROWTH AND ACCUMULATION

A. Erinç Yeldan

INTRODUCTION

With the embarkment of the 1980 adjustment reform program, Turkey has rested its development strategy on the model of export-led growth based on private initiative. Commensurate with a series of reforms implemented through the 1980s, both the domestic commodity markets and foreign trade regime have been liberalized, and the economy has entered into a process of integration with the world markets. The theoretical underpinning of the new strategy was based on the orthodox approach. This argues that, in an economy in which world (efficiency) prices were not distorted through trade restrictions, and in which capital accumulation was guided by the profit motive one would achieve the optimum allocation of productive resources. For restoration of macro balances, this theoretical perspective has rested its short-run stabilization policies on the monetarist prescription of domestic credit restraint to control the excess commodity demand. This was supplemented by a series of policy reforms to achieve longer-term adjustment by changing the structure of the economy toward an outward orientation, and by providing an increased role for the private sector and market forces. The policy elements of the reform have been extensively debated in the literature and shall not be dealt with here.[1] Instead, this chapter will address a less understood aspect of structural adjustment—namely, that of changed patterns of income distribution and acquisition of economic surplus during adjustment by the industrial and financial capitalist classes, through various forms of price and nonprice coercive income transfer mechanisms.

The emergence of new modes of expropriation of economic surplus and their policy design have not been expressed openly as underlying objectives of the reform. However, such discourse on the distributional reality has been a synergistic component of the economic rationale of the postadjustment era. Indeed, reconstruction of the domestic economy and functioning of the labor market were shaped in this period through political authoritarianism, depoliticization and demobilization of the labor force (Cizre-Sakallıog˘lu, 1991). The bargaining power of labor was severely curtailed through a series of articles set forth in the new Constitution of 1982, and the new Labor Code of 1983. In the meantime, the rural economy has witnessed severe erosion of real income of the peasantry and intensification of the transfer of resources from villages to the urban industrial centers. The Turkish peasantry has faced a severe decline in its relative terms of trade as a consequence of the dramatic withdrawal of administrative price supports on agricultural products. This price scissors effect (Mutlu, 1990) has severely deteriorated the rural sector's economic power and has led to an enormous transfer of surplus toward industrial and financial capital.

The purpose of this chapter is to investigate and analytically depict the economic basis of these dramatic swings in surplus transfer in the Turkish economy throughout the adjustment era, addressing itself to three sets of issues: (1) the phases of the economic reconstruction and the subsequent changes (and reversals) of its accompanying polity as witnessed throughout the 1980s; (2) the reformation of this economic structure for consolidating the power basis of capital in the product and factor markets; and (3) the emerging patterns of capital accumulation and the mode of disposition of the economic surplus by the capitalist classes. These issues will be respectively covered under the three subsequent sections of the chapter, with the fourth section providing summary conclusions and comments.

PHASES OF STRUCTURAL CHANGE AND POLICY MIX

Table 6.1 summarizes important aspects of the Turkish adjustment process of 1980–90. A thorough review of the realized production and accumulation patterns and the policy parameters suggests three distinct phases of growth in the domestic economy: Phase 1 covers the 1980–82 subperiod and is characterized by hesitant resumption of GDP growth, a rapid increase in manufactured exports, and decline in private investment along with intensification of capacity use in the manufacturing industry. Thus, this subperiod reveals a pure reorientation of the economy toward foreign markets based on static stabilization of the domestic commodity and financial markets. The exchange rate is observed to be the main policy instrument of this phase, with a profound cumulative real depreciation of 28 percent. In the domestic financial markets, interest liberalization brings forth positive rates of return to savings and causes an increase in the share of interest/rent incomes in total value added (see also Özmucur, 1991a).

Based on an index value of 100 for 1980, the real wage rate is observed to be sustained initially, and there is a slight deterioration in the level of real profits. From the point of view of capital owners, these processes should be attributed to

Table 6.1

Production, Accumulation and Distribution in Turkey, 1980–90

	Stabilization			Growth via external adjustment					Cyclical growth "reform fatique"		
	1980	1981	1982	1983	1984	1985	1986	1987	1988	1989	1990
I. Production and accumulation											
Annual Growth Rate:											
1. GDP	−1.0	3.6	4.5	3.9	6.0	4.2	7.3	6.5	4.6	0.4	8.1
2. Agriculture	1.7	0.1	6.4	−0.1	3.5	2.4	7.9	2.1	8.0	−11.5	11.3
3. Manufacture	−6.0	9.5	5.4	8.7	10.2	5.5	9.6	9.9	1.8	3.2	10.1
4. Commerce	−4.1	7.4	4.6	6.9	8.0	4.6	9.4	9.9	3.8	5.8	12.1
5. Finance	1.8	1.9	1.6	0.5	4.5	3.5	3.7	3.6	4.7	1.8	3.5
Private Manufacturing:											
6. Productivity[a,b]	100	109	117	114	115	121	147	163	156	—	—
7. Exports[a]	100	230	405	649	725	891	758	1107	1301	1144	1269
8. Investment[a]	100	101	97	95	98	107	122	113	105	90	115
9. Capacity (%)	51	62	66	69	72	73	73	75	75	75	76
II. Distribution and Prices											
10. Wage rate[c]	100	107	103	94	78	72	63	79	61	74	—
11. Real profits											
Industry[d]	100	97	96	109	154	215	176	229	202	185	—
Banking	100	120	94	167	293	279	476	662	708	485	611
12. Real exc. rate	100	104	115	125	141	136	130	109	109	93	70
13. Interest (%)[e]	−33	2.9	7.8	6.7	−4.5	7.6	12.6	5.9	−3.6	−2.1	−3.1
14. Producer Prices											
Private Man.	100	131	166	219	323	453	613	860	1546	2530	3637
Public Man.	100	131	165	213	311	451	576	702	1219	2033	3241
15. Domestic terms of trade[f]	100	92	84	87	88	87	99	—	—	—	—

Sources: Rows 1-5, 7, 8: State Planning Organization, Annual Programs; Rows 6, 9, 10: State Institute of Statistics (SIS) Manufacturing Industry Surveys; Row 11: Petrol–Iş, 1990 and Türkiye Bankalar Birligi, *Bankalarımız*, various issues; Row 12: OECD, 1991, Table M; Rows 13, 14: SIS, Monthly Bulletin of Statistics; Row 15: Mutlu, 1990, Table 3.

[a] Index (1980=100) based on 1980 prices

[b] Private Manufacturing value added per labor employed, deflated by the private producer price index

[c] Annual wage payments per labor in manufacturing, deflated by CPI

[d] Total profits of 500 largest industrial firms deflated by the producer price index

[e] Annual average of the 1-year time deposits, deflated by CPI

[f] Terms of trade between the prices received by farmers and the prices paid by them for current inputs and capital goods

the costs of adjustment under the changed direction of the economy operating with a positive rate of interest and redirected incentives.

Phase 2 of the Turkish adjustment process exhibits sustained rapid growth—especially in manufacturing—and spans 1983 through 1987. What is peculiar about this phase is the continuation of rapid export expansion and increased productivity gains in the manufacturing industry. The enigma of the period is the meager performance of private investment. At a time of accelerated growth opportunities provided by the external economy, the retardation of private accumulation signals a nonconformity in the process of surplus disposition. As will be argued in the following section, the drastic fall in real wages and expansion of real profits clearly manifest the prevailing mechanism of surplus extraction of this period. The pattern of private accumulation will be examined at more length in the third section; however, our discussion so far clearly suggests that the consumerist tendencies of the capitalist class have outweighed its entrepreneurial spirit throughout the adjustment era, along with more receptive attitudes toward Western lifestyles based on consumerism.

Phase 3 of the Turkish adjustment history covers the period since 1988, and reveals a subperiod during which political rationalities finally come to grips with the economic realities of the markets (Öniş, 1991). The limits of orthodox stabilization based on price incentives and surplus extraction via wage suppression seem to have been reached, and the economy enters a period of cyclical growth. The faltering growth performance of the economy is accompanied by weakened managerial activity of the bureaucracy due to "reform fatigue" (Ersel, 1991), and what at face value seems to be a reversal of the standing macro policies.

The inflation rate gained momentum starting in 1987. Even though it was never publicly announced, there were indications that the authorities used the foreign exchange rate and the rate of interest as antiinflationary tools. The real exchange rate appreciated and the real rate of interest turned negative. An important aspect of the culminating pressures of inflation became more apparent: As observed, until 1985, the series of private and public manufacturing producer price indexes moved almost together. However, beginning in 1986, the spread between the two indexes widened in favor of the private sector. Furthermore, over the 1980–88 period, the index of private producer prices exceeded that of the nominal wage rate by 54 percent.[2] This observation suggests that the private sector was able to sustain its mode of surplus acquisition in this period via a process that can be termed the "supra-economic (rent)-inflation" fed upon producer mark-ups over prime costs (Yeldan, 1991).

THE NEW ECONOMIC STRUCTURE OF POWER

According to the supposition of the orthodox theory, as domestic industries integrate with world markets, there will be efficiency gains obtained from the optimal use of resources, and consequently productivity of labor will also increase. Again, according to the theory, it is expected that such gains will translate into real wage increases, and the share of labor in the value added of export sectors will rise, given the presumed high labor intensities of these sectors.

However, the industrialization experience of many developing countries does not confirm this unidirectional comovement that the theory proposes. For instance, de Janvry and Sadoulet (1983) provide evidence that, under the strategy of export-led growth, countries such as Brazil, Mexico and the Philippines have witnessed worsening income distribution concurrent with rapid growth, while in some others such as South Korea and Taiwan—at least in the initial phases of export promotion—income distribution and growth progressed simultaneously. On the other hand, the small number of studies conducted for Turkey (see e.g., Celasun, 1989) suggest a tendency toward worsening income distribution (at the functional level) along with industrial growth (see Figure 6.1 and Table 6.1).[3]

Thus, the proposition of the orthodox theory, based on the unidirectional principle of "open economy" →→ gains in productivity →→ improvement in the distribution of income, has historically been realized in certain countries, while in some others this expectation has failed to materialize. Based on this observed insufficiency in explaining factor income shares, I reject the orthodox presumption that the rate of profit is a payment/return to a scarce productive input, capital. Rather, following Bowles, Gordon and Weisskopf (1986), I adopt the working hypothesis that profits are a residual obtained by deduction from net value added the costs of wages and of other primary factors. This deduction is made possible by the power of the capitalist class over other economic agents based on its private ownership of capital and other assets in the production process. Thus, in this framework, profits are treated not as a market-determined rate of return, but rather as a socially determined entity, shaped and molded by the policy decisions and the structural parameters of the given social-economic formation.

Furthermore, as Bowles, Gordon and Weisskopf (1986: 136–37) note, capitalist profits can be materialized only through capital owners' dealings with economic agents other than the capitalist class itself; trade in final commodities is a zero sum game between buyers and sellers—gains of one group necessarily result in losses for the other.

In the context of the Turkish adjustment process, one can identify three main mechanisms for creating and sustaining of profit income for the capitalist class: The first is determined by the position of the capitalist class against labor and other primary factors of production; the second is based on the resolution of the integration process between the domestic and foreign markets through movements of the exchange rate and flows of financial capital; the third mechanism is due to the process of surplus creation based on the position of the capitalist class vis-à-vis the state, through the exercise of power of the state apparatus in the formation of income shares in the economic sphere.

Figure 6.1
Capital's Position Toward Wage-Labor and the Rural Economy in Turkey, 1980–90

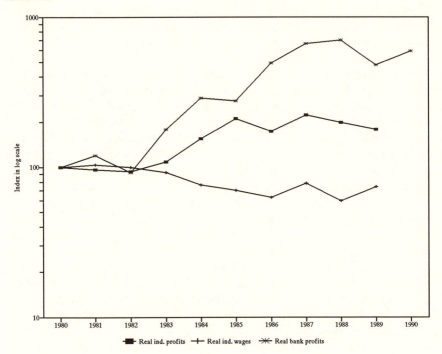

Source: Table 6.1

Surplus Extraction from Wage-Labor and the Peasantry

After the 1980 price reform and especially with the restrictive articles of the 1982 Constitution and the new Labor Code of 1983,[4] there was a dramatic erosion in the relative position of wage-labor vis-à-vis capital. As claimed in Yeldan (1989), under export-led growth, creation of an "exportable surplus" would require suppression of domestic demand. Another reason for the hostility toward labor incomes under export-led growth is related to the role of wages in costs of production. For an explanation of the nature and extent of this process, I examine the trends in real wages and profits within the manufacturing sector.

The behavior of these two key indicators of income distribution can be seen from the left-vertical axis of Figure 6.1. As clearly seen, the decline in the real wage rate reached almost 40 percent between 1980 and 1988, while real profits (as reported by the largest 500 companies) almost doubled. While it is a widely recognized fact that the data on factor income shares are limited in scope and suffer from severe shortcomings, many independent researchers agree on the severe decline of the share of wage income and the rise of the nonlabor component of manufacturing value added in the 1980s. Özmucur (1991a, 1991b), for instance, argues that the share of nonwage income in nonagricultural value added has increased from 65 percent in 1980 to 72 percent in 1991. In a similar vein, Boratav (1990: 207) reports that the share of wages in manufacturing value added has fallen from its peak of 38.7 percent in 1979 to 22.4 percent in 1985.

Unfortunately, as the latest data on manufacturing series at the time of writing reach only 1988, one cannot deduce the extent of the significant wage increases that occurred during the 1989–91 set of collective bargaining agreements. Limited available data from independent sources reveal, however, that even though significant gains in real wages have been realized in this period, they were not sufficient in general to compensate for the erosion that had taken place during the previous eight years. Gerni (1991), for example, has found that after hitting its trough of 48.8 in 1988, the index (1980 = 100) of public sector employee income (wages plus other remuneration) reached only 77 in 1990. Clearly, it can be argued on many grounds that there has been a severe intensification of direct surplus transfer by way of suppression of wage income in the post-1980 structural adjustment period.

Another set of indicators with regard to the position of capital in the process of commodity production concerns the relationship between urban capital and the rural economy. As an indicator of the relative purchasing power of the rural and urban sectors, I plot the index of agriculture's terms of trade on the right-vertical axis of Figure 6.1. Here again, even though the available data are limited, one can see the severe decline of agriculture's terms of trade.

It can be argued that because Turkey is not a major importer of food, agricultural prices are determined primarily in domestic markets and also by the government's price support policy. Thus, cutbacks in price supports, the provision of generous export incentives directed almost exclusively to manufacturing and the severe reduction of the purchasing power of urban workers, with a consequent fall in the real demand for food, caused a substantial fall in the relative net price of the agricultural economy (Celasun & Rodrik, 1989). As measured by the implicit GNP deflator, the deterioration of the agricultural terms of trade from 1977 (the first year of the economic crisis) to 1986 amounts to 53 percent. As Boratav (1990) rightly argues, this collapse is comparable only to the one experienced during the Great Depression. This process clearly manifests the magnitude of a phenomenal resource transfer within the domestic economy, from the rural to the urban sectors.

Surplus Creation Under the New Trade Regime

The process of outward orientation initiated in 1980 has opened new venues of surplus creation for the capitalist classes. The major instruments of foreign trade policy under adjustment have been the exchange rate and direct subsidies to exporters. In addition, the international donor agencies have made an important contribution to the adjustment process by providing financial assistance through Structural Adjustment Loans, debt relief and technical aid. In 1980, resource transfer to the domestic economy through such aid represented 4.7 percent of GDP, with Turkey singly accounting for nearly 70 percent of the total volume of debt rescheduled internationally by the developing countries in the 1978–80 period (Celasun & Rodrik, 1989). Even though the cost of such transfers has been quite high—as the direction of resource transfer was reversed after 1984 and added significant pressure on public finance—their timely availability has eased the external pressures on the domestic economy.

Figure 6.2 portrays the behavior of the above- mentioned instruments during the adjustment period. As depicted on the left–hand scale, the real exchange rate depreciated by almost 40 percent until 1985, after which this trend was reversed. Subsidies on exports were also significant, averaging around 25 percent of export value during the 1981–85 period, reaching a peak of 34.2 percent in 1983. The most important component of the export subsidy was the production tax rebates, which accounted for about half of the total subsidies granted in 1982 and 1983, and as much as 75 percent in 1984 (Milanovic, 1986). After 1984 there was an overall tendency toward scaling down the tax rebates, with a view to eventually remove them altogether. In addition to its burden on the central government budget, the rebate scheme was held responsible for "export-oriented rent seeking," through overinvoicing of exports and the so-called "fictitious exports."[5]

Export promotion was also hailed at the institutional level, on the basis of its record in creating and reorganizing the structure of major export companies and giving them the status of Foreign Trade Companies (FTCs). FTCs were built on the East Asian model of export promotion, and were designed to function on a centralized scale as the long arm of the domestic economy in reaching foreign markets, especially those in the Middle East (Öniş, 1992). Those FTCs that that were able to meet specific export volume targets were granted additional subsidies by the government, leading to a bias in the conduct of the export promotion policy in favor of large producers. Although this pattern of export orientation based on FTCs was clearly in conflict with the stated stance of the state toward a liberal market economy based on price rather than administrative incentives (Öniş, 1992), it was in direct conformity with the mode of surplus creation for the capitalist class.

Figure 6.2
Capital's Position Toward the External Economy in Turkey, 1980–90

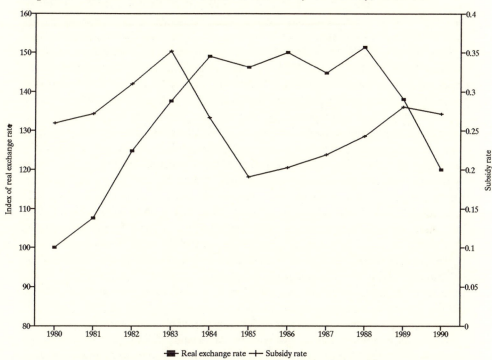

Source: Subsidy rate from Aktan, 1991; Exchange rate data from OECD, 1991.

Surplus Creation and Surplus Transfer by the State

One of the major undertakings of the state in the Turkish socioeconomic environment that has emerged during the adjustment process has been directed toward achieving conformity between the economic rationale of the market forces and the political realities of the policy-making process. In so doing, significant reorganization of the state apparatus was needed. First and foremost, the political rationale of the adjustment efforts substantiated the continued presence of the state as both a productive and a regulating agent in economic affairs. As thoroughly discussed in Öniş (1991: 32–33), state involvement in the economic sphere continued in various forms: through the significant role played by the public enterprise system as a producer and employer in manufacturing; through the dominance of government securities and bonds in the financial system; and through the administration of a complex incentive system of subsidies and grants, often implemented by different layers of a firmly centralized bureaucracy.

Figure 6.3 portrays two key parameters of the incentive system. The left-hand vertical axis depicts the amount of aggregate investment subject to incentive certification by the government in real 1980 prices. Real value of investment under the incentive certification system, after fluctuating around 300 billion lira between 1980 to 1984, jumped to the plateau of 750 billion lira in the second half of the decade. In the meantime, the number of incentive certificates increased rapidly from 573 in 1980, to 1031 in 1983 and 3141 in 1990. The decrease in the real value of incentives granted in 1990 should mostly be attributed to the erosion caused by accelerating inflation rather than a change in the stance of successive governments toward entrepreneurial support.[6]

Concurrently, the incidence of tax evasion on corporate incomes has increased, and a process of surplus creation has resurfaced through tax allowances, exemptions and other forms of incentives granted to capital owners to retain their otherwise taxable income. The right vertical axis of Figure 6.3 depicts the share of corporate taxation in the government's total budget revenues in the 1980s. In the initial phases of the adjustment process there is a gradual increase in capital's tax share. After 1986, however, it falls continuously, to reach 7.2 percent in 1991. What is more striking about these figures is not the direction of movement of the corporate tax share, but its sheer minuscule level in absolute terms. The tax share of capital in total budget revenues reached a peak of only 14 percent in 1984, and averaged around 9.1 percent over the decade as a whole. If one is to regard this ratio as the contribution of capital to the revenue base of the civil society, one can infer that a substantial resource transfer from noncapital incomes toward capital owners has continued during the adjustment period. Yeldan (1989) reports, for instance, that the Turkish lira value of the tax rebates granted to manufacturing alone stood at 11.5 percent of the total consolidated budget revenues of the government in 1984. Clearly, the state's incentive policies in investment and export promotion combined have resulted in a sizable transfer of income to the capitalist classes, especially in the second half of the decade.

Thus, fed from the above-mentioned three sources (through wage suppression, commercial policy and fiscal policy), economic surplus in the Turkish economy in the adjustment period of the 1980s was generated, administered and directed toward capital, often through coercive measures. The economic rationale of outward orientation has given substantial leverage to the state in implementing its policies, in suppressing the domestic absorption capacity, and in biasing incentives toward nonagricultural commodity producers and the financial sectors.

Summarizing these observations, in lieu of the three-phase characterization of the adjustment process, I see that surplus creation under phase 1 (pure stabilization) seems to have occurred through foreign trade policies, that is, export subsidies and the real exchange rate. In phase 2 (growth and external adjustment), while this mechanism in the first phase still prevails, the main attribute of surplus creation now rests on primary distributional relations of production by way of wage repression and resource transfer from the rural economy through price

Figure 6.3
Capital's Position Toward the State in Turkey, 1981–90

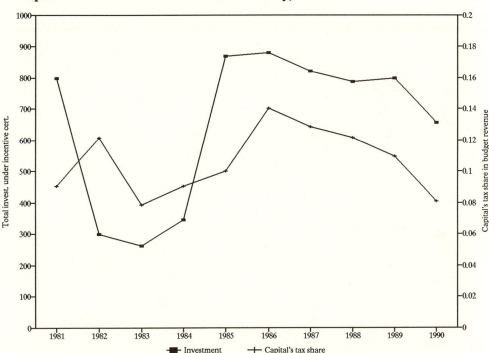

Source: Total investment under incentive certification data from SPO, *Annual Programs*;
Capital's tax share in total budget revenues data from the *General Directory of Treasury
and Foreign Trade*.

scissors. As clearly depicted in Figure 6.1, the gap over the wage-profit frontier
opens up in 1983 and rapidly widens over this phase. Finally, Phase 3 (cyclical
growth) is characterized by a more lenient stance toward labor and the working
classes in general. Consequently, the nature of surplus acquisition seems to have
changed, with the main mechanism now being founded upon the indirect processes
of (non)taxation.

The following section draws on some of the observed anomalies of the pattern
of disposition of surplus thus created, and portrays the economic rationale of the
realized mode of accumulation.

CONFLICTING PATTERNS OF ACCUMULATION

The post-1980 process of structural adjustment was aimed at the reorientation
of incentives toward private sector–led accumulation, to replace the public

Table 6.2
Distribution of Fixed Capital Investment, 1983–90 (Selected Years, Percent)

| | P r i v a t e | | | | P u b l i c | | | |
	1983	1985	1987	1990	1983	1985	1987	1990
Traded Sectors	49.9	46.6	38.7	39.2	63.3	54.6	46.3	38.9
Agriculture	12.2	8.9	6.9	4.4	8.3	5.8	8.9	8.8
Mining	1.3	1.4	1.5	1.3	9.6	10.1	3.7	3.5
Manufacturing	35.0	33.5	25.6	25.3	18.6	14.1	6.5	4.2
Tourism	0.7	2.2	3.8	6.4	0.6	1.1	2.4	1.5
Energy	0.7	0.6	0.9	1.0	26.2	23.5	24.8	21.4
Non-Traded Sectors	50.0	53.5	61.2	60.8	36.7	45.4	53.8	61.1
Transport & Commun.	16.9	17.9	12.4	13.6	22.5	28.5	32.6	34.2
Housing	28.4	30.3	43.9	41.3	1.5	2.4	1.5	3.5
Other	4.7	5.3	4.9	5.8	12.7	14.5	19.5	22.4

Source: State Planning Organization, *Annual Programs*, various years.

sector–led development strategy of the previous decades. Concomitant with this change of philosophy, the state's share in total fixed investment has receded, as the volume of public investment grew at an average annual rate of only 1.8 percent during the 1980–90 period. Private investment, on the other hand, did not show the buoyancy expected by the liberalization paradigm, and attained only about half the rate of growth of the precrisis period, returning to its precrisis level only after 1986 (Rittenberg, 1991).

Furthermore, a definite trend has been observed in the sectoral distribution of gross investment. Throughout the period under consideration, both public and private investment decisions shied away from manufacturing and other traded sectors and moved toward nontraded activities. The share of manufacturing in total private investment fell by 10 percentage points over the decade (Table 6.2), with housing, with its promise of rent-based opportunities for sizable profits, emerging as the sector most favored by private investment.

From a dynamic, growth-oriented perspective, this observation signals a very important deficiency in the industrialization strategy. Just as the overall growth strategy was based on increased manufactured exports, physical capital investments shifted away from manufacturing, adversely affecting the growth potential of manufactured exports.

This nonconformity between the export and accumulation targets of the adjustment experience is portrayed in Figure 6.4. Based on the data given in Table

Figure 6.4
Structural Schema of Surplus Extraction and Disposition
During Structural Adjustment in Turkey

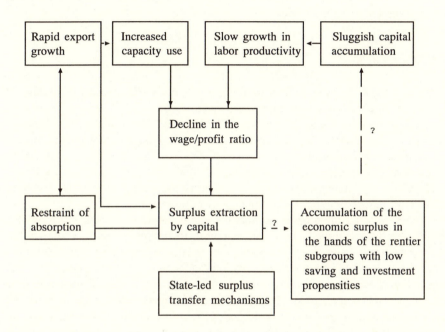

6.1, it can be argued that the increase in exports is sustained directly by more intensive use of installed capacity and suppression of real domestic absorption. Restraint of the absorption capacity facilitates the extraction of economic surplus and its acquisition by capital owners. At the same time, the slow pace of capital accumulation slows down the rate of growth of labor productivity and may lead to further regression of wage incomes.

In this process, one final question is why increased capitalist incomes in the aggregate do not translate into increased capital investments. Boratav and Türel (1988) argue that the slowing pace of capital accumulation in the manufacturing sector is the result of the redistribution of the economic surplus into the hands of the rentier and other tertiary subgroups having low saving and investment propensities. In fact, data in Table 6.1 suggest that the profitability of the banking system has surpassed that of the industrial sector during the adjustment era, with real profits of the private commercial banks increasing by as much as sixfold over the 1980–90 period. The real profitability index of the industrial sector, however, is observed to rise by 2.6 times. Concurrently, interest income has claimed more than a third of industrial value added, and total interest income as a proportion of gross domestic product has increased to 14.1 percent in 1988, from its initial level of 1.9 percent in 1980 (State Planning Organization [SPO] Annual Program, various years). Interest income is observed to have increased elevenfold in real terms over the 1980–88 period.

CONCLUSION

The Turkish adjustment experience through the 1980s narrates a process of how, in a dualistic economy trapped between the needs of the domestic industry for integration with the world markets and the painful distributional requirements of such a reorientation, the state apparatus became the bastion of privilege for rent seeking groups. Rent seeking involved both direct mechanisms, such as obtaining more favorable export subsidies (leading to significant overinvoicing practices), and indirect mechanisms, such as tax evasion, macro pricing policies and recoding of existing legislation in crucial spheres of economic life.

I have rejected the proposition that the rate of return to capital, vis-à-vis the profit rate, is determined purely by economic forces operating in a competitive market of neutral incentives, and argued instead that economic surplus as the basis of profits was shaped and molded by various social and economic processes, often necessitating active state involvement. Finally, I have emphasized the basic inner conflict of such a mode of surplus transfer, namely the nonconformity between the industrialization targets and the emerging pattern of accumulation. This leaves us with the task of finding plausible alternatives for reconciling realities of policy making with the economic structure in a structurally adjusting indigenous economy.

NOTES

The author wishes to express his gratitude to Hikmet Uluğbay, Osman Zaim and Erol Balkan for their comments and help in gathering valuable supplies of data, and to Alper Yılmaz for research assistance.

1. For a thorough policy assessment of the reform package, see Şenses (1983); for an economic analysis of the new commercial regime, see Baysan and Blitzer (1991). Celasun and Rodrik (1989) and the series of papers in the edited volume of Arıcanlı and Rodrik (1990) provide in– depth analysis of the postreform Turkish economic development. For a political-economic portrayal of the Turkish adjustment experience from an interest group viewpoint, see Yeldan and Roe (1991), Öniş (1991, 1992) and Heper (1991).

2. Yeldan (1991, Table 6.1).

3. Yeldan (1990) also analyzes the adverse movement in the (functional) distribution of income along with manufacturing export growth and accumulation within the concept of "disarticulated" growth process.

4. See Cizre-Sakallıog¨lu (1991) for a thorough depiction of the political environment surrounding capital-labor relations after the 1980 reform.

5. See Yeldan and Roe (1991) for an analysis of the rent-seeking environment under an open trade regime, and Öniş (1992) for an extensive discussion of the political economy underlying the rent-seeking practices during the early 1980s.

6. SPO, Annual Program, various years. For further documentation of the postreform investment incentive system, see Güvemli (1991).

7

LIBERALIZATION, TRANSNATIONAL CORPORATIONS AND FOREIGN DIRECT INVESTMENT IN TURKEY: THE EXPERIENCE OF THE 1980S

Ziya Öniş

INTRODUCTION

The structural adjustment program introduced in Turkey in 1980 placed major emphasis on foreign direct investment as a source of capital inflow and technology transfer. The overall liberalization of the trade and payments regime, a process that has gathered momentum during the post-1983 period, has been accompanied by a number of specific changes designed to attract larger inflows of foreign direct investment. A cursory examination of the data reveals that the new economic strategy implemented since 1980 has been quite effective in attracting foreign investment, although a large gap continued to exist between the authorized and actual inflows. The cumulative total of foreign direct investment authorized during the 1950–70 period had been recorded as $229 million. Yet, during the 1980–90 period, the cumulative total of FDI authorized emerged as $6,189.9 million. A similar pattern is revealed with respect to the number of enterprises involved. A total of 91 companies had been in operation in Turkey in 1979, of which 76 were based in manufacturing and 14 in services. By the end of 1990, however, a total of 1,813 companies were in operation of which 508 were in manufacturing, 1,224 in services and the remainder in agriculture and mining. Hence, in retrospect, a striking transformation can be detected with respect to both the magnitude and pattern of FDI in the 1980s as compared with the pre-1980 import-substitution era. This chapter seeks to provide a broad and critical evaluation of Turkey's foreign investment record and to draw some lessons from the Turkish experience that might be of wider comparative interest.

THE GLOBAL CONTEXT: THE RENEWED IMPORTANCE OF
FOREIGN DIRECT INVESTMENT IN THE 1980s

An adequate understanding of the Turkish experience with FDI in the 1980s ought to take into consideration the profound changes that have recently occurred concerning the operation of transnational companies as well as their relations with less developed countries at the global level. In the context of developing countries as a whole, the past decade has been characterized by a marked liberalization of policies toward foreign investment, with the old policy of confrontation with the transnational corporations being replaced by a more pragmatic approach (Cable & Persaud, 1987; Page, 1987).

Several forces account for the radical shift in the attitude of LDC governments toward foreign investment. First, LDCs have collectively experienced slow economic growth and low levels of capital accumulation in the 1980s, which have been accompanied by a process of continued widening of the technological gap vis-à-vis the industrial countries (United Nations Center on Transnational Corporations [UNCTC], 1988). With the notable exceptions of certain newly industrializing countries in Asia, they have become progressively less attractive sites for investment by TNCs. At the same time, the heavy debt burden of the LDCs and the consequent need to service foreign debt dramatically limited the funds available for capital formation. The commercial banks had established themselves as the principal engine of capital flow to the LDCs in the 1970s. Yet, in the aftermath of the debt crisis, the commercial banks became increasingly reluctant to expand their lending to LDCs. Consequently, the LDCs and the international community have progressively turned their attention to TNC investment as a means of restoring capital inflows (UNCTC, 1988).

The initial response of the multinational corporate community when the debt crisis hit the LDCs has been to cut the level of annual investment by more than 25 percent (Moran, 1988). Hence, rather paradoxically, a marked slowdown occurred in the growth rate of FDI at a time when LDCs needed them most as a source of structural adjustment and technology transfer for export-oriented development. The indications are that FDI is not likely to provide a sufficiently large financial flow to make up for the contraction of lending from the transnational banks and official development aid. TNCs by themselves cannot facilitate the process of structural adjustment in the direction of export-oriented industrialization that most developing countries need. (Cable & Persaud, 1987; Moran, 1988).

A broad examination of the pattern of investment by the TNCs during the past decade reveals several interesting trends. Historically, FDI flows among the developed market economies have been much larger than those between developed market economies and LDCs. The evidence suggests that during the course of the 1980s the gap has grown even wider. In 1985, FDI flows to nonoil LDCs accounted for a mere 16.2 percent of total global foreign investment. A progressively greater share of TNC activity appears to be concentrated in developed market economies. Particularly significant is the concentration of TNC investment in Europe in anticipation of the free market conditions expected to materialize by the end of 1992 (UNCTC, 1988).

Another key characteristic relates to the expansion of TNCs through a variety of institutional arrangements, many of which involve little or no investment of capital. TNCs have made increasingly greater use of nonequity arrangements such as licensing agreements and subcontracting and of limited equity arrangements such as joint ventures, which allow the firm to maintain an economic presence without incurring the full risks associated with direct investment (Oman, 1984; UNCTC, 1988; Cable & Persaud, 1987). The new forms of investment that emerged during the 1980s have a rather striking ramification. They suggest that TNCs per se are not likely to become a major source of capital transfer as a substitute for bank lending and official aid.

Another trend that deserves emphasis is the declining importance of the United States as a major source of foreign investment. In fact, the U.S. TNCs appear to have increasingly turned inward to their home market in recent years. In contrast, Japan has emerged as the third largest investor after the United States and the United Kingdom during the last decade. Japan's rise as a major source of FDI has been based on the fact that it has established a strong competitive advantage for a range of technologically advanced products. The outstanding technological change in the 1980s has involved the application of microelectronics- based information technologies to manufacturing systems and to handling information in the service sectors. Parallel to these changes, and essential to their effective implementation, innovations have occurred in the organization and management of production that stress flexibility, quality and cooperation. These organizational changes, which are frequently referred to as flexible specialization, inherently contradict the logic and principles of the mass production model (UNCTC, 1988; Schmitz, 1989).

The indications are that the world is on the threshold of a new technological era that offers novel possibilities for rapid growth. Information technologies have been incorporated into the production processes of almost all sectors of the economies of industrial countries. Furthermore, discoveries in biotechnology and new materials appear to be on the verge of being translated into commercially viable products and technologies. The emergence of new technologies accentuates the role of the TNCs as a major vehicle of technology transfer to developing countries. The emergence of new technologies, however, tends to undermine the traditional advantage of LDCs in attracting investment, in the sense that labor costs per se are becoming increasingly less relevant to the location decisions of TNCs (Broad & Cavanagh, 1988).

Another major trend in the 1980s involved the dramatic increase of investment in services. By the mid-1980s, about 40 percent of the world stock and half of the annual flows were in finance- and trade-related services. A significant portion of

FDI flows to developing countries represents investment in offshore financial centers.

When we examine FDI flows to LDCs, we observe a striking concentration in the activities of TNCs in a limited number of highly developed newly industrializing countries and "near NICs." During the last fifteen years, five countries (Brazil, Indonesia, Malaysia, Mexico and Singapore) have received 50 percent of all foreign direct investment, while the 41 low-income LDCs (excluding China and India) have received only 2 percent (Moran, 1988). The heavy concentration of TNC investment in NICs continued during the 1980s, although in the aftermath of the debt crisis there has been an increasing shift of FDI flows away from the major Latin American LDCs to the Asian NICs. The pattern clearly suggests that the majority of LDCs, even if they implement highly liberal policies toward FDI, are unlikely to benefit from the new wave of transnational investment that originated during the course of the 1980s.

Yet another insight that emerges from an examination of global trends is that the new production technologies have reduced direct labor costs, while "just-in-time" inventory systems have frequently made location more important. Hence, these changes appear to undermine the comparative advantage of developing countries in many assembly operations. The exceptions to this general rule are those countries that have large domestic markets or those with close proximity to advanced country markets. Clearly, Turkey falls under this exceptional category and can potentially be a major beneficiary of the new wave of transnational investment.

THE MACRO-INSTITUTIONAL ENVIRONMENT AND FOREIGN DIRECT INVESTMENT IN TURKEY

The institutional framework and the structure of incentives governing foreign direct investment in Turkey have been radically transformed during the post-1980 period. In retrospect, the liberalization of the foreign investment regime has constituted a sphere in which government policy has been characterized by a high degree of consistency, thereby confirming that the attraction of foreign investment was a major priority of the structural adjustment program initiated in 1980. From a comparative perspective, it would be instructive, therefore, to examine the nature of the incentives provided to FDI and the associated changes in the institutional environment.

It is widely recognized that the pre-1980 era had been characterized by a highly restrictive and protectionist trade and payments regime, which, in turn, provided a strong bias in favor of import substitution and production for the internal market (Krueger, 1974). Similarly, the foreign investment regime displayed a rather restrictive pattern, a fact that has been extensively documented (Erdilek, 1982). Many investigators have drawn attention, however, to the existence of a highly paradoxical situation with respect to the foreign investment regime. The Foreign Investment Law (Law 6224) introduced in 1954 had provided the basic legal framework for FDI throughout the 1954–80 period. Even a casual examination of the provisions of this law suggests that it was, in principle, a liberal piece of legislation, designed to create a favorable environment for FDI. This law contained no obvious restrictions on the sectors in which FDI might take place, nor on FDI profit transfers and interest payments or repatriation of FDI capital. Yet, in practice, the vagueness in the formulation of Law 6224 had lent itself to a variety of interpretations which, in turn, provided the rationale for extensive intervention and regulation of FDI activity at the implementation stage. The vagueness of the law can be illustrated with reference to clause (A), which stated that FDI might be permitted provided that it (a) aided the country's economic development; (b) was active in a field that was open to Turkish private enterprises; and (c) did not possess any monopoly or special privileges. It is self-evident that an apparently liberal FDI regime could at the same time provide the basis of a highly interventionist and tightly regulated FDI environment.

In practice, the regime that emerged during the 1960s and 1970s displayed the following characteristics: (1) Foreign investors were subjected to discriminatory treatment vis-à-vis domestic firms in the implementation of investment credit incentives. They were also subjected to restrictions concerning their ability to transfer profits abroad. (2) Significant pressures were exerted on individual firms to increase local equity participation and to expand exports. (3) Foreign investors were subjected to considerable delays in the initial stages of obtaining the approval for setting up their operations in Turkey. The delays were magnified by the extremely fragmented bureaucratic structure. Several government agencies were involved in the process of authorizing FDI, including the Ministry of Commerce, the State Planning Organization, the Ministry of Finance and the Ministry of Industry and Technology, with little coordination of their activities. The fragmented bureaucratic structure not only obstructed the process of foreign investment but also undermined considerably the government's ability to monitor and regulate effectively the activities of foreign investors. Hence, the foreign investment regime was in many ways typical of the majority of LDCs that had pursued restrictive import-substitution strategies during the 1960s and 1970s. It was a regime based essentially on confrontation and mutual distrust between the government and foreign investors, a regime that was clearly not conducive to the goal of attracting large inflows of foreign investment (Erdilek, 1982).

This extremely restrictive regime has been progressively dismantled during the course of the 1980s, and has been replaced by a highly liberal regime. In analyzing the changing environment for FDI in the post-1980 period, however, a firm distinction ought to be drawn between two specific phases. During the first phase, corresponding to 1980–83, significant steps were taken in the direction of replacing the import-substitution strategy with an outward-oriented regime. Key relative prices including the exchange rate, interest rates and the product prices of state enterprises were deregulated and import quotas were largely dismantled.

The major moves toward liberalization of the economy occurred following the retransition to parliamentary democracy in November 1983. Significant reductions in the effective rates of protection as well as the removal of restrictions on the capital account and the payments regime in December 1983 and January 1984 constituted the immediate measures of the newly elected Motherland Party government (Nas & Odekon, 1988; Olgun, Togan & Akder, 1988). Parallel to the reform of the trade and payments regime, specific measures in the direction of liberalizing the FDI regime were introduced during the post-1983 phase. The landmark in the context of FDI reform involved the reorganization of bureaucracy, effectively in 1984, with a single organization, the Foreign Investment Department of the State Planning Organization, assuming responsibility for authorizing applications for foreign investment and for monitoring the subsequent performance of foreign investors. A highly unified bureaucratic structure emerged, which substantially eliminated the delays and ambiguities associated with the highly fragmented structure that had characterized the pre-1980 era. In fact, the unified bureaucratic structure in the foreign investment field contrasted sharply with the fragmented and incoherent nature of policy making that characterized other major spheres of economic policy in the 1980s, such as the administration of export incentives (Öniş, 1992).

Another major shift in the direction of liberalizing the FDI regime involved the specific legislation on the formation of free trade zones in 1985. The major objective of this law was to encourage export-oriented foreign investment in prespecified regions of the country. These regions or free zones would be exempt from most of the provisions applying to FDI activity outside the free zones. The major benefit offered by the free zones involved exemption from Turkish taxes. Furthermore, Turkish labor laws would not be applicable in the free trade zones for a 10-year period, which meant that the regions would be free from strike activity. All payments in the free trade zones have to be made in Central Bank–designated hard currencies. The first free trade zone was opened in Mersin in January 1987 (DPT, 1987; Erdilek, 1988; Ilkin & Tekeli, 1987).

1986 marked the climax of the FDI liberalization process. As a result of the changes introduced, 100 percent foreign ownership became feasible for all foreign investors in all sectors of the economy. Disincentives for foreign ownership in the form of attempts to impose local equity participation were eliminated. The minimum export requirements that had been imposed on foreign firms, but not on domestically owned firms, were removed (YASED, 1986; Erdilek, 1988). Another fundamental step involved the elimination of fiscal discrimination against foreign investors. The Turkish personal and corporate income tax legislation were modified and became much more favorable to foreign investors. Finally, the scope of the Foreign Investment Department of the State Planning Organization was considerably expanded. The department was empowered to receive and approve applications up to $50 million, even in cases where the application involved 100 percent foreign ownership. Applications exceeding $50 million, however, still required approval by the Cabinet.

The basic principle underlying the government's philosophy toward foreign investment, namely the equal treatment of domestic and foreign firms, became firmly established through the series of steps introduced in 1986. It is important to emphasize that the new Turkish foreign investment regime does not embody any specific measures that involve positive discrimination in favor of foreign investors, such as tax holidays. In this respect, the Turkish FDI regime differs considerably from the FDI regimes of many developing countries, particularly countries in Southeast Asia (Mehmet, 1990).

Finally, the FDI regime in Turkey involved a major institutional innovation in the form of the "build-operate-transfer" (BOT) model that has attracted widespread international attention (DPT, 1987; Dinç, 1989). Many investigators had identified transport and communications as the major bottlenecks confronting the Turkish economy during the early 1980s. In fact, public investment has progressively shifted, as part of the structural adjustment program, away from manufacturing into infrastructural activities in order to relieve this constraint. The evidence suggests, however, that infrastructural projects within the public sector are characterized by long gestation lags with a corresponding amplification in costs (Öniş & Özmucur, 1991). The BOT model was a direct response to the endemic problems of prolonged investment projects within the public sector. The model was designed to attract foreign investment to the construction of infrastructural facilities and thereby transfer some of the burden imposed on the public sector to the private sector. The proponents of the BOT model claim that it embodies several distinctive advantages. The consortium of firms undertaking the projects has an obvious built-in incentive to complete the project as rapidly as possible so that it can reap the benefits of operating the project. Significant economies in costs can be established as companies seek to obtain their inputs from the cheapest source possible. Parallel to the gains in efficiency, a major advantage of the scheme is that it constitutes an additional source of finance for priority projects.

TURKEY's FOREIGN DIRECT INVESTMENT PERFORMANCE IN THE 1980s: THE EMERGING PATTERN

The unfavorable environment we have outlined had resulted in extremely low levels of foreign investment by international standards in the pre-1980 period. The evidence clearly indicates a considerable deterioration in FDI performance during the 1974–79 phase. The escalating political and economic crisis of the late 1970s undoubtedly exercised a negative influence over foreign investment during the second half of the decade (Table 7.1). Aggregate figures disguise, however, the

Table 7.1

Foreign Investment Authorizations in Turkey in the Pre-1980 Era, 1961–79 (In Millions of Dollars)

	Annual FDI	Cumulative FDI
Until 1960	17.3	17.3
1961-1970	88.6	105.9
1971-1973	91.8	197.7
1974	-7.7	190.0
1975	15.1	205.1
1976	8.9	214.0
1977	9.2	223.2
1978	11.7	234.9
1979	-6.4	228.5

Source: DPT, 1987.

high degree of sectoral concentration of foreign capital in the pre-1980 era. A casual examination of the data based on authorized FDI reveals that FDI was heavily concentrated in the manufacturing sector, and within the manufacturing sector four key sectors, namely, the automotive industry, chemicals, rubber and electrical and electronic products, accounted for more than two-thirds of the total stock of foreign capital (Table 7.2). Hence, foreign capital performed a key role in the development of important branches of the manufacturing industry oriented toward the internal market.

In evaluating the foreign investment performance in the post-1980 era, we need to distinguish between two quite separate phases. In spite of a certain improvement in FDI performance on average, relative to the pre-1980 era, inflows of FDI displayed a highly unstable pattern during the first half of the 1980s (Table 7.3). Moreover, the initial spurt in FDI reflected to a significant degree voluntary conversion of nonguaranteed foreign commercial credits and convertible Turkish lira deposits into FDI (Erdilek, 1988). It is clear that the sustained increases in FDI flows occurred in the second half of the 1980s, with the increase being particularly pronounced during the 1988–90 period (Table 7.3). The actual inflows of FDI jumped from an annual average of $128.4 million during 1980–87 to $406 million in 1988, $738 million in 1989, $789 million in 1990, $910 million in 1991 and $912 million in 1992. However, the data on authorized FDI clearly exaggerate, by a significant margin, the magnitude of actual FDI flows that the economy has been able to attract in the post-1980 era.

Table 7.2
Sectoral Distribution of Foreign Capital in the Pre-1980 Era, End of 1977 (Percent)

A. Manufacturing	88.3
Food, Beverages and Tobacco	6.1
Rubber	9.0
Chemicals	18.9
Automotive Industry	27.9
Electrical & Electronics Industry	12.8
B. Services	10.8
Tourism	8.7
Banking	2.1
C. Agriculture and Mining	0.9

Sources: Ministry of Commerce data as given in Uras, 1979.

In analyzing the sectoral distribution of FDI, we need to recognize from the outset that our data are based on authorized rather than realized FDI, and that a quite different pattern might have emerged if data on actual inflows had been available. With this qualification in mind, a broad examination of the sectoral distribution of the authorized FDI reveals that the increase in FDI flows relative to the pre-1980 era was accompanied by a marked shift away from manufacturing into services during the post-1980 period (Table 7.4).

It is interesting that the shift toward services occurred in the early 1980s and subsequently the distribution of annual FDI between manufacturing and services has remained fairly stable. A further disaggregation at the sectoral level points toward a profound transformation in both the annual flows and the total stock of FDI within the manufacturing sector. The most recent evidence based on data for 1989 reveals that food and beverages and iron and steel stand out as the most favored sectors, followed by automotive equipment and textiles. A striking trend concerns the dramatic decline in the share (in total authorized FDI) of the major import-substituting sectors, such as automotive equipment and automotive components, and a corresponding increase in the share of food and beverages, textiles, and iron and steel that constituted Turkey's principal export-oriented industries in the post-1980 period (Table 7.5). A similar pattern emerges from the sectoral distribution of the total stock of foreign investment at the end of 1989 (Table 7.6). Finally, by the end of 1989, almost one-half of the total stock of foreign capital was concentrated in services, with tourism and banking emerging

Table 7.3
Authorized Versus Realized FDI in Turkey, 1980–90 (In Millions of Dollars)

| | Authorized FDI | | Actual Inflow | |
	Annual	Cumulative	Annual	Cumulative
1980	97.0	97.0	35.0	35.0
1981	337.5	434.5	141.0	176.0
1982	167.0	601.5	103.0	279.0
1983	102.7	704.2	87.0	366.0
1984	271.4	975.6	162.0	528.0
1985	234.5	1,210.1	158.0	686.0
1986	364.0	1,574.1	170.0	856.0
1987	536.5	2,110.6	171.0	1,027.0
1988	824.5	2,935.1	406.0	1,433.0
1989	1,470.5	4,405.6	738.0	2,171.0
1990	1,784.0	6,419.0	739.0	2,910.0

Source: DPT, 1990.

as the key subsectors in which the inflows of FDI were particularly pronounced during the post-1980 period (Table 7.6).

THE FOREIGN INVESTMENT BOOM OF 1988–90: AN EXPLANATION

1988 marked a decisive turning point in Turkey's FDI performance. A proper assessment of this impressive pattern, however, requires a comparative perspective. In terms of the ratio of the stock of FDI to GDP, the Turkish record falls considerably short of the LDC average and a selected group of LDCs (Table 7.7). In terms of annual inflows, Turkey's experience in recent years compares favorably with that of South Korea, a leading NIC that has traditionally maintained a relatively restrictive stance toward foreign investment. If we exclude South Korea, the performance of the principal Latin American and Asian NICs, including Thailand (a country that has emerged as a major second-generation NIC1988 during the 1980s) are superior to the Turkish case (Table 7.8). The problem of interpretation and comparison is complicated, however, by the fact that the upsurge of FDI in Brazil and Mexico during 1988–89 reflects extensive debt-equity swaps and, hence, is not a totally voluntary process.

The recent surge of foreign investment in Turkey provides some support for the hypothesis that the domestic policy environment and the nature of the system

Table 7.4
Sectoral Distribution of Authorized Foreign Investment in Turkey, 1980–90
(Percent)

	Manufacturing	Agriculture Mining	Services
1980	91.5	0.0	8.5
1981	73.1	0.5	26.4
1982	59.0	1.8	39.2
1983	36.6	0.0	13.4
1984	68.5	2.3	29.2
1985	60.9	4.6	34.5
1986	53.1	4.9	42.0
1987	51.0	2.5	46.5
1988	58.7	3.9	37.4
1989	61.3	1.4	37.3
1990	64.0	6.3	29.7
Average	61.4	2.4	36.2

Source: DPT, 1987, 1990, 1991.

of incentives are critical variables that determine the magnitude and pattern of FDI inflows to a particular economy. Many investigators have pointed out that Turkey has always possessed a number of country- or location-specific advantages that rendered Turkey potentially attractive to foreign investors. These country- or location-specific advantages include a substantial industrial and infrastructural base, a large domestic market and a highly suitable geographic position for export-oriented FDI in terms of close proximity to the key markets in the European Community, the Middle East, and the former Soviet Union and Eastern European socialist countries. Turkey's substantial natural endowments in tourism constituted another important location-specific advantage. From an orthodox, neoclassical perspective, therefore, the inability of Turkey to take advantage of her country- or location-specific advantages with respect to foreign investment in the past can be attributed to the unfavorable policy environment as characterized by a significant degree of bureaucratic interventionism. Additional support for the orthodox perspective is provided by the fact that the acceleration of inflows of foreign investment occurred, not in the early stages of the structural adjustment program, but only after the introduction of the specific set of measures that drastically altered the FDI environment during the 1984–86 period. A secondary

Table 7.5

Sectoral Composition of Authorized FDI in Turkish Manufacturing, 1989 (Percent)

	Sector's Share in Total FDI	Sector's Share in Total FDI in Manufacturing
Chemicals	6.5	9.6
Food & Beverages	10.5	15.6
Electrical & Electronics	3.0	4.5
Iron & Steel	6.0	8.9
Automotive Equipment	3.9	5.8
Textiles	3.7	5.5
Automotive Components	1.0	1.5
Total Manufacturing	67.4	100.0

Source: DPT, 1990.

factor to emphasize is the steady decline in real wages in Turkey at least until early 1989, at a time when significant increases in real earnings had occurred in countries such as South Korea. By the second half of the 1980s, Turkey provided a more favorable environment for export-oriented FDI as compared to South Korea on the basis of differences in labor costs (ILO, 1987).

Yet, in our judgement, the orthodox explanation that underlines the importance of a changed policy environment provides an important, and yet only a partial, explanation of the foreign investment boom of 1988–90. A closer investigation of recent trends reveals a more complex process than we have hitherto described. It seems that the drastic changes in the global environment in the second half of the 1980s also provided an impetus to foreign investment in Turkey. The following changes in the geopolitical environment are of particular significance: (1) the movement toward a complete economic union of Western Europe by the end of 1992; (2) the enormous political and economic changes taking place in the former Soviet Union and Eastern Europe, involving political and economic liberalization; and (3) the dramatic rise of Japan as a world power and as a major source of foreign investment.

A merger boom occurred in Western Europe during the 1980s, as companies prepared themselves for the single European market projected to materialize by the end of 1992. The surge in foreign investment in Turkey during 1988–90 may also be explained, in part, by a similar merger boom involving a number of partnership and joint venture agreements between the leading Turkish

Table 7.6

Sectoral Composition of the Stock of Foreign Capital in Manufacturing and Services in Turkey, End of 1989 (Percent)

	Sector's Share in Total Capital	Sector's Share of Total Foreign Capital in Manufacturing
A. Manufacturing		
Chemicals	12.5	24.5
Food & Beverages	8.3	16.3
Electrical & Electronics	6.9	13.5
Iron & Steel	4.6	9.1
Automotive Equipment	4.2	8.2
Textiles	3.4	6.6
Automotive Components	1.4	2.8
Miscellaneous	9.7	19.0
Total Manufacturing	51.0	100.0
B. Services		
Trade	10.4	23.3
Tourism	15.5	34.7
Banking	8.8	19.7
Miscellaneous	10.0	22.3
Services	44.7	100.0

Source: DPT, 1990.

conglomerates and foreign investors, a process that allowed the former to upgrade their technological base and augment their marketing capacities. The underlying motive for these mergers appears to have been mutual interest in trying to take advantage of the process of global restructuring that has gathered momentum at the end of the 1980s. From the foreign investors' point of view, Turkey appears to be a particularly attractive location to be employed as an export base and a point of entry into markets in the European Community, the Middle East and the potentially lucrative markets in the former Soviet Union and Eastern Europe. The additional advantages of a large internal market, low labor costs and the absence of European Community–style rigorous technological regulations have increased the attractiveness of Turkey from the point of view of European investors. There

Table 7.7
Share of FDI Stock in GDP in Selected LDCs, 1985 (Percent)

LDCs	8.7	Chile	14.9
Indonesia	5.9	Mexico	8.9
S.Korea	6.4	Peru	15.4
Philippines	28.6	Brazil	13.9
Thailand	6.1	Turkey	0.8
Argentina	12.9	Turkey[a]	1.1

Sources: United Nations Center on Transnational Corporations, 1988; DPT, 1990.
[a] 1989 figure

are also indications that the Japanese companies are interested in using Turkey as an export base and as a platform for expanding into the Western European markets in the course of the 1990s. Yet, the current contribution of the Japanese companies to foreign investment in Turkey is only marginal. Japanese firms accounted for 4.5 percent of the total stock of FDI and 4.9 percent of the total annual authorized inflow in 1989. The first Toyota plant in Turkey, which is expected to start production in the near future, could well signal a wave of Japanese investment in Turkish manufacturing industry.

The foreign investment boom of 1988–90 reflected another striking, but at the same time less favorable, trend. This involved the take over of medium- and small-scale domestic firms in financial difficulties by foreign investors to increase their control over the internal market. It is a well-documented fact that, with the exception of large conglomerates with close organic links to commercial banks, the majority of Turkish firms have weak financial structures characterized by extremely high debt-equity ratios and a high degree of dependence on short-term loans from commercial banks for working capital requirements (ISO, 1989; Yaser, Weed & Marchesini, 1988). The Turkish economy experienced a "mini-crisis" in the aftermath of the general elections of November 1987, due to a loss of fiscal discipline and overexpansion of the economy in the preelection period. The disequilibrium was manifested in the form of currency substitution away from the Turkish lira into dollar-denominated deposits, which resulted in a steady expansion of the gap between the official and the black-market exchange rate. The February 1988 measures designed to restabilize the economy following the mini-crisis accentuated the financial difficulties of a large number of domestic manufacturing firms. In the aftermath of these measures, firms were confronted with a relatively stagnant internal market, accelerating inflation, and high loan rates of interest. Consequently, mergers with foreign companies or direct acquisitions of domestic companies by foreign investors emerged as the principal

Table 7.8
Inflows of FDI in Selected Countries, 1988, 1989 (In Millions of Dollars)

	1988	1989
Turkey	406	738
Brazil	1,794	744
Mexico	635	1,852
S.Korea	720	453
Thailand	1,082	1,650
Singapore	2,710	3,963

Sources: International Financial Statistics, various issues; DPT, 1990.

solution through which many small or medium-scale companies could resolve their financial difficulties. An increasing proportion of FDI during this period assumed the form of increases in equity and portfolio investment, while a progressively smaller proportion was directed toward building new capacity and the modernization of plant and equipment (Table 7.9).

Is the boom in FDI of 1988–90 sustainable and does it provide the beginnings of a much larger wave of transnational investment in the Turkish economy during the course of the 1990s? Given its geographical location and level of development, Turkey is clearly in a favorable position vis-à-vis the majority of LDCs to capitalize on the process of global restructuring. Yet, in an era of intense competition to attract foreign investment, transnational corporations are particularly sensitive to the policy environment of the host country. Hence, steady increases in inflows of FDI to Turkey will be conditional on the sustainability of economic reforms, which in turn is crucially dependent on the ability to maintain a stable political and macroeconomic environment. Persistently high rates of inflation in recent years have been a particular source of concern for foreign investors. The fact that foreign investors have not perceived Turkey's macroeconomic and political trajectory as sufficiently stable and predictable may well account for Turkey's inability to attract even larger inflows of FDI in recent years, an inability that is clearly reflected also by the large discrepancy between authorized and actual inflows.

FOREIGN INVESTMENT AND THE CASE FOR INDUSTRIAL POLICY

As we have argued above, Turkey's foreign investment policy has been transformed from a highly interventionist approach in the 1960s and 1970s to a

Table 7.9
Distribution of FDI in Turkey According to Type of Investment, 1980–89
(Percent)

	Building New Capacity, Modernization of Plant and Equipment	Increases in Equity and Portfolio Investment
1980	74.4	25.6
1981	51.6	48.4
1982	58.1	41.9
1983	65.7	34.3
1984	73.9	26.1
1985	66.3	33.7
1986	73.7	26.3
1987	55.7	44.3
1988	48.1	51.9
1989	46.0	54.0

Source: DPT, 1990.

liberal regime involving equal incentives for domestic and foreign investors, with minimal bureaucratic intervention or regulation. The FDI environment in the pre-1980 era restricted the volume of foreign investment and also minimized its contribution to Turkey's economic development. The type of FDI that was attracted under the pre-1980 regime was primarily oriented toward the domestic market and hence was incapable of generating significant volumes of export. Furthermore, the highly protectionist trade and payments regime and the associated inefficiency in the allocation of resources substantially reduced the net benefits from FDI from the point of view of national welfare. Compared to their domestic counterparts, foreign-owned enterprises relied disproportionately on domestic financing, were generally more import dependent and had a smaller propensity to export, with a higher orientation toward the expansion of domestic consumption of consumer durable goods (Erdilek, 1982). Admittedly, the concentration of foreign investment in certain key areas of manufacturing industry, such as automotive components, resulted in significant learning effects over time, which enabled Turkey to export manufactured products on a significant scale in the post-ISI phase in the 1980s.

While we do recognize that extensive regulation of FDI is likely to be counterproductive, we believe that a free market approach, which is synonymous with a passive industrial policy, also embodies important limitations in terms of maximizing the developmental contribution of FDI. The policy makers should be concerned with both the composition of foreign investment and the composition of the manufacturing sector. As indicated earlier, the increase in FDI flows into Turkey during the 1980s has been associated with a drastic rise in the share of the services sector, which was concentrated mostly in banking and tourism. In 1989, for example, services accounted for nearly 40 percent of the actual stock of FDI. Clearly, this pattern is to some extent a reflection of global trends. Furthermore, the nature of services has changed a great deal during the last decade, with many branches of services emerging as complementary to manufacturing. Nonetheless, for policy makers preoccupied with the developmental impact of foreign investment, as measured by its contribution toward technology transfer and indigenous learning, the heavy weight of services in the annual flows and total stock of FDI represents a distorted and lopsided structure.   During the next decade, one of the objectives of industrial policy should be to shift the balance of FDI flows increasingly in favor of manufacturing. What is required are subtle and indirect forms of FDI regulation as part of a broader industrial strategy, which at the same time links foreign investment explicitly to the strategy of export expansion and export deepening.

The case for an active industrial strategy, designed to identify and subsidize key sectors or subsectors of manufacturing industry with dynamic comparative advantage, rests on the following grounds: (1) In recent years, a process of relative deindustrialization has been occurring in Turkey due to the combination of two forces. First, as public investment has steadily shifted away from manufacturing into infrastructural activities such as transport, communications and energy, the private sector has failed to fill the gap generated by the retreat of the public sector from manufacturing. The share of manufacturing in private investment has declined in recent years, reflecting the shift in favor of construction activities, notably housing (Öniş, 1989). (2) Rapid export expansion has been a major success story of the early 1980s. Yet, the process of export expansion has been based primarily on the diversion of existing capacity, created under import substitution, toward production for external markets. Furthermore, export growth has been heavily concentrated in a small number of sectors such as food and beverages, textiles, clothing, and iron and steel, with 63.1 percent of exports in 1987 originating from resource-intensive and labor-intensive industries (OECD, 1990). As these are the very industries that are subject to heavy protection in advanced country markets, they have only very limited growth prospects. Moreover, most of the expansion in world trade in recent years has been taking place, not in resource-intensive, labor-intensive or scale-intensive industries, but in differentiated goods and science-based industries (Dahlman, 1990). Hence, the sustainability of rapid export growth in Turkey depends on the ability to diversify the export base and also substantially expand investment in new export industries (Öniş, 1989; Şenses, 1989b; Rodrik, 1988).

The problem is aggravated by the fact that, in order to maintain competitiveness in international markets, even traditional export industries such as textiles and clothing require substantial restructuring through new investment in flexible technologies (Kırım, 1990b). These considerations suggest that the introduction of new technologies as a means of accomplishing the restructuring process necessary for attaining international competitiveness in key sectors of the economy should emerge as the fundamental guiding principle of foreign investment policy. An active industrial policy designed to encourage specific sectors or subsectors of manufacturing would be perfectly consistent with the principle of the equal treatment of domestic and foreign investors as embodied in the current foreign investment regime.

CONCLUDING OBSERVATIONS

Several interesting lessons can be drawn from our broad account of the Turkish experience with FDI during the last decade. A major lesson is that the transnational companies are highly sensitive to the macroinstitutional and policy environment of the host country. The recent surge of FDI flows to Turkey may, to a significant extent, be attributed to the transformation of incentives through the liberalization of trade and payments regimes, elimination of bureaucratic controls and of discrimination in favor of domestic investors, and to a lesser extent comparatively low labor costs. What is also striking in the Turkish case is that the foreign investors started to respond with a considerable time-lag following the inception of economic reforms in 1980 and only after a drastic shift of incentives. The pattern suggests that the foreign investment decision is crucially dependent not only on the change of incentives but on the sustainability of the new incentive regime which, in turn, depends on the stability of the macroeconomic and political environment. The importance of the confidence factor also points toward another important lesson, namely, that FDI and capital inflows from commercial banks are complementary phenomena. FDI flows assumed significant proportions only after the restoration of balance of payments equilibrium and the reestablishment of Turkey's creditworthiness in international financial markets during the post-1983 period.

By similar logic, Turkey's failure, in spite of important country- or location-specific advantages, to attract larger inflows of FDI during the 1980s may be attributed to the fact that foreign investors do not as yet regard the macroeconomic and political environment as sufficiently stable. The important general message that emerges, therefore, is that a drastic shift in incentives in favor of foreign investment per se will not generate large inflows of FDI, if foreign investors have serious doubts concerning the sustainability of policy reforms.

A balanced interpretation of Turkey's FDI performance in the 1980s ought to take into consideration the far-reaching changes that have occurred with respect to the pattern of TNC activity at the global level. Particularly relevant in this context are the increasing importance of new forms of transnational investment, which tend to minimize the direct capital contribution of the foreign investor, as well as the growing importance of transnational activity in services. Finally, the liberalization process affects not only the magnitude but also the composition of FDI. Foreign investment may play a key role in the process of industrial restructuring via the introduction of new, flexible technologies. The ability to capitalize on this process, however, requires sector-specific policies as well as a general improvement in incentives governing foreign investment.

NOTE

This chapter was completed while the author was a Visiting Fulbright Fellow at the Center of International Studies, Princeton University. Financial support from the Council of International Exchange of Scholars and the Boğaziçi University Research Fund is gratefully acknowledged. The author would like to thank Fikret Şenses and Arman Kırım for encouraging him to write this chapter and for their detailed and constructive comments on the preliminary draft of the study, and Feyzi Baban for his able assistance.

8

THE PUBLIC ENTERPRISE SECTOR IN TURKEY: PERFORMANCE AND PRODUCTIVITY GROWTH, 1973–1988

Süleyman Özmucur and Cevat Karataş

INTRODUCTION

The public enterprise sector in Turkey has grown at a significant pace since the 1950s. It has contributed a large proportion of gross domestic capital formation and has made a marked impact on production, employment and savings. The public enterprise sector absorbs a huge portion of the government's financial resources and is responsible for a major part of the country's external debt.

Various estimates of financial profitability ratios and factor productivity measures have shown that the public enterprise sector is relatively inefficient as compared to the private sector. The purpose of this chapter is to test this hypothesis for various manufacturing industries in Turkey. Financial profitability is the most commonly used yardstick to measure enterprise performance and to estimate efficiency. However, as indicators of public enterprise performance, all financial profitability ratios share some important shortcomings. Therefore, three alternative profitability rates, namely, rate of return on turnover, rate of return on equity, and rate of return on total assets, will be used to measure financial returns to the providers of public funds. The chapter also provides a detailed overview of the macroeconomic role and impact of public enterprises in Turkey. An attempt is made to examine the economic contribution of the public enterprise sector in terms of value added, employment, investment, savings and its role in the money supply. A larger section of the study will focus on the relative efficiency of public enterprises based on profitability and total factor productivity estimates.

Lacking incentives for good performance, bound by bureaucratic procedures and controls and subject to patronage and government interference, public enterprises in Turkey have, on the whole, shown poor results. In addition to poor investment decisions, there are many reasons why public enterprises have not performed up to expectations. Obviously, some of these reasons are institutional while others are technical and financial.

In recent years, because of the wave of privatization in both developed and developing countries, a number of research works have concentrated on analysis of performance of public and private enterprises using the criterion of productive efficiency (Millward, 1986). However, there is no satisfactory evidence to suggest that public enterprises in developing countries have had a lower level of technical efficiency than private firms operating at the same scale of operation (Kirkpatrick, 1987b). There are only a few examples of entirely comparable public and private sector enterprises that enable the analyst to isolate the effect of ownership on productive efficiency from factors such as scale of operation and product mix (Cook & Kirkpatrick, 1988: 5). It is therefore difficult to generalize that the performance of public enterprises is inferior to similar enterprises in the private sector. In fact, it has been emphasized that while the economic performance of public enterprises has been poor, they have the potential to achieve considerable improvements in efficiency.

In this context, it is illuminating to refer to some of the studies on Turkey that have attempted to establish the degree of poor performance in the public sector. Krueger and Tuncer (1982), in their analysis of the manufacturing sector in Turkey, discovered that even though the average rate of total productivity growth in public enterprises was higher than in private enterprises in both 1963 and 1976, 10 private enterprises out of 14 showed greater efficiency in terms of capital and labor usage per unit of output than the corresponding public enterprises.

In his study of productivity and growth in the Turkish manufacturing sector, Özmucur (1988: 26–30) concluded that

the post-1980 economic system has not been accompanied by an increase in the growth of total factor productivity, but that there was a marked improvement in labor productivity both in the public and private manufacturing sectors. Similarly, capital productivity has improved in the context of the public sector. However, the contributions of the material input variable have been substantial in both sectors.

He also demonstrated that

during the period 1979–85, labor and capital productivity of the private manufacturing sector was much higher than the public manufacturing sector; while total factor productivity growth in the same period was negative for the private sector (-0.8 percent) and considerably higher for the public manufacturing sector (2.8 percent). (Özmucur, 1988: 30)

Yıldırım (1989: 80), who analyzed the performance of both public and private enterprises operating in different manufacturing branches in Turkey for the 1963–83 period, concluded that the public enterprises had a greater TFP growth than did the private enterprises; and that the difference in TFP growth between public sector and private sector can be attributed to the differences in capital stocks per worker and size of the firms in both sectors.

It has been asserted with some vigor that public enterprises' low performance in most developed and developing countries cannot be attributed solely to public ownership. It is often argued that this may instead be due to factors such as a weakening of incentives associated with public ownership and political interference or due to most of them operating under monopoly conditions that do not permit free entry and competition (Kirkpatrick, 1987b: 5).

The evidence available indicates that private enterprises are more subject to market discipline than public enterprises. In other words, competitive market conditions may force the management of private enterprises to be efficient in both resource allocation and productivity to a greater degree than the management of public enterprises. Clearly, the management of private enterprises holds a relatively large degree of financial autonomy to undertake economic activities, while public enterprise management is provided with limited financial autonomy and power. In most cases, pricing, investment and employment policies of public enterprises are dictated by supervising ministers or the government.

It is now widely recognized that public enterprises, in the context of LDCs, have been used as a policy device to reduce unemployment, protect low income groups, combat inflation and encourage further industrialization by supplying low-cost inputs.

In attempting to assess performance, one faces the difficult task of selecting the appropriate criteria. The best that can be done is to examine dimensions of performance that are of relevance for a more general evaluation, while recognizing that no single measure is likely to be of decisive importance. For instance, although profitability may be a key measure of success for a firm operating in a competitive market that is free of externalities, it cannot be so regarded in cases where the firm enjoys significant market power.

THE MACROECONOMIC ROLE AND IMPACT OF PUBLIC ENTERPRISES

From 1930 onward, a new economic strategy was developed in Turkey to stimulate the process of industrialization through newly established State Economic Enterprises (Kepenek, 1990; Aysan & Özmen, 1981; Economic and Social Studies Conference Board (ESSCB), 1968). The poor industrialization record of the private sector by then, lack of entrepreneurship, and particularly the adverse effects of the Great Depression, were the main factors behind the adoption of the policy of etatism (Okyar, 1965; Hale, 1980). This was followed by the introduction of three successive industrialization programs, covering the 1934–38, 1939–43 and 1947–51 periods. The new policy comprised (1) an industrialization strategy of import substitution with protective foreign exchange and trade policies;

(2) the establishment of a number of State Economic Enterprises that were to play a crucial role in industrialization efforts; and (3) the financial policy of transferring resources from agriculture to industry via taxation and pricing policies.

In principle, the SEEs were expected to concentrate their activities in areas such as heavy industry, where the private sector was reluctant to invest. The dominant view at the time was that the SEEs would wither away as soon as the private sector got stronger economically and was ready to take over.

The SEEs in Turkey produce the bulk of industrial inputs comprising raw materials, energy supply and virtually all major basic materials and services. They also play a key role in the production of basic consumer goods and the purchase, stock and sale of cereals. Through their extensive banking activities they provide credits for agriculture, housing, and handicraft and small-scale industries.

Gross Value Added Contribution

Within the public enterprise sector the SEEs' value added, which accounted for 34 percent of total industrial value added in 1979, fell to 28 percent in 1980 and further to 25 percent in 1982. Later, their share in total industrial value added increased to 31 percent in 1984 and 26 percent in 1987 (Table 8.1, Özmucur & Karataş, 1990).

In a broader sense, the average annual rate of growth of gross value added (GVA) of public enterprises was 9.6 percent during the 1982–87 period, as against 5.8 percent for GNP during the 1981–88 period (State Institute of Statistics [c]). In 1987, within the public sector, high growth sectors were led by chemicals, petroleum, coal, and rubber and plastic (31%), paper and printing (23.8%), earthenware products (16.7%) and textile, clothing, and leather sectors (15.8%), followed by food, beverages and tobacco (13.4%), paper and printing (11.4%) and chemicals, petroleum, coal and rubber products (11.1%).

Distribution of Large Manufacturing Value Added

The share of the public enterprise sector in manufacturing value added declined from 42.6 percent in 1976 to 37.4 percent in 1984 (State Institute of Statistics [b]). The public large manufacturing sector (establishments with 10 or more workers) accounted for 40.4 percent of the total in 1980 and 37.4 percent in 1984. The share of the public sector decreased in 1983 and 1984. If firms with 10 to 24 employees are included for these years, the increasing importance of the private sector would have been even more pronounced.

The public enterprise sector's share in GDP is high relative to that of other countries. As a proportion of GDP, gross value added of SEEs was 13 percent in

Table 8.1

State Economic Enterprises (SEEs) and Their Share in Total Value Added, Employment and Investment, 1987

Sector	Value Added (Billion TL.)				Employment (1000)				Fixed Investment (Billion TL.)			
	Turkey	SEE's	SEE's Share in Total	SEE's Sectoral Share	Turkey	SEE's	SEE's Share in Total	SEE's Sectoral Share	Turkey	SEE's	SEE's Share in Total	SEE's Sectoral Share
Agriculture	9532.3	38.1	0.4	0.4	9335	11	0.1	1.4	1129.8	19.3	1.7	0.4
Industry	16847.5	4442.1	26.4	52.2	2282	444	19.5	54.8	4498.4	2885.4	64.1	66.3
Mining	1060.0	807.6	76.2	9.5	129	92	71.3	11.4	399.0	319.3	80.0	7.3
Manufacturing	13597.0	2484.6	18.3	29.2	2008	281	14.0	34.7	2197.1	1183.3	53.9	27.2
Energy	2190.5	1149.9	52.5	13.5	145	71	49.0	8.8	1902.3	1382.8	72.7	31.8
Trade	9326.2	268.3	2.9	3.2	876	21	2.4	2.6	10.7	0.2		
Transportation & Communication	5323.0	1389.6	26.1	16.3	592	178	30.1	22.0	3303.7	1393.7	42.2	32.0
Financial Inst.	1468.4	801.1	54.6	9.4	250	71	28.4	8.8		39.7		0.9
Services, Construc and others	7212.1	1571.5	21.8	18.5	3215	85	2.6	10.5	5196.3[a]	116.9[b]		2.7
Total	49709.6	8510.7	17.1	100.0	16550	810	4.9	100.0	8931.9	4348.9	48.7	100.0
Government Service	3219.0	0.0	0.0									
GDP (factor prices)	52928.6	8510.7	16.1									
Subsidies (-)	485.2	10.2	2.1									
Indirect Taxes	5855.7	2667.7	45.6									
GDP(purchasers' pr	58299.1	11168.2	19.2									

Source: Başbakanlık Yüksek Denetleme Kurulu, 1989: 30, 32, 174.

[a] Includes housing, tourism, health, education and others

[b] Includes 46.3 billion lira of Social Security Institutions and 62.5 billion lira of other institutions

1978, which dropped to 12 percent in 1980 and leveled off at 11 percent in 1981, 1982 and 1983. However, between 1983 and 1987 there was an upward trend in the contribution of the SEEs to GDP, which increased to 14 percent in 1984 and 18 percent in both 1986 and 1987 (Özmucur & Karataş, 1990).

Capital Expenditures of Public Enterprises

Public sector investment accounted for 10.9 percent of GNP in 1980. This rose to 11.7 percent in 1985 and peaked at 13.4 percent in 1986. On the other hand, public investment accounted for 53 percent of total investment in the second five year plan period (1968–72) and 54 percent in 1987.

The share of SEEs in total investment rose from 30.8 percent in 1979 to 38.9 percent in 1980. However, this figure dropped to 35.9 percent in 1983, before increasing to 40.0 percent in 1985. The share of SEEs in public investment also showed a similar trend, increasing from 53 percent in 1979 to 68 percent in 1985.

During the 1968–77 period, investment in manufacturing constituted nearly one-half (47%) of capital expenditures of the SEEs. Investment in the energy sector ranked second (21%), while other economic services (transport and communication) ranked third (State Planning Organization). Investment allotted to agriculture was less than 1 percent during the same period. The big share of the energy sector in public capital expenditures was due to the government policy of developing alternative sources of energy in response to the oil price increases of the 1970s.

During the 1980–88 period, on the other hand, the level of public investment did not decline, but priorities in the allocation of investment resources showed a considerable change. For instance, public investment in manufacturing, which accounted for 26 percent of total public investment in 1979, dropped to 18.7 percent in 1984 and 5.9 percent in 1988. The largest proportion of SEEs' investment during the 1984–88 period was devoted to the transport sector, which saw its share increase from 25 percent to 32 percent (Özmucur & Karataş, 1990).

Public investment devoted to the energy sector showed a slight increase, rising from 23.7 percent in 1981 to 24.8 percent in 1988. During the 1978–83 period, public investment devoted to education and health was very low, with the share of the former falling from 8.2 percent to 4.0 percent and the latter from 2.3 percent to 1.4 percent. However, there was a slight increase in the share of both sectors during the 1984–88 period.

Clearly, compared to previous five year plans, less attention was paid to these activities during the fourth five year plan (1979–83) and the fifth five year plan (1985–89) periods.

On the other hand, capital expenditures in agriculture were largely devoted to irrigation.

Employment Impact of the Public Enterprise Sector

The contribution of the SEEs to total employment increased steadily during the 1980–88 period. In 1980, the level of employment in SEEs (including administrative personnel) rose from 540,793 in 1980 to 580,225 in 1983, 722,012 in 1986 and 810,000 in 1987 (Table 8.1).

The share of SEEs in total employment, which was 3.5 percent in 1980, increased to 4.4 percent in 1986 and almost 5.0 percent in 1987.

Government Savings and Other Sources of Funding the Public Sector

Government savings represented 7.1 percent of GNP in 1984 and over 7.6 percent in 1988, contributing almost 45 percent of the economy-wide savings in 1984 (Table 8.2).

The self-financing ratio (i.e., ratio of savings to investment) of the public enterprise sector was generally high, averaging 67 percent during the 1980–85 period. The savings investment gap of the sector was 6.2 percent of GNP in 1980 but declined to 2.7 percent in 1988. The public enterprise sector's deficit averaged 3.7 percent of GNP during the 1980–85 period (Özmucur & Karataş, 1990).

The public enterprise sector's deficits during the 1980–87 period were financed largely by government contributions through budgetary assistance and subsidies. The budgetary burden of public enterprises was larger than the government budget deficit during the 1980–86 period. The budgetary burden of public enterprises was met by increasing government revenues and/or cutting down on other government expenditures, or was passed forward into higher budget deficits to be financed through borrowing or money creation. A comparison of the growth rates of the fiscal burden and government budget deficits indicates that an increase or decrease in the fiscal burden is associated with a corresponding movement in the same direction in the national budget deficit.

As the ratio of the public enterprise sector's deficit to GNP increased between 1983 and 1986, there was a parallel increase in the budget deficit-GNP ratio. Although there was a reduction in the deficits of SEEs from 1984 onward, they still contributed to rampant inflation, mainly through raising the prices of their products above their production costs, thus causing cost-push inflation.

Financial requirements of the SEEs were responsible for a major inflationary spiral during the pre-1980 period. However, in the post-1980 period there was a switch to deregulation of SEE prices and elimination of the automatic link between the SEEs' financial requirements and the government budget deficit and the Central Bank (Öniş and Özmucur,1988b: 74). Apparently, the SEEs were forced to operate as autonomous commercial entities and were allowed some freedom in determining their product prices.

Table 8.2
Summary Statistics on Private and Public Manufacturing

	Average Shares		Average Growth Rates				Price/	Capital/
	Labor	Capital	Labor	Capital	Value	TFP	Cost	Output
Private Sector								
Sector : 31 – Food								
1973–76	35.0	65.0	–0.3	13.3	3.1	–5.4	1.149	0.165
1976–79	32.7	67.3	0.1	8.4	5.6	–0.1	1.183	0.223
1979–82	24.6	75.4	8.0	8.3	18.3	10.2	1.232	0.222
1982–85	21.8	78.2	4.1	11.5	–4.0	–13.8	1.246	0.234
1973–85	28.1	71.9	2.9	10.3	5.5	–2.8	1.202	0.210
Sector : 32 – Textiles								
1973–76	38.7	61.3	7.6	22.0	7.4	–9.0	1.271	0.296
1976–79	30.6	69.4	0.5	10.7	8.3	0.7	1.345	0.365
1979–82	27.8	72.2	4.0	1.7	0.2	–2.1	1.364	0.422
1982–85	27.4	72.6	4.3	15.5	5.4	–7.0	1.318	0.380
1973–85	31.4	68.6	4.1	12.2	5.3	–4.4	1.320	0.364
Sector : 33 – Wood products								
1973–76	31.2	68.8	0.8	18.9	9.0	–4.2	1.336	0.305
1976–79	35.9	64.1	5.4	7.9	–5.3	–12.3	1.378	0.455
1979–82	34.8	65.2	4.6	7.0	3.7	–2.4	1.293	0.530
1982–85	31.5	68.5	4.0	2.3	1.2	–1.6	1.252	0.482
1973–85	33.3	66.7	3.7	8.9	2.0	–5.1	1.317	0.437
Sector : 34 – Paper products								
1973–76	28.8	71.2	0.3	6.5	8.9	4.2	1.424	0.292
1976–79	25.8	74.2	1.5	–5.5	–3.3	0.4	1.415	0.263
1979–82	26.0	74.0	7.1	4.0	5.0	0.2	1.403	0.205
1982–85	29.8	70.2	2.9	18.1	0.5	–13.1	1.418	0.323
1973–85	27.8	72.2	2.9	5.4	2.7	–2.1	1.422	0.277
Sector : 35 – Chemicals								
1973–76	24.1	75.9	4.2	14.4	–0.2	–12.1	1.318	0.233
1976–79	21.0	79.0	0.9	6.3	9.5	4.4	1.363	0.250
1979–82	20.8	79.2	2.6	3.2	–2.3	–5.3	1.384	0.275
1982–85	20.5	79.5	1.2	13.7	–0.8	–11.9	1.304	0.288
1973–85	21.6	78.4	2.2	9.3	1.5	–6.3	1.337	0.262

In recent years a shift occurred, not in the absolute size of the SEE financial requirements, but in their sources of financing. From 1982 onward, the share of budgetary transfers in the total financing of SEEs declined considerably, from 49 percent in 1983 to 30 percent in 1987 (Özmucur & Karataş, 1990). Similarly, the share of SEEs in Central Bank credits was reduced from a peak of 32 percent in

Table 8.2 Continued

| | Average Shares | | Average Growth Rates | | | | Price/ | Capital/ |
	Labor	Capital	Labor	Capital	Value	TFP	Cost	Output
Private Sector								
Sector : 36 – Non–metallic products								
1973–76	30.8	69.2	8.7	33.8	16.6	–9.4	1.457	0.527
1976–79	30.2	69.8	2.0	3.0	–2.9	–5.6	1.483	0.656
1979–82	25.7	74.3	2.3	3.5	11.3	8.1	1.548	0.646
1982–85	26.4	73.6	5.3	2.0	–3.7	–6.5	1.520	0.590
1973–85	28.6	71.4	4.5	9.8	5.0	–3.3	1.506	0.605
Sector : 37 – Basic metals								
1973–76	32.4	67.6	12.5	29.8	23.6	–0.6	1.204	0.205
1976–79	25.9	74.1	4.0	7.3	0.7	–5.8	1.253	0.242
1979–82	27.2	72.8	3.0	15.0	8.5	–3.2	1.239	0.323
1982–85	19.5	80.5	3.3	12.0	13.0	2.8	1.229	0.281
1973–85	26.5	73.5	5.6	15.7	11.2	–1.9	1.230	0.261
Sector : 38 – Machinery								
1973–76	31.1	68.9	4.5	11.9	12.3	2.7	1.291	0.150
1976–79	28.1	71.9	4.7	10.8	–1.9	–11.0	1.309	0.174
1979–82	31.5	68.5	3.1	1.8	8.4	6.2	1.344	0.231
1982–85	24.9	75.1	3.3	14.6	8.4	–3.5	1.340	0.191
1973–85	28.7	71.3	3.9	9.7	6.6	–1.4	1.321	0.185
Public Sector								
Sector : 31 - Food								
1973–76	28.7	71.3	4.1	4.4	8.9	4.6	1.514	0.227
1976–79	36.9	63.1	7.6	9.8	–4.4	–13.4	1.299	0.234
1979–82	32.2	67.8	–4.3	2.2	27.4	27.3	1.379	0.252
1982–85	19.0	81.0	–0.7	6.1	2.7	–2.1	1.587	0.212
1973–85	28.9	71.1	1.6	5.6	8.0	3.6	1.448	0.232
Sector : 32 - Textiles								
1973–76	54.6	45.4	2.7	8.8	1.7	–3.7	1.281	0.523
1976–79	55.3	44.7	–1.5	1.0	–3.2	–2.8	1.216	0.627
1979–82	54.9	45.1	–2.9	4.8	–1.7	–2.3	1.217	0.713
1982–85	53.0	47.0	0.9	8.5	–2.6	–7.0	1.214	0.757
1973–85	55.2	44.8	–0.2	5.7	–1.4	–3.9	1.230	0.657
Sector : 33 - Wood products								
1973–76	59.0	41.0	8.1	14.0	8.1	–2.5	1.165	0.136
1976–79	65.2	34.8	–4.8	32.2	–1.3	–9.3	1.211	0.293
1979–82	50.8	49.2	–1.4	9.3	2.8	–1.0	1.262	0.380
1982–85	40.4	59.6	3.0	–1.9	22.8	22.7	1.337	0.366
1973–85	52.2	47.8	1.1	12.7	7.7	1.1	1.256	0.286

Table 8.2 Continued

	Average Shares		Average Growth Rates				Price/	Capital/
	Labor	Capital	Labor	Capital	Value	TFP	Cost	Output
Public Sector								
Sector : 34 - Paper products								
1973–76	41.1	58.9	4.5	1.2	9.6	7.0	1.290	1.336
1976–79	53.1	46.9	–2.4	–0.1	–21.8	–20.4	1.166	1.358
1979–82	67.4	32.6	2.0	0.5	15.0	13.5	1.088	1.408
1982–85	41.5	58.5	3.8	–0.3	9.7	8.3	1.243	1.127
1973–85	49.2	50.8	2.0	0.3	2.0	0.9	1.210	1.319
Sector : 35 - Chemicals								
1973–76	2.8	97.2	5.6	–5.6	–1.0	4.4	1.935	0.350
1976–79	10.5	89.5	9.6	–2.3	–29.3	–28.3	1.374	0.332
1979–82	9.0	91.0	3.5	–1.2	54.6	55.4	1.455	0.291
1982–85	4.7	95.3	3.2	–7.1	–17.1	–10.5	1.425	0.159
1973–85	6.1	93.9	5.4	–4.1	–2.7	0.8	1.550	0.279
Sector : 36 - Non-metallic products								
1973–76	38.0	62.0	5.9	12.5	10.4	0.4	1.307	0.541
1976–79	46.2	53.8	1.6	5.6	–9.8	–13.6	1.252	0.710
1979–82	39.9	60.1	–3.5	–3.9	10.2	13.9	1.313	0.600
1982–85	41.5	58.5	5.4	32.4	–3.6	–24.8	1.291	0.762
1973–85	41.2	58.8	2.3	10.9	1.4	–5.9	1.302	0.665
Sector : 37 - Basic metals								
1973–76	37.5	62.5	14.8	8.9	–7.4	–18.5	1.524	1.432
1976–79	33.7	66.3	5.8	6.5	10.2	3.9	1.613	1.499
1979–82	50.6	49.4	–4.1	0.7	–18.2	–16.4	1.332	1.686
1982–85	47.5	52.5	0.5	1.8	15.2	14.0	1.173	1.229
1973–85	40.6	59.4	4.0	4.4	–1.0	–5.2	1.415	1.416
Sector : 38 - Machinery								
1973–76	67.3	32.7	–2.0	0.0	–7.9	–6.6	1.126	0.916
1976–79	56.4	43.6	1.6	–0.6	14.2	13.5	1.155	0.737
1979–82	65.9	34.1	–4.7	–1.7	3.6	7.3	1.200	0.840
1982–85	46.1	53.9	3.9	12.5	–6.4	–14.9	1.244	0.685
1973–85	59.8	40.2	–0.4	2.4	0.5	–0.3	1.174	0.790

1979 to 11.7 percent in 1986 and 21 percent in 1987. Nevertheless, a progressively greater proportion of SEE financing was secured through external borrowing (foreign project loans), whose share in total financing increased from 35 percent in 1984 to almost 68 percent in 1987. Therefore, it is safe to infer that a significant link exists between the financing requirements of the SEEs and the intensification of the external debt problem.

FINANCIAL PERFORMANCE INDICATORS FOR THE PUBLIC ENTERPRISE SECTOR

Financial performance is the most commonly used yardstick to measure enterprise performance and assess efficiency. However, all financial profitability ratios share the following shortcomings: First, they do not take into account the social objectives of public enterprises. Second, under noncompetitive market conditions, high financial profits may not genuinely reflect an efficient enterprise operation, but may simply result from above- normal profits being made because of the firm's monopoly power. Finally, financial profits do not take into account the implicit subsidies such as tariff concessions, granted to public enterprises. Therefore, while financial performance may be indicative of public enterprise efficiency, it should be used with some caution in evaluating public enterprise performance.

In this section, three alternative profitability ratios are used to measure the financial returns to the providers of public enterprise funds. These consist of the rate of return on sales revenue (ROSR), rate of return on total assets (ROA), and rate of return on equity (ROE). The ROSR is the profits to sales ratio, which measures the rate of profit accruing per unit of sales revenue. ROE represents the rate of profit accruing to the stockholders of the corporation, which is generally regarded as the measure of private profitability. Finally, ROA is the ratio of management profit to total assets, where management profit is defined as net income before income tax. ROA measures the rate of profit resulting from the use of funds in the purchase of both fixed and current assets. ROA uses total assets in the denominator, as they represent the aggregate resources at the disposal of the firm.

The following figures are related to the largest 500 corporations, both in the public and private sectors.

Both ROSR and ROE of public enterprises recorded steady growth during the years 1983, 1986 and 1988. For instance the public enterprise sector's rate of return on sales revenue, which was 8.0 percent in 1983, increased to 8.4 percent in 1986 and 11.5 percent in 1988 (Istanbul Sanayi Odası, 1984: 68–71, 1987: 70–73, 1989: 68-71). It should be noted that ROSR for the entire private sector, which was 8.5 percent in 1983, fell to 7.8 percent in 1986, before recovering to 9.8 percent in 1988. Thus, the financial performance of public sector enterprises during the 1983–88 period was slightly better than the performance of private sector enterprises. ROSR during the 1983–88 period was 9.5 for public enterprises as opposed to 8.7 percent for the private sector. Finally, ROE averaged 42.9 percent for the public enterprise sector and 56.2 percent for the private sector during the same period.

Özmucur (1989) exhibits the financial performance of both public and private sectors from the standpoint of major industries included in the survey. The public industrial subsectors that recorded a steady growth and high ROSRs in 1986 were mining (34.0%), forestry products (36.0%), stone and earthenware (20.0%) and food, beverages and tobacco (13.2%). The public sector industries that showed a relatively poor performance in the same year included paper and paper products (2.1%), automotive industry (3.3%), electricity (4.0%), basic metals (6.0%) and chemicals, petroleum products and plastics (6.8%).

The public sector industries that continued to show relatively better financial profitability (ROSR) in 1988 included mining and quarrying (59.0%), basic metals (23.3%), paper and paper products (26.5%), stone and earthenware (14.2%), chemicals, petroleum products and plastics (7.8%) and automotive industry (15.1%). The public industries that registered a poor performance in 1988 included metal products and machines (2.3%) and food, beverages and tobacco (5.5%) (Istanbul Sanayi Odasi, various years).

According to the ROE measure, the public industries that emerged as the most profitable in 1986 included textiles and clothing (337%), forestry and wood products (143%), stone and earthenware (96.2%) and mining and quarrying (65%). Most sectors showed improving ROEs in 1988, especially public industries such as mining and quarrying (214%), stone and earthenware (138%), paper and paper products (99%), basic metals (78%) and automotive industry (44.8%). Public industries that recorded consistently positive ROEs both in 1983 and 1986, but experienced a deterioration in 1988, included sectors such as food, beverages and tobacco, forestry and wood products, and metal products and machinery.

Within the private sector, the major industrial groups that recorded a notable improvement in ROEs during the same period were automotive industry, paper and paper products, wood products, chemicals and petroleum products, textiles and clothing and food and beverages. Apparently, aggregate ROE of public industries increased consistently during the 1983–88 period, except for a slight drop in 1986.

Three public sector industries, namely paper and paper products, nonmetallic products and basic metals, recorded negative average rates of return on total assets in 1983, while other industries exhibited positive but insignificant rates. The operational losses of the paper, stone and earthenware and basic metal industries in 1983 were 12.7 billion lira, 2.5 billion lira and 20.3 billion lira, respectively. On the other hand, mining and quarrying had the highest ROA in 1983 (12.0%). During 1986, the highest ROA was obtained in forestry and wood products (29.3%) and stone and earthenware (26.2%), followed by textiles and clothing (22.5%), food and beverages (16.6%) and mining and quarrying (12.7%). In the same year, the poorest performance was recorded in paper and paper products (-8.8%), automotive industry (1.9%), electrical machinery (1.2%) and basic metals (2.2%).

In 1988, the highest ROAs were observed for mining and quarrying (36.8%), stone and earthenware (29.5%), basic metals (20.3%) and paper and paper products (18.6%). The poorest performance was observed in electrical machinery, metal products and machinery, automotive industry and textiles and clothing industries. In aggregate terms, over the same period (1983, 1986 and 1988), the average ROA for the public enterprise sector was 6.7 percent, as opposed to over 10.0 percent for the private sector. Inasmuch as interest rates exceeded the sectoral profitability margin, public enterprises faced large liquidity problems.

TOTAL FACTOR PRODUCTIVITY

Growth in total factor productivity was calculated using Divisia indexes (Özmucur and Karataş, 1990). Two data sets were used:

1. State Institute of Statistics, Results of Manufacturing Surveys or Censuses. Survey data include material inputs, output, value added, wage bill, number of workers and investment. Gross profit (including depreciation and indirect taxes), which is to be used in profitability calculations, is computed as the difference between value added and wage bill. Capital stock figures, which are calculated using the perpetual inventory method, are taken from Özmucur (1988).

2. Istanbul Chamber of Industry (ISO) data on the 500 largest industrial establishments covering the 1983–88 period. Because major steps toward import liberalization were taken in 1984, it was necessary to analyze the post-1984 period. ISO data enable us to do that. Although the number of establishments is low, especially if sectoral differences are to be studied, their share in total industrial output is over 40 percent (in some sectors 100 percent) (Özmucur, 1989).

Table 8.3 shows that the average overall rate of total factor productivity growth for public manufacturing industry was -9.0 percent during 1973–79, 7.6 percent during 1979–85, and -1.0 percent during 1973–85. The negative TFPG in the 1970s was due to the fact that there was a dramatically low utilization of capacity resulting from an acute shortage of foreign exchange and raw materials.

On the other hand, TFPG in the private manufacturing sector was constantly negative, where it was -4.6 percent in 1973–79, -2.5 percent in 1979–85 and -3.6 percent in 1973–85. This outcome was again due to extremely low capacity utilization. Consequently, TFPG for total manufacturing industry was negative (-5.4%) for 1973–79, -1.9 percent for 1973–85, but positive 1.7 percent for the 1979–85 period. Taking 1979 as a base year has, no doubt, influenced the magnitude of TFPG in the 1979–85 period.

Examining the sectoral rate of TFPG in the public sector, we observe that in the 1973–85 period textiles -(3.9%), nonmetallic products (-5.9%), basic metals (-5.2%), and machinery (-0.3%) indicated a negative TFPG, while sectors such as food (3.6%), wood products (1.1%), and paper products (0.9%) demonstrated positive but very low growth rates (Table 8.2).

Within the private sector, all sectors recorded negative TFPG. Besides, in the 1982–85 period, while in the private sector TFPG was excessively negative for food (-13.8%), textiles (-7.0%), paper products (-13.1%), chemicals (-11.9%), nonmetallic products (-6.5%) and machinery (-3.5%), TFPG in the public sector

Table 8.3
Total Factor Productivity Growth Using Value Added

	Average Shares		Average Growth Rates				Contribution of Factors		
	L^a	C^b	L	C	W^c	VA^d	TFP	L	C	TFPG
Sector : 3 – Total Manufacturing – Private										
1973–76	31.6	68.4	5.1	18.9	14.5	8.3	–6.2	19.4	155.9	–75.3
1976–79	27.5	72.5	2.0	7.8	6.2	3.3	–2.9	16.3	170.7	–87.0
1979–82	26.7	73.3	4.1	4.2	4.2	5.6	1.4	19.3	55.2	25.5
1982–85	24.1	75.9	3.7	12.4	10.3	3.5	–6.8	25.5	266.0	–191.5
1973–79	29.1	70.9	3.5	13.2	10.4	5.8	–4.6	17.7	162.3	–80.0
1979–85	25.6	74.4	3.9	8.2	7.1	4.6	–2.5	21.8	133.8	–55.6
1973–85	27.5	72.5	3.7	10.7	8.8	5.2	–3.6	19.7	149.8	–69.5
Sector : 3 – Total Manufacturing – Public										
1973–76	19.8	80.2	4.8	1.8	2.4	0.4	–2.0	258.1	379.0	–537.1
1976–79	30.6	69.4	4.1	2.7	3.2	–12.2	–15.4	–10.2	–15.5	125.8
1979–82	29.6	70.4	–3.2	0.3	–0.7	24.8	25.5	–3.8	0.9	102.9
1982–85	20.0	80.0	1.2	2.8	2.5	–5.8	–8.3	–4.2	–38.2	142.5
1973–79	25.2	74.8	4.5	2.2	2.8	–6.2	–9.0	–18.3	–27.3	145.6
1979–85	25.9	74.1	–1.0	1.5	0.9	8.4	7.6	–3.1	13.5	89.5
1973–85	24.8	75.2	1.7	1.9	1.8	0.9	–1.0	47.7	161.8	–109.5
Sector : 3 – Total Manufacturing – Total										
1973–76	25.5	74.5	5.0	8.1	7.3	4.3	–3.0	29.7	140.9	–70.6
1976–79	28.6	71.4	2.7	5.0	4.4	–3.4	–7.7	–23.2	–107.2	230.4
1979–82	27.6	72.4	1.5	2.2	2.1	13.1	11.1	3.2	12.4	84.4
1982–85	22.3	77.7	2.9	7.9	6.8	–0.6	–7.4	–102.4	–950.6	1153.0
1973–79	27.0	73.0	3.8	6.6	5.8	0.4	–5.4	266.9	1226.5	–1393.4
1979–85	25.6	74.4	2.2	5.0	4.3	6.0	1.7	9.5	62.2	28.3
1973–85	26.1	73.9	3.0	5.8	5.1	3.2	–1.9	25.1	135.2	–60.3

[a] L: Labor
[b] C: Capital
[c] W: Weighted
[d] VA: Value Added

attained remarkable growth in wood products (22%), basic metals (14%) and paper products (8.3%). During the same period, the public industries that showed negative TFPG included food, textiles, chemicals, nonmetallic products and machinery.

TFPG in the 500 largest firms was positive during the 1985–88 period (Table 8.4), averaging 6.1 percent for the private, and 3.2 percent for the public sector. Within the public sector, food (-9.2%), textiles (-0.6%), wood (-18.6%) and machinery (-9.4%) recorded negative TFPG rates during the 1985–88 period. Within the private sector, the paper and paper products sector was the only sector with a negative TFPG rate (-3.8 %).

Comparison of TFPG rates and profit rates reveals a positive correlation in the private sector and a negative correlation in the public sector. One can infer, however, that high rates of profit in the public sector cannot be explained only by TFPG; high rates of increase in product prices were also a factor.

LIBERALIZATION AND TRENDS IN TOTAL FACTOR PRODUCTIVITY AND PROFITABILITY

Two regressions are used to study the trends in and impact of economic liberalization:

$$Y_t = a + bt$$
$$Y_t = a + bD,$$

where
Y_t = profitability or TFPG
t = year
D = dummy variable (= 1 or 0).

Using data for the 1974–85 period, it is possible to study the impact of liberalization on profitability and TFPG. With liberalization, the former is expected to decline and the latter to increase. Tables 8.5 and 8.6 present trend lines and regressions on "liberalization" dummy variables.

There is no discernible trend in TFPG during the 1974–85 period. Liberalization (a dummy variable for the 1981–85 period is used as a proxy) has no significant effect on TFPG (Table 8.5).

On the other hand, price-cost ratios show a trend in some sectors. Within the private sector, there is a positive trend in food (0.01), nonmetallic minerals (0.011) and machinery (0.006), and a negative trend in wood products (-0.013). Within the public sector there is a positive trend in wood products (0.022) and machinery (0.015), and a negative trend in basic metals (-.038).

In price-cost ratio regressions on the liberalization dummy variable constant terms are significant at the 5 percent level. The constant term indicates the price-cost ratio for the 1973–80 period. The average ratio for the private sector is 1.33, with large variations among sectors (food 1.18, paper 1.427, nonmetallic minerals 1.472, basic metals 1.234). The average ratio for the public sector is 1.301. The

Table 8.4
Profitability and Total Factor Productivity in Five Hundred Largest Firms

Average for the Period	Sector	Average Shares in Net Value Added		Average Growth Rates (%)				Profitability Indicators			
		Labor	Capital	Labor	Capital	Val.Add.	TFP	Profit/ Sales	Profit/ Equity	Profit/ Assets	Capital/ Output
Private Sector											
1983–85	Food	39.8	60.2	−0.8	2.9	2.7	1.3	2.9	25.9	4.0	0.290
1985–88	Food	32.7	64.8	5.7	7.3	13.9	7.2	5.0	50.4	7.0	0.298
1983–85	Textiles	46.9	53.1	1.3	4.8	4.2	1.1	7.6	26.8	8.1	0.598
1985–88	Textiles	40.1	59.3	5.0	11.8	17.5	8.5	9.2	37.6	10.6	0.536
1983–85	Wood	39.8	60.2	−5.6	−13.6	−8.3	2.1	6.5	18.6	8.7	0.424
1985–88	Wood	43.4	61.4	−3.9	−13.1	−7.1	2.0	6.2	26.7	9.3	0.314
1983–85	Paper	36.9	63.1	5.1	−29.1	4.4	20.9	11.7	37.4	13.0	0.771
1985–88	Paper	34.8	63.6	24.7	16.4	15.5	−3.8	7.9	28.5	10.3	0.499
1983–85	Chemicals	35.9	64.1	−1.1	8.2	−6.8	−11.7	5.7	35.2	12.5	0.236
1985–88	Chemicals	32.8	66.0	−0.2	3.9	14.9	12.3	6.0	49.2	13.6	0.232
1983–85	Non-metallic	44.5	55.5	5.2	3.4	6.8	2.7	11.7	29.1	11.8	0.757
1985–88	Non-metallic	36.6	66.4	8.7	14.8	17.6	5.0	15.6	52.5	16.7	0.665
1983–85	Basic metals	38.0	62.0	15.6	21.5	6.7	−12.5	4.2	24.1	6.5	0.311
1985–88	Basic metals	31.0	67.4	3.0	9.7	16.6	9.0	4.6	27.2	7.0	0.351
1983–85	Machinery	41.7	58.3	−0.6	17.6	8.9	−1.1	8.2	40.6	10.1	0.290
1985–88	Machinery	37.1	63.2	2.0	3.6	5.4	2.4	7.1	46.6	9.9	0.272
1983–85	Auto	43.5	56.5	−3.4	12.7	−12.4	−18.1	5.2	25.5	7.7	0.327
1985–88	Auto	40.2	56.6	9.3	8.0	19.0	10.5	6.6	42.9	11.2	0.329
1983–85	Total Industry	41.0	59.0	1.3	5.4	1.8	−1.9	6.6	31.8	9.3	0.370
1985–88	Total Industry	35.6	64.0	4.8	9.8	14.1	6.1	7.8	44.5	11.3	0.360

Table 8.4 Continued

Average for the Period	Sector	Average Shares in Net Value Added		Average Growth Rates (%)				Profitability Indicators			
		Labor	Capital	Labor	Capital	Val.Add.	TFP	Profit/ Sales	Profit/ Equity	Profit/ Assets	Capital/ Output
Public Sector											
1983–85	Food	64.6	35.4	–5.6	11.8	63.7	63.1	6.0	22.5	8.1	0.220
1985–88	Food	58.4	47.8	7.2	–0.1	–5.0	–9.2	10.0	34.9	12.4	0.223
1983–85	Textiles	72.3	27.7	–4.6	–6.8	–0.1	5.1	5.1	22.0	5.5	0.459
1985–88	Textiles	63.7	44.8	–7.1	8.0	–2.2	–0.6	5.3	94.4	9.4	0.476
1983–85	Wood										
1985–88	Wood	27.4	80.2	–4.1	32.0	3.5	–18.6	36.3	119.7	27.2	0.176
1983–85	Paper										
1985–88	Paper	105.3	–73.9	–5.4	–7.1	42.9	48.2	1.7	7.5	1.2	1.828
1983–85	Chemicals	35.2	64.8	31.8	–4.0	17.7	9.2	5.2	33.6	7.9	0.338
1985–88	Chemicals	24.1	66.7	–3.7	21.9	44.5	28.7	7.1	41.3	11.4	0.401
1983–85	Non–metallic	86.9	13.1	–16.5	74.9	32.6	37.1	3.1	–4.4	0.3	0.789
1985–88	Non–metallic	49.5	60.0	–7.6	–1.3	8.2	12.6	16.3	72.6	23.8	0.567
1983–85	Basic metals	105.2	–5.2	–17.2	30.0	16.6	36.2	1.0	–3.5	–0.3	1.226
1985–88	Basic metals	53.3	36.8	6.7	4.6	37.6	31.9	9.8	19.7	8.0	1.308
1983–85	Machinery	50.3	49.7	–14.1	14.6	–1.8	–2.0	7.8	21.6	6.1	0.248
1985–88	Machinery	48.1	51.4	–3.0	0.8	–10.5	–9.4	5.5	13.5	4.0	0.610
1983–85	Auto										
1985–88	Auto	97.2	5.6	–6.3	22.3	–1.6	3.9	6.0	8.3	3.2	0.957
1983–85	Total Industry	58.1	41.9	1.8	45.4	33.3	13.3	7.2	21.8	7.3	0.548
1985–88	Total Industry	38.4	57.2	1.3	15.2	13.0	3.2	8.9	22.9	7.7	0.890

127

Table 8.5
Liberalization and Total Factor Productivity Growth and Price-Cost Ratios

| | Total Factor Productivity Growth | | Price-Cost Ratio | |
	constant	Dummy8185	constant	Dummy8185
Private				
food	1.886	−6.965	1.181 *	0.063 *
clothing	−4.637	1.695	1.320 *	0.002
wood	−6.381	4.851	1.362 *	−0.106 *
paper	2.590	−11.948	1.427 *	−0.012
chemicals	−4.466	−0.792	1.348 *	−0.038
non-metal	−5.973	8.614	1.472 *	0.066 **
basic met	−5.520	11.846	1.234 *	−0.007
machinery	−2.386	7.303	1.307 *	0.037 **
pooled	−3.111	1.792	1.331 *	0.001
Public				
food	−2.759	18.745	1.359 *	0.189 **
clothing	−2.111	−2.811	1.235 *	−0.031
wood	1.320	14.180	1.218 *	0.096
paper	−0.753	10.733	1.190 *	0.021
chemicals	−13.744	102.656	1.488 *	0.019
non-metal	−0.233	−9.525	1.272 *	0.061
basic met	−5.847	11.99	1.517 *	−0.330 *
machinery	7.703	−5.04	1.131 *	0.094 *
pooled	−2.053	17.616	1.301 *	0.015
Private and Public				
pooled	−2.026	9.704	1.319 *	0.0078

* significant at the 5 percent level
** significant at the 10 percent level

price-cost ratio is above the average in the food (1.359), chemicals (1.488) and basic metal (1.517) industries. This is expected, because the state has a monopoly in these sectors.

The results on the 500 largest firms show some differences as far as changes and trends are concerned. When there are not a sufficient number of observations for a sectoral study, figures for aggregates only are given. Evidently, there is a positive trend in TFPG in the private sector during the 1983–88 period. The public sector, on the other hand, reveals no discernible trend in TFPG (Table 8.6).

In the analysis, three profitability measures are used. In the private sector, the profit–sales ratio does not show an upward trend during 1983–88. Profit-assets and profits–equity ratios exhibit an upward trend in both the private and public sectors. This is an important result as far as the use of funds is concerned. With high rates of interest and high cost of borrowing, firms had to utilize their equity or assets more efficiently; that is, to generate more sales with the same amount of assets or equity.

Using the regression on the dummy variable (which is equal to 1 during 1985–88 and equal to 0 for the period 1983–84), it is possible to test whether there is a change in the level of TFPG and profitability. Apparently, there is a significant increase in TFPG in the private sector. TFPG increased from -30.2 percent during the 1983–84 period to an average of 2.2 percent during the 1985–88 period. Meanwhile, the increase in TFPG in the public sector is not significant. There are differences in shifts in profitability. In the private sector, there is no significant change in profit-sales nor profits-assets ratios, but a positive change (10.12) in the profits-equity ratio. In contrast, the public sector realized a significant change in all three profitability indicators. These results also indicate that in the postliberalization period, public sector profits are more likely to be the result of price increases reflecting its monopoly power.

DETERMINANTS OF TOTAL FACTOR PRODUCTIVITY AND PROFITABILITY

Basic Models and Tests

As in Roberts (1988) and Froutan (1990), the basic model to be examined is:

$$P_{it} = f (K_{it}, M_{it}, H_{it}, D_i, D_t),$$

where P_{it} is the price-cost ratio for industry i in year t.

The numerator of P_{it} equals the value of production in industry i (value of sales plus change in final goods inventories). The denominator equals the sum of payments to labor (wages, salaries and benefits) and expenditures on intermediate inputs. This definition is one plus the cost price margin used by Roberts (1988) and Froutan (1990). M_{it} is the measure of import penetration in industry i in time t.

Table 8.6
Trends in Total Factor Productivity Growth and Profitability, 1983–88
(Five Hundred Largest Firms in Turkey)

| | Trends in TFPG & Profitability | | Liberalization & TFPG and Profitability | |
	constant	time	constant 1985-88	Dummy
Private				
TFPG	−19802.4 *	9.969 *	−30.191 *	32.413 *
Profits/S	−803.3	0.408	7.632 *	−0.047
Profits/A	−1774.7 *	0.899 *	9.731 *	0.887
Profits/E	−10503.5 *	5.309 *	30.069 *	10.121 **
Public				
TFPG	−8463.6	4.267	−4.896	20.550
Profits/S	−4399.5 *	2.220 *	4.332	6.553 **
Profits/A	−5227.4 *	2.637 *	2.273	8.901 *
Profits/E	−23313.8 *	11.758 *	3.034	42.722 *
Private and Public				
TFPG	−14976.0 *	7.542 *	−19.124 *	27.870 *
Profits/S	−2543.2 *	1.285 *	6.079 *	3.156
Profits/A	−3392.5 *	1.713 *	6.221 *	4.675 *
Profits/E	−16549.4 *	8.352 *	17.347 *	25.626 *

* significant at the 5 percent level
** significant at the 10 percent level

It equals the value of competing imports for industry i as a share of the total sales of industry i. Total industry sales equal the total sales of domestic producers plus the value of imports.

K_{it} is a measure of the capital intensity of the domestic producers in industry i in year t. It is constructed as the end-of-year capital stock of the domestic producers in industry i divided by the real output of the domestic producers. It is necessary to include the capital-output ratio as an explanatory variable in the margin regressions because the dependent variables include payments to fixed factors.

M_{it} is the measure of import penetration in industry i in time t. It equals the values of competing imports for industry i as a share of the total sales of industry

i. Total industry sales equal the total sales of domestic producers plus the value of imports.

H_{it} is the Herfindahl index for industry i in year t. It is the sum of the squared plant market shares. Each plant's market share is the ratio of the plant's value of production to total production of the domestic industry.

D_i is a set of dummy variables to distinguish omitted industry-specific effects that do not vary over time.

D_t is a set of dummy variables to distinguish the years in data.

These are included to control for any year-specific influences, such as macroeconomic factors that are likely to affect all industries.

The empirical model that was used to explain the rate of industry productivity growth is:

$$\dot{T}_{it} = f\ (Q_{it},\ M_{it},\ H_{it},\ D_i,\ D_t)$$

$\dot{T}_{it}$ is the total factor productivity growth.

Q_{it} is the rate of growth of real industry output. If there are scale economies in production then expansion of demand for the industry's output can allow firms to exploit these economies and lower their average production cost. This would result in positive rates of productivity growth.

The growth in the share of competing imports, measured as a share of total sales of industry, is included to control for the effect that import competition may have on the efficiency of the domestic industry. A common argument is that increased import competition should result in less slack among domestic producers, and this would appear as a positive effect on the rate of productivity growth.

Nevertheless, there are some problems in applying this model to Turkish data. First, industrial concentration ratios are not available for every year (There was only the Tekeli et al. (1983) study at the time of writing). There is also no distinction between competitive and noncompetitive imports. Almost 80 percent of imports are investment goods and raw materials. These imports, by reducing bottlenecks in production and increasing capacity utilization, may lead to higher price–cost margins and TFPG. These data problems have forced us to use the modified models:

$$\dot{T}_{it} = f\ (Q_{it},\ L_t,\ D_i,\ D_t)$$

$$P_{it} = f\ (\ K_{it},\ L_t,\ D_i,\ D_t)$$

where L_t is the liberalization dummy, which has the value 1 for the 1981–85 8period and 0 for the 1973–80 period.

Our purpose here is to study the determinants of the price–cost ratio (or profitability) and TFPG. We have also attempted to explain the differences, if any, among manufacturing subsectors, between public and private sectors, and between the pre- and postliberalization periods.

Profitability

In price-cost regressions it appears that the capital-output variable is not significant and has the wrong sign in the private sector (Table 8.7). There are differences among manufacturing subsectors, as indicated by high F ratios for sector dummy variables as a group. There are also significant differences between the public and private sectors. These indicate that most of the explanatory power of the basic model derives from the industry dummy variables, as in Froutan (1990: 20). Similar conclusions can be drawn for the public sector, although there are significant differences between them, as indicated by a high F ratio (Table 8.7).

The regression results based on the 500 largest firms of Turkey for the period 1983–88 indicate similar results. Profitability, which is measured as the ratio of pretax balance sheet profits to total sales revenue, is related to the capital–output ratio (fixed assets given in the balance sheet/total sales) and sector and time dummy variables. In both private and public sectors, time and sector dummies are highly significant. These reinforce the view that profitability cannot be explained only by capital-output ratio. Obviously, there are sector- and time-specific factors to consider. Admittedly, concentration ratios and macroeconomic incentives that were omitted because of lack of data may emerge as important factors (Table 8.8).

Total Factor Productivity Growth

TFPG regressions in general provide more satisfactory results (Tables 8.9 and 8.10). The value added growth variable is significant in all regressions. These results clearly indicate that firms have taken advantage of economies of scale and lowered their average production costs. However, there are notable differences among the public and private sectors as far as industry- and time- specific factors are concerned. Evidently, time dummies are significant in the private sector, while sector dummies are significant in the public sector.

Results on the 500 largest firms also indicate a close relationship between output growth and TFPG. Time dummy variables seem to be significant, and with one exception have shown an increase compared to the base year 1983. It is interesting to note that there are no differences between the public and the private sectors in this regard (Table 8.10).

Table 8.7
Price-Cost Ratio Regression Results (Turkish Manufacturing Industries, 1974–85)

Variable	Private	Public	Pooled
Constant	1.176 *	1.527 *	1.361 *
Capital/output ratio	–0.012	0.004	–0.054
Dummy variables			
year 1975	–0.019	–0.087	–0.0529
year 1976	0.009	–0.047	–0.01916
year 1977	0.059 *	–0.117	–0.02941
year 1978	0.067 *	–0.117	–0.023
year 1979	0.035	–0.167 *	–0.061
year 1980	0.076 *	–0.142	–0.026
year 1981	0.048 *	–0.074	–0.011
year 1982	0.050 *	–0.086	–0.018
year 1983	0.042	–0.095	–0.026
year 1984	0.033	–0.107	–0.037
year 1985	–0.007	–0.046	–0.025
sector 32	0.116 *	–0.217 *	–0.034
sector 33	0.114 *	–0.180 *	–0.026
sector 34	0.217 *	–0.243	0.019
sector 35	0.126 *	0.059	0.094 *
sector 36	0.297 *	–0.141	0.100 *
sector 37	0.025	–0.064	0.017
sector 38	0.116 *	–0.269 *	–0.061
Adjusted R^2	0.790 *	0.232 *	0.058
see	0.047	0.169	0.150
D.W.	1.172	1.297	0.961
rss	0.2	2.2	3.9
F	19.77	2.5	1.6
n	96	96	192
F ratios for group of parameters			
Time dummies	0.60	0.40	0.20
Sector dummies	29.10 *	5.10 *	3.60 *
Time & sector	12.60 *	2.30 *	1.50
Private & public differences			4.97 *

* significant at the 5 percent level

Table 8.8
Profitability (Profit/Sales Revenue) Regression Results (Five Hundred Largest Firms, 1983–88)

Variable	Private	Public	Pooled
Constant	2.210	−1.233	2.053
Capital/output ratio	4.851	0.228	−3.742
Dummy variables			
year 1984	1.042	9.488 *	5.431
year 1985	−0.713	10.287 *	4.837
year 1986	−1.007	8.319	3.853
year 1987	2.454 *	9.079 *	5.844 *
year 1988	2.784 *	14.309 *	8.789 *
sector 32	3.160	−2.388	2.052
sector 33	2.248	28.199 *	14.584 *
sector 34	3.626 *	−9.357	1.613
sector 35	1.928	−1.176	0.463
sector 36	7.068 *	3.680	8.023 *
sector 37	0.178	−1.371	1.613
sector 381	3.440 *	−1.094	1.642
sector 384	1.870	−3.411	0.969
Adjusted R^2	0.561 *	0.549 *	0.244 *
see	2.478	8.753	8.245
D.W.	1.802		
rss	239.4	2835.1	6185.9
F	5.85	5.4	3.4
n	54	52	106
F ratios for group of parameters			
Time dummies	3.33 *	2.26 *	1.90 *
Sector dummies	2.54 *	5.37 *	3.77 *
Time & sector	3.18 *	4.85 *	3.21 *
Private & public differences			5.13 *

* significant at the 5 percent level

Table 8.9
Total Factor Productivity Growth Regression Results (Turkish Manufacturing Industries, 1974–85)

Variable	Private	Public	Pooled
Constant	–11.403 *	–4.678	–7.940 *
Output growth	0.875 *	0.962 *	0.957 *
Dummy variables			
year 1975	–0.056	–5.946	–3.539
year 1976	0.922	1.293	0.004
year 1977	6.337	–5.742	–0.225
year 1978	6.182	3.226	4.028
year 1979	10.832 *	1.838	6.829 *
year 1980	10.785 *	3.462	7.309 *
year 1981	11.167 *	6.128	8.129 *
year 1982	2.094	4.614	2.679
year 1983	3.877	1.487	2.662
year 1984	4.869	–0.521	1.802
year 1985	1.829	–5.006	–1.782
sector 32	–2.649	1.811	–0.437
sector 33	–0.572	–2.422	–1.350
sector 34	1.040	3.536	2.385
sector 35	–1.039	8.324 *	3.815
sector 36	–1.483	–3.744	–2.635
sector 37	–5.320	–0.006	–2.947
sector 38	–0.897	3.677	1.262
Adjusted R^2	0.746 *	0.977 *	0.953 *
see	7.993	8.385	8.829
D.W.	1.597	1.752	1.500
rss	4855.6	5342.8	13407.6
F	15.71	212.0	203.8
n	96	96	192
F ratios for group of parameters			
Time dummies	2.09 *	1.64	2.74 *
Sector dummies	0.67	2.49 *	1.73
Time & sector	1.50	2.10 *	2.39 *
Private & public differences			2.39 *

* significant at the 5 percent level

Table 8.10
Total Factor Productivity Growth Regression Results (Five Hundred Largest Firms, 1983–88)

Variable	Private	Public	Pooled
Constant	–58.879 *	–55.066 *	–57.381 *
Output growth	0.594 *	0.553 *	0.551 *
Dummy variables			
year 1984	65.952 *	66.771 *	66.558 *
year 1985	49.846 *	59.636 *	54.483 *
year 1986	61.327 *	63.404 *	63.897 *
year 1987	59.067 *	58.363 *	59.982 *
year 1988	60.030 *	49.636 *	55.520 *
sector 32	–2.126	–6.194	–4.059
sector 33	–3.528	–11.985	–7.597
sector 34	–12.603	29.450	8.378
sector 35	3.113	3.006	3.058
sector 36	–1.274	2.626	0.731
sector 37	–5.823	15.155	4.883
sector 381	1.728	–19.848	–8.968
sector 384	–8.615	6.365	–4.981
Adjusted R^2	0.663 *	0.606 *	0.644 *
see	20.309	35.494	28.057
D.W.	2.892		
rss	16085.8	41574.5	68488.0
F	8.45	6.16	14.1
n	54	48	102
F ratios for group of paramete			
Time dummies	13.70 *	3.53 *	13.17 *
Sector dummies	0.37	0.92	0.49
Time & sector	4.93 *	1.91	5.15 *
Private & public differences			0.9

* significant at the 5 percent level

STRUCTURAL CHANGE IN PROFITABILITY AND PRODUCTIVITY

Structural Change in Profitability

Chow tests for structural change indicate that there are important differences between price-cost and capital-output ratios during the pre- and postliberalization periods.

The coefficient of the capital-output ratio is 0.098 for the 1974–80 period and 0.197 for the 1981–85 period. For the public sector, the corresponding coefficients are -0.01 and -0.14. The negative sign accentuates the fact that public enterprises are more concentrated in capital-intensive and nonprofitable industries (Özmucur & Karataş, 1990).

Chow tests for structural changes also indicate that there are differences between profitability (profits/sales) and capital–output (fixed assets/total sales) ratios during the pre- and post-1984 import liberalization periods in the private sector, but not in the public sector.

Structural Change in Total Factor Productivity Growth

The results of Chow tests also show that there are structural changes during the pre- and post-liberalization periods. The value added growth coefficients are 0.78 and 1.22 for the private, and 0.87 and 0.96 for the public sectors during the two periods under consideration (Özmucur & Karataş, 1990).

Chow tests based on data for the 500 largest firms also support the hypothesis that there are structural changes both in the private and public sectors as far as the relationship between TFPG and value added growth are concerned. We should note that, due to an insufficient number of observations, time and sector dummies are excluded from the public sector regression.

CONCLUSION

The overall rate of TFPG for public manufacturing industry was -9.0 percent in 1973–79, 7.6 percent in 1979–85, and -1.0 percent in 1973–85. The negative TFPG in the 1970s was due to the fact that there was a dramatically low utilization of capacity, resulting from the acute shortage of foreign exchange and raw materials.

TFP growth in the private manufacturing sector was constantly negative: -4.6 percent in 1973–79, -2.5 percent during 1979–85 and -3.6 percent during 1973–85. This outcome was again due to extremely low capacity utilization. Consequently, TFPG of total manufacturing industry was negative: -5.4 percent for 1973–79, -1.9 percent for 1973–85, but positive (1.7 percent) for the 1979–85 period. Taking 1979 as a base year has, no doubt, influenced the magnitude of TFP growth during the 1979–85 period.

From the sectoral rates of TFPG in the public sector, we can infer that during the 1973–85 period textiles, nonmetallic products, basic metals, and machinery indicated a negative TFPG, while sectors such as food, wood products and paper products demonstrated positive but very low growth rates.

During the same period, within the private sector, all sectors portray negative TFPG. Besides, in the 1982–85 period, while in the private sector TFPG was excessively negative for food (-13.8%), textiles (-7.0%), paper products (-13.1%), chemicals (-11.9%), nonmetallic products (-6.5%) and machinery (-3.5%), TFPG in the public sector had attained remarkable growth in wood products (22%), basic metals (14%) and paper products (8.3%). During the same period, public industries that showed negative TFPG included food, textiles, chemicals, nonmetallic products and machinery.

TFPG in the 500 largest firms was positive during the 1985–88 period, at 6.1 percent for the private and 3.2 percent for the public sector. Calculations for the 1983–85 period were also provided for the sake of comparison. Within the public sector, food (-9.2%), textiles (-0.6%), wood (-18.6%) and machinery (-9.4%) recorded negative TFPG rates during the 1985–88 period. Within the private sector, the paper and paper products sector was the only sector with a negative TFPG rate (-3.8%).

It is also interesting to compare TFPG and profit rates. In the private sector, there is a positive correlation between the TFPG and profit (profit/sales) rates. In contrast, in the public sector there is a negative correlation between the TFPG and profit rates. High rates of profit in the public sector cannot be explained only by productivity growth rates; high rates of increase in product prices are also a contributing factor.

Even those public industries that are based on indigenous resources (e.g., paper, sugar, food processing, textiles, cement) did not seem to have been able to utilize their potential capacity. There is a need to correct the uneconomic input-output relationship through rationalization and increase in capacity utilization. In addition, protection provided by the government spoils the performance of firms by encouraging them to relax their cost-reducing efforts. Despite considerable trade liberalization, infant industries continue to get protection through the government's trade restrictionist policy.

Most public industries have a tendency to relax cost-reducing efforts. It will be reasonable to introduce stringent measures to augment economic performance. Some public sector enterprises are not eager to introduce improvements and take advantage of available opportunities, although it would be profitable to do so, and would not contradict any socioeconomic objectives of the government.

It is expedient to consider how new investments can be better planned and implemented to allow economically efficient production in textiles, paper and paper products, nonmetallic products, basic metals and machinery. This will obviously necessitate a detailed investigation of the specific causes of technical and economic inefficiency.

Insofar as incentives for investment in manufacturing industries are concerned, adequate account should be taken of interdependence of measures and their effects on resource allocation and internal efficiency.

NOTE

We would like to thank Osman Sarı, Ayşe Mumcu, Alpay Filiztekin, Emre Alper and Barkan Öz for data collection, and Professor Fikret Şenses for improving presentation.

9

SUBCONTRACTING PRACTICE IN THE TURKISH TEXTILE AND METAL-WORKING INDUSTRIES

Mehmet Kaytaz

INTRODUCTION

Small and medium-scale manufacturing enterprises (SMEs) and their role in the industrialization process of developing countries have attracted a great deal of interest, particularly from governments and international organizations. Another point of interest is the relations between small and larger enterprises, especially subcontracting relations. The positive contribution of subcontracting to industrialization, primarily in the Japanese case, is well documented (Shinohara, 1968: 72–77; Watanabe, 1971; Sato, 1988). Several governments, considering subcontracting as a course of promoting industrialization, developed particular policies to increase subcontracting relations in selected sectors (Watanabe, 1974; Hill, 1985; Kashyap, 1988: 677–78).

As in other developing countries, very little is known about subcontracting in Turkey. The few available studies suggest that the extent of subcontracting relations between larger and smaller establishments is limited.[1] In a study carried out by the State Planning Organization in 1970, it is reported that only a small percentage of small firms produced intermediary goods; it was 3, 8, 8, and 19 percent in Van, Konya, Gaziantep and Bursa, respectively (DPT 1971, vol. 1:23). Even then, it is not clear if these percentages were output produced purely under a subcontract. A study on subcontracting in the automotive industry found that during the 1970–72 period there were approximately 350 firms that received subcontracts, with the estimated share of subcontracts accounting for less than 20 percent of the value of total output (Kıraç, 1973: 157). In a study conducted in Bursa, where two car factories are located, the findings indicate that subcontracting practice is far less than would be expected both in scope and nature (Gupta, 1981: 83–115). This result is not surprising, since most of the subcontract-receiving firms in the automotive industry are in Istanbul. On the other hand, there is evidence from Bursa that in some sectors subcontracting is practiced extensively among smaller firms and that commercial subcontracting is widespread, particularly in textiles.[2]

The objective of this chapter is to examine the extent and nature of subcontracting relations in the textile and metal-working industries in Turkey. A question to be considered in this chapter is whether the subcontracting relationship promotes the development of SMEs. This question will be studied with reference to the type of subcontracts, financial and technical assistance of the subcontract offering establishments, exclusivity, and expectations and economic performance of subcontractors. The data come from a survey conducted by the author in the Istanbul and Kocaeli region in September–November 1989.

In this study, the size of an establishment is measured in terms of employment. Those establishments with a total work force of 10–99 are defined as SMEs.[3] Those with a work force of 100 or more are classified as large scale enterprises (LSEs). The terms establishment, enterprise, and firm are used interchangeably throughout the chapter.

Subcontracting is defined in this study as a commercial agreement between two parties where "the party offering subcontract requests another independent enterprise to undertake the whole or part of an order it has received instead of doing the work itself, while assuming full responsibility for the work vis-a-vis the customer" (Watanabe 1971: 56). Subcontracting involves more than an off-the-shelf purchase (Watanabe, 1971: 54); the enterprise receiving the subcontract produces in accordance with the specifications provided by the counterpart. The parties involved in a subcontract are referred to as counterparts, those offering subcontracts as principal, and those receiving subcontracts as subcontractors.

The data sources and methodology are discussed in the next section. The third section presents the survey findings and the last section gives a summary of the findings and discusses the policy implications.

DATA

The data used in this study come from a larger survey covering the following sectors: food (311), textiles (321 and 322), wood products (332), printing (341), and metal-working (381, 382, 383 and 384), with the number in parantheses indicating the corresponding International Standard Industry Classification (ISIC) numbers. Only the results pertaining to textiles and metal-working are included here.

The universe of the establishments covered in the survey was defined as those firms in the Istanbul-Kocaeli region employing at least 10 persons in the aforementioned sectors. The main sources for the address lists of establishments were Chambers of Industry, the Industrial Development Bank of Turkey, and the Association of Textile Exporters.

The number of establishments to be interviewed in each sector was determined by stratified random sampling based on each sector's proportional share in the total number of establishments. The firms were asked for an interview. Those that refused or had stopped their activities were replaced again by random sampling. In some cases, if the interview could not be conducted when the interviewer visited the establishment, another establishment in the same area was visited and the person in charge was interviewed.

The interviews for the survey were conducted using two different questionnaires: one for LSEs and one for SMEs. They included questions on the entrepreneurs' background and work experience, on firm profile and production activities, on input and output markets, on relations with other firms, on problems faced by firms and on firms' policy and program proposals.

The limitations of field surveys are well known. In order to complement and to verify some of the survey findings, the author has carried out extensive and in-depth interviews with some selected producers. In selecting these successful, reliable producers, assistance was received from acquaintances and larger firms dealing with these producers. The interviews were conducted without a formal questionnaire. The respondents were guided around some general topics about the industry and specific topics about their business and were asked to comment on them.

Of a total of 423 establishments that were visited, information about only 341 is included in the survey results. Of these establishments 105 are in textiles and 134 are in metal-working. In textiles, 91 of the establishments are defined as SMEs; for metal-working this figure is 119. The sampling ratios, which were calculated by using the total figures given in the 1985 Census of Industry and Business Establishments (State Institute of Statistics, 1988a: 11–129; 1988b: 140–45), covering all establishments in Turkey, are as follows: in textiles, 4.9 percent and 5.2 percent for SMEs and LSEs, respectively; in metal-working, 5.5 percent and 4.5 percent for SMEs and LSEs, respectively.

FINDINGS

The firms in the sample show a variety of interfirm relations SMEs are classified into four groups according to subcontracting relations: those establishments that are not involved in subcontracting, those receiving subcontracts (subcontractor), those offering subcontracts (principal) and those both offering and receiving subcontracts. In both sectors a large proportion of establishments is involved in some form of subcontracting relation (Table 9.1). In textiles those establishments offering subcontracts constitute the largest group, while in metal-working those both offering and receiving subcontracts are the largest group, though there is not a significant difference between the groups. In the case of LSEs, textiles have a considerably larger proportion of subcontract-offering firms,

Table 9.1

Distribution of Firms in Textiles and Metal-Working by Subcontracting Relations, Export Share and Average Employment

Sector Subcontracting relation	Textiles				Metal- working			
	Freq.	Percentage %	Export share[a]	Size[b]	Freq.	Percentage %	Export share[a]	Size[b]
Small and Medium Scale Enterprises								
Non-subcontracting	18	19.8	24	38	27	22.7	10	34
Subcontract offering	35	38.5	54	45	31	26.1	40	36
Subcontract receiving	20	22.0	6	28	27	22.7	15	35
Subcontract offering and receiving	18	19.8	16	35	34	28.6	35	28
Total	91	100.0	100	38	119	100.0	100	33
Large Scale Enterprises								
Subcontracting	9	64.3		255	4	26.7		717
Non-subcontracting	5	35.7		294	11	73.3		435
Total	14	100.0		294	15	100.0		510

[a] Export share: proportion of exporting firms to the total number of firms in the sector
[b] Size: 1988 level of total employment

whereas in metal-working, nonsubcontracting firms are dominant. In textiles, clothing manufacturing firms have a larger proportion of subcontract-offering firms than in weaving.[4]

In both sectors, subcontract-offering SMEs have the highest proportion of exporting firms to the total number of firms in the sector; in metal-working the distribution of the share of exporting firms is more even than in textiles (Table 9.1).

Subcontract-offering SMEs are the largest establishments in both sectors; in textiles differences in size are significant, but not in metal-working.[5] Exporting firms have a relatively larger size. The distribution of firms by size exhibits the standard dichotomy of large principal and small subcontractor in textiles, particularly in clothing, while in metal-working there are smaller firms that offer subcontracts to larger firms. In some cases this is also true for textiles, such as large textile-dyeing firms receiving subcontracts from smaller firms.

For LSEs, the average share of subcontracting in total cost is 38 and 4 percent in textiles and in metal-working, respectively; the median figures are not much

Table 9.2
Reasons for Offering Subcontracts in Textiles and Metal-Working (Percent)

	Small and Medium-Scale		Large-Scale	
	Textiles	Metal-Working	Textiles	Metal-Working
Insufficient capacity	86.2[a]	71.9	88.9	50.0
Shortage of labor	39.2	22.8	-	-
Cost saving	23.5	240.4	44.4	50.0
Availability of counterparts	19.6	31.6	-	-
Adjustment to cycles	2.0	7.0	33.3	75.0
Long-term transactions	-	-	11.1	25.0
Specific technology	-	-	22.2	25.0

[a] Due to respondents citing more than one response, percentages may add up to more than 100

different from the average figures. For SMEs offering subcontracts, the average and median share of subcontracting in total cost in textiles is about 20 percent, while in metal-working the average is 21 percent and the median is 15 percent.

Reasons for Subcontracting and Types of Subcontracts

In both textiles and metal-working, a large proportion of the subcontracting firms, both small and large, consider insufficient capacity as the main reason for offering subcontracts (Table 9.2). Otherwise, there are differences between sectors and between smaller and larger firms. Adjustment to business cycles emerges as a more important factor in larger firms than in smaller firms. In general, reasons other than insufficient capacity have a higher ranking in metal-working than in textiles. In clothing, the shortage of labor is a considerably more important reason than in weaving.

The differences between the two sectors become even more apparent when we consider the type of subcontracts (Table 9.3). In textiles, the main type of subcontract is for the manufacture of a specific production process, while in metal-working it is for the manufacture of components and parts. Other types of subcontracting have a relatively minor place in both sectors. In textiles, subcontracted work is mainly in the form of the processing of cloth, such as dyeing, printing or sewing a specific part of a wearing apparel. The larger firms, mostly exporters, subcontract mainly for sewing a specific part or the whole of a

Table 9.3
**Distribution of Firms by Subcontract Types in Textiles and Metal-Working,
Export Share and Average Employment**

Subcontract types	Textiles			Metal - working		
	Percen-tage %	Export share[a]	Size[b]	Percen-tage %	Export share[a]	Size[b]
Small and Medium-Scale Enterprises						
Subcontract Receiving Firms						
Specific process	63.2	-	35	26.2	-	43
Component production	23.7	-	19	60.7	-	30
Assembly	2.6	-	66	8.2	-	18
All	10.5	-	26	4.9	-	16
Total	100.0	-	31	100.0	-	32
Subcontract Offering Firms						
Specific process	62.7	70.6	46	48.6	23.130	
Component production	25.5	20.6	30	37.8	53.8	36
Assembly	5.9	5.9	32	7.3	15.4	31
All	5.9	2.9	48	6.3	7.7	24
Total	100.0	100.0	41	100.0	100.0	32
Large Scale Enterprises						
Specific process	88.9	-	269	50.0	-	1317
Component production	11.1	-	153	50.0	-	117
Total	100.0	-	270	100.0	-	717

[a] Export share: proportion of exporting firms to the total number of firms in the sector
[b] Size: 1988 level of total employment

wearing apparel when they have limited time to meet orders. In textiles, subcontractors doing assembly work, and representing only a small proportion of the total number of establishments in the group, have the largest average size. This also confirms the existence of large subcontractors and small principals in this sector.

In the small and medium segment of metal-working, larger firms subcontract the manufacture of parts. These are firms producing essentially machinery, vehicles and household goods. Smaller firms subcontract the production of a specific process such as machining, turning, milling, grinding or spot-welding, more than the production of parts and components. In the large segment of the sector, subcontract types have equal weights.

Watanabe (1971: 56) defines "capacity-oriented" subcontracting, where the subcontracting parties produce similar products and are competitive by nature. This type of subcontracting is likely to be temporary, since the principal may increase its plant capacity in the future. On the other hand, "specialized subcontracting," or more generally "economic subcontracting" (Watanabe, 1971: 56; World Bank 1980, vol. 3: 44) is more conducive to development. In this case, the principal finds it more profitable to subcontract rather than undertake investment, either because the quantity subcontracted does not justify investment and investment costs are high or the subcontractor has a superior technology.

Insufficient capacity being the main reason for offering subcontracts suggests that subcontracting practice in Turkey is temporary rather than developmental. This seems to be true particularly in textiles. In the small and medium-scale segment of the industry this reason in some cases overlaps with cost saving and lack of specific technology. For firms such as those in dyeing textiles, the subcontracts are specialization oriented. The majority of subcontracts these specialized firms receive come from smaller firms, as larger ones have their own dyeing facilities. In metal-working, on the other hand, subcontracts are more specialization oriented. The fact that adjustment to business cycles, specific technology and long-term transactions rank high among the reasons for offering subcontracts in this sector implies that subcontracting practice in metal-working is more developmental than in textiles. The percentage of respondents citing the availability of counterparts, that is, the existence of firms ready to receive subcontracts, as one of the reasons for offering subcontracts is significantly higher in metal-working than in textiles. This may be considered as another indication of the more developmental nature of subcontracting in metal-working, since the availability of subcontractors has been an important element in the Japanese subcontracting experience.

Cost saving as a reason for offering subcontracts suggests economic subcontracting (Table 9.2). However, in some cases cost saving means time saving; in this case it is highly likely that subcontracting is temporary. The duration of contracts and delivery time provide some indirect evidence in this respect. In textiles, median delivery time is 10 days, while in metal-working it is 15 days.

Exclusivity

Exclusivity was one of the important aspects of the Japanese subcontracting experience. The relationship between the subcontract-offering and -receiving firms was a close and stable one; often the latter was almost an extension of the former.[6] The survey results show that this type of relationship is rather limited in Turkish manufacturing. Subcontract-offering firms prefer to have more than one subcontractor for a given component, mainly because they desire to have a stable supply source in case of delays and disagreements and more room for maneuver in price determination. Subcontractors, considering that in price negotiations they will be in a weaker position, also prefer to work for more than one counterpart. Furthermore, subcontractors, depending on the type of product or process they are producing,

 prefer to market their goods independently whenever possible. One major reason for this is that their production capacity is usually more than necessary to meet the demand of a single counterpart.

The average and median number of counterparts for a subcontractor are 23 and 5, respectively. These figures do not differ significantly across sectors. On the other hand, the number of LSE counterparts is relatively smaller; in textiles the average and median number of LSE counterparts are 7 and 1, respectively; in metal-working these figures are 8 and 3, respectively. In the Japanese experience it was often the case that one subcontractor worked solely for a single principal.

For SMEs offering subcontracts, the average number of counterparts is 7.5 and 8.8 in textiles and metal-working, respectively; the median figures are 3 and 4, respectively. For LSEs offering subcontracts, the average and median figures are 29 and 20 in textiles, and 10 and 7 in metal-working, respectively. The majority of establishments receiving subcontracts from LSEs are those employing 10–49 workers. The average number of counterparts is 21 and 5 in textiles and metal-working, respectively.

In textiles, the average share of subcontracts in total sales is 78 percent, while in metal-working it is 64 percent. On the other hand, the median share of subcontracts is higher in both sectors: 100 and 83 percent in textiles and metal-working, respectively. The average share of the largest customer is about 34 percent in both sectors.

Assistance

Strong linkages between subcontract-offering and -receiving establishments are necessary for subcontracting to foster industrialization. The technological linkages are especially important in this respect. In the Turkish case, the linkages do not seem to be very strong. A sizable proportion of subcontractors do not receive any form of assistance from the subcontract-offering establishments (Table 9.4). In both textiles and metal-working, supply of raw materials is the major form of linkage between the firms. This may give an advantage to the subcontractor in securing supplies in an inflationary environment and may provide pecuniary economies of scale.[7] In textiles, this is also somewhat due to the nature of the production process. On the other hand, supply of raw materials in metal-

Table 9.4
Assistance and Technical Guidance Received by Subcontractors in Textiles and Metal-Working (Percent)

	Textiles	Metal-working
	Assistance	
Supply of raw materials	34.3	33.9
Technical guidance	25.7	37.5
Management guidance	2.9	7.1
Financial assistance	22.9	39.3
No assistance	20.0	21.4
	Technical Guidance	
Dispatch of personnel	33.3	47.6
Training	22.2	38.1
Provision of blue-prints	44.4	52.4

[a] Due to respondents citing more than one response, percentages may add up to more than 100

working means higher quality and cheaper inputs.[8]

Technical guidance as a form of assistance has an important place in both sectors, especially in metal-working. Technical guidance is given in the form of dispatch of personnel such as engineers and technicians, training of the employees of subcontractors and provision of blueprints and samples. Although the last type of technical guidance, which is the major type in both sectors, can hardly be called assistance, it may create some initial technological spin-off in some cases (Hill, 1985: 252–53).

Subcontract-offering foreign joint ventures seem to be providing more technical guidance than domestic principals. This is true for both sectors.

A large proportion of subcontractors, 61 percent in textiles and 88 percent in metal-working, report that they make an effort to improve their technology. In both sectors, purchase of new machinery is regarded by about 60 percent of the subcontractors as the main form of technological improvement. The second major form is R&D in textiles and technical training in metal-working. On the other hand, the subcontractors do not have a clear idea about the nature of the assistance they desire from counterparts. Most of them are not aware of the benefits technical guidance can bring. Consequently, financial assistance is the main type of help they desire; only about 12 percent want more technical guidance. The dispatch of personnel and training are the major types of technical assistance the establishments desire.

An improvement in quality control is an area in which the subcontract-offering firms seem to have made some positive contribution. In both sectors the rejection rate has fallen in the last five years, especially in metal-working where about 50 percent of the subcontractors reported a drop. Improvement in quality control is also evidenced by the subcontractor's perception of the reason for his selection by the counterpart. More than half of the subcontractors in the sample attribute this to their being stringent on quality requirements. The largest drop in rejection rate occurred in establishments receiving subcontracts from foreign joint ventures or from firms producing for export markets.

An indirect form of technological diffusion is the movement of skilled workers. Although it was not possible to obtain direct evidence on this point from the survey, the previous jobs of entrepreneurs provide some information. In both sectors, more than 30 percent of the subcontractors had worked in the same sector as employees before establishing their own business. This suggests that there is some degree of technological diffusion through former employees starting their own business and taking subcontracts. These are usually technicians or engineers who had an early retirement or went into partnership and resigned before retirement.

About one-half of subcontractors in both sectors consider the subcontracts they receive as regular and stable. Another 30 percent find the orders not regular and quantities not stable. About three-fourths of subcontractors in both sectors consider that the principal adheres to the agreement conditions. Usually payment conditions, that is, delay in payments, is the area in which the principal is regarded as not adhering to the agreement conditions.

Prospects for Subcontracting

Most of the establishments in the sample increased their average level of employment during the 1983–88 period (Table 9.5). The growth of employment in textiles is higher than in metal-working; in the former, employment increased on the average by 10.2 employees between 1983 and 1988, while in the latter this increase was 5.1 employees. However, the distribution of the increase in employment in textiles is more skewed than in metal-working; the median levels of growth are one and three employees in textiles and metal-working, respectively. In both sectors, the highest growth in employment took place in subcontract- offering firms. However, in textiles this increase is statistically significant, while in metal-working it is not. In both sectors, establishments not involved in subcontracting have the second largest increase, and establishments both offering and receiving subcontracts have the lowest increase in employment.

Table 9.5

Average Labor Productivity, Wage Rate and Employment Growth in Textiles and Metal-Working by Subcontracting Relations

Sector Subcontracting relation	Textiles			Metal-Working		
	Productivity	Wage rate	Employment growth	Productivity	Wage rate	Employment growth
Non-subcontracting	49.8	4.7	8.3	33.1	4.7	5.4
Subcontract offering	50.7	5.5	18.4	37.2	6.0	7.2
Subcontract receiving	21.7	4.8	6.6	55.5	5.9	4.2
Subcontract offering and receiving	41.3	5.2	1.6	37.7	6.8	3.7
Total	42.8	5.1	10.2	40.6	5.9	5.1

Note: Productivity: ratio of gross output to total employment, in million lira.

Wage rate: ratio of annual wage bill to total employment, in million lira.

Employment growth: difference between 1988 and 1983 levels of total employment

The findings on labor productivity (ratio of gross output to total employment) present an interesting picture. In textiles, establishments offering subcontracts have the highest level of labor productivity, while subcontractors have the lowest level. In metal-working, on the other hand, subcontractors have the highest level of productivity, with nonsubcontracting establishments having the lowest. The establishments with higher levels of productivity are also generally larger and younger firms, producing also for export markets.[9]

It seems that the same kind of relationship exists between establishment size and average wage rates. Usually, larger firms pay higher wages. In textiles, the distribution of wage rates supports the idea of subcontracting as disguised wage labor; in metal-working this does not seem to be true, as wage rates in subcontract-offering and in subcontract-receiving firms are not significantly different.

In both sectors, more than 60 percent of the subcontractors find the existing subcontracting relations satisfactory. In textiles, 51 percent and in metal-working, 58 percent of the subcontractors intend to expand subcontracting. Thirty-two percent and 23 percent of subcontractors in textiles and metal-working, respectively, plan to keep the extent of subcontracts at the existing level. The views of subcontract offering firms, on the other hand, are slightly different. Principals consider delays in delivery as the major problem in textiles, while low quality is viewed as the main problem in metal-working. In both sectors, they also identify the insufficient number of counterparts as an important problem. In textiles, about one-third of the establishments plan to increase the volume of subcontracts, while in metal-working this figure is about 50 percent.

CONCLUSIONS AND POLICY IMPLICATIONS

The findings show that the sectoral differences in the nature and extent of subcontracting are significant. In textiles there is more subcontracting than in metal-working; however, in the latter, subcontracting has more of a developmental character. This result is suggested by the insufficiency of capacity being the main reason for offering subcontracts, a lower level of assistance as well as a lower level of employment growth, and significantly lower wage rates and productivity in subcontract-receiving establishments in textiles than in metal-working.

In metal-working, the higher level of technical guidance and financial assistance indicate stronger interfirm linkages than in textiles. However, the existing level of linkages and assistance is not sufficient for diffusion of technology, which is a primary aspect of a faster rate of industrialization through subcontracting.

Until recently, other than individual efforts of a small number of official or semiofficial organizations in Turkey, there has been no explicit policy of encouragement for subcontracting. Government policies toward SMEs have been very general, in the form of providing cheaper loans and assisting in the establishment of industrial districts. In 1990, the Small and Medium Industry Development Organization (SMIDO) was established, with the aim of creating a suitable environment for entrepreneurship, providing technical and managerial training, assisting in obtaining information and technology and strengthening subcontracting relations. SMIDO conducts its activities through regional centers by providing consultancy, guidance and support in technical, administrative and financial matters. To the author's knowledge, the details of the activities of SMIDO for strengthening subcontracting relations have not yet been specified.

The existing level of subcontracting in textiles and metal-working seems to be not much different from those developing countries where subcontracting was encouraged in particular sectors. It seems possible to increase the level of subcontracting and promote industrialization in Turkey by comprehensive and complementary policies. These policies should aim at both SMEs and LSEs and provide an environment that encorages subcontracting.

The policies for SMEs should aim at increasing their technical, managerial and financial capabilities. Possible measures to this end would include "reduced import duties on machinery for subcontractors, accelerated depreciation allowance on equipment to facilitate subcontractors' acquisition of capital assets, provision of industrial extension services, materials testing equipment and industrial estate facilities" (World Bank, 1980, vol. 3: 46–47). These measures would directly influence SMEs, regardless of whether they receive subcontracts from smaller or larger firms, and decrease the degree of captive or exploitative subcontracting. Indeed alongside the technical and financial capacities, managerial capacities should also be developed. The results indicate that most of the entrepreneurs in the sample obtained and developed their technical skills at their jobs and are not aware of the importance of management skills. SMIDO plans to overcome this deficiency through advisory services in the regional centers. The strengthening of SMEs would create a favorable environment where LSEs would find reliable subcontractors. If the production processes are suitable, the availability of subcontractors would influence LSEs' investment plans toward offering more subcontracts. Furthermore, the subcontracting relations among smaller firms, the volume of which is already high, would become even stronger and more productive.

A significant proportion of subcontractors in the sample find the existing relationship not to their advantage and consider it as exploitative. The establishment of a regulation or arbitration board to tackle this problem would increase the advantages of subcontracting.

The policies aimed at LSEs to increase subcontracting would include the requirement by the government "that larger firms receiving public contracts must subcontract specified portions of the work to SMEs" (World Bank, 1980, vol. 3: 44). The State Economic Enterprises may also play a greater role in encouraging subcontracting. Another measure would be to provide special investment incentives to LSEs that include subcontracting in their investment projects. These measures should be applied selectively and only after a careful study of the sector and the particular production process; otherwise, they may create inefficiencies, as happened in a number of developing countries.

The policies enumerated above should be complemented by other policies. In both sectors, export orientation seems to be a major factor in increasing the volume of subcontracts, as exporting sectors have a higher proportion of subcontract-offering firms. It seems that, given a limited domestic market, production for exports encourages subcontracting. The continued promotion of exports as a major policy would therefore establish even stronger subcontracting relations. Furthermore, stringent quality requirements for the competitiveness of exports in world markets may also increase the linkages between counterparts. The findings show that this is evident, particularly in the manufacture of clothing.

For the above policies and measures to be successful, a stable flow of raw materials of required quality and achievement of standardization in components and parts are essential.

NOTES

I am grateful to the Institute of Developing Economies of Tokyo, Japan for financing the survey. I thank Dr. Ali Eşref Turan of Yönelim, who provided invaluable assistance in the conduct of the survey and Ümit İzmen of Boğaziçi University, who assisted in various stages of the survey. My thanks also go to the editor of this book for invaluable comments and criticisms.

1. A report by the Statistical, Economic, and Social Research and Training Center for Islamic Countries (1987: 77–78) gives brief summaries of the studies conducted on the relations between the larger and smaller firms. This paragraph draws heavily on that report.

2. Bademli (1977: 237–41) notes that the relations among smaller firms are more in the nature of a "social cooperation" than subcontracting. Çınar, Evcimen and Kaytaz (1988: 287–301) and Kaytaz, Evcimen and Cinar (1989: 4–6) give examples of commercial subcontracting in textiles and industrial subcontracting in iron-casting.

3. The total work force of an establishment covers the owner(s), unpaid family workers and paid workers. State Institute of Statistics of Turkey in its surveys and censuses until 1983 classified establishments with a total work force of fewer than 10 as "small"; afterwards, this definition included those with a work force of fewer than 25. Recently, establishments with a work force of one to nine employees were classified as "very small," and those with 10–49 employees as "small." Otherwise, there is no official uniform definition of small–scale manufacturing establishments. Consequently, different public bodies dealing with small establishments use different classification criteria. The classification adopted in this study follows the proposals of a committee sponsored by the State Planning Organization (DPT, 1989: 55–56). This is also in line with the definition of small and medium-scale firms used in many other developing countries.

4. The size of the sample is sufficient to distinguish between characteristics of the two subsectors in textiles, namely manufacture of textiles (321) and manufacture of wearing apparel except footwear (322). When referring to the entire sector the term textiles will be used; the former subsector will be referred to as weaving and the latter as clothing.

5. The significance tests of the differences between means of different groups are based on analysis of variance and multiple comparisons using Duncan's statistic. Both tests are done at a 5 percent level of significance unless otherwise stated.

6. For some issues such as exploitation in the subcontracting process in developing countries see Schmitz (1982: 435–37).

7. See Hill (1985: 253–54) for a discussion of the implicit assumption of imperfect markets.

8. In many sectors, production of intermediate goods is carried out by State Economic Enterprises. In recent years, due the insufficiency of investment in these enterprises, there were bottlenecks in meeting the increased demand. This led to a decline in quality or to resorting to imports of these goods. Since SMEs' orders are small in quantity, they can neither order directly from the State Economic Enterprises nor import directly. Consequently, they probably pay higher prices and get lower quality in return (see DPT, 1989: 150–51).

9. In both sectors, labor productivity follows a U-shaped curve; that is, in firms with a total work force of 10–24 it is higher than in firms with a work force of 25–49, and the larger firms have the highest productivity. This is in line with the results of another study (Kaytaz et al., 1989: 4–6).

10

Changing Spatial Distribution and Structural Characteristics of the Turkish Manufacturing Industry

Ayda Eraydın

INTRODUCTION

In the last two decades the production system in the world has undergone important changes. While Fordist production, which defined the characteristics of the postwar period, faced several problems marked by a slowdown in productivity (Lipietz, 1986; Storper, 1990; Schoenberger, 1988; Harvey, 1989), a new form of accumulation and a flexible, post-Fordist production system have emerged.

Although there are discussions related to the future of the post-Fordist production system, in particular whether this mode of production will become dominant (Sayer, 1989; Cooke, 1988) or will stay as a section of the production system, there is wide agreement on the importance of its impact on labor and production relations.

In sharp contrast with mass, Fordist production, which is defined by Taylorist separation of managerial and manual work, task fragmentation, standard commodity production and large markets based on a considerable middle-income class, post-Fordist production is characterized by small batch production, flexibilities in production and labor relations and production for small market niches.

In the late Fordist period, the newly industrializing countries were the new points of attraction for the multinational enterprises that were looking for new locations. However, a flexible production system and a regime of accumulation define a new set of conditions for different countries, including peripheral ones. The spatial implications of this new system of production are different from the previous production system.

There are two different views on the spatial impact of flexible forms of production. The first group of views (Leborgne & Lipietz, 1988) emphasize the possibilities of decentralization in the context of complementarity between center and periphery[1]. It is claimed that the work force of flexible production units will tend to be polarized in a core of highly qualified workers with multiple skills, cooperating closely with the service-class employees in research and development, managerial and marketing functions. In this context, a semiperiphery is characterized by semiskilled, low-wage, flexible workers, and a periphery by part-time jobs (Cooke, 1988). This situation results in the fragmentation of the work force (Albertsen, 1988) according to the character of production by spatial units. Decentralization and networking across the field of operations are toward minimizing innovation costs (R&D, testing, etc.) through strategic alliances or special linkages that can also foster decentralization tendencies.

According to the second point, the new production systems have dynamics for concentration. It is argued that the spatial dynamic of flexible production seems to be the opposite of the late-Fordist "explosive-implosive" dissolution of regions into global-local networks (Albertsen, 1988). Similarly, Storper and Scott (1988) claim that flexible production recreates spatial agglomeration, normally outside the strongholds of Fordist production and rigidly organized labor. Flexibility contradicts spatial decentralization because of high costs of transactions within and between large and small firms. Dependencies on pools of highly skilled and multiskilled labor and need for highly complex subcontracting relationships further reinforce spatial clustering (Amin & Robins, 1990: 13). Accordingly, intensifying flexibility and vertical disintegration of organizational structures is expected to lead to locational convergence and spatial agglomeration.

Within the new geography of flexible accumulation, the fundamental observation is the change of the priority areas of industrial development (Scott, 1988), both at an international and national scale. The new industrial districts and new localities to which industry looks are quite different from during the Fordist era.

First, in the transition from Fordism to flexibility, a functional logic of organizational structure gives way to a new territorial logic based on the centrality and importance of industrial districts. The main theme offered by various discussions of post-Fordist production is a very coherent account of the proliferation of industrial districts by disintegration of production structures.

At this point, an important question is whether these industrial districts will replicate the existing districts, or whether we need to foresee the industrial district formation within a different perspective.

In the formation of new industrial districts, learning advantages of network systems are expected to be crucial, not only to small firms but also to an increasing number of large corporations that are imitating and allying with other firms in order to survive within flexible conditions.

Second, the industrial restructuring thesis and the transformation to a post-Fordist type of production have been responsible for the revival of locality studies (Sayer, 1991; Warde, 1988). The demonstration that industrial organization had profound effects at various spatial levels directed attention to the localities where people ultimately experience these changes in their everyday life. One analytical problem that then arises is related to the impact of restructuring on local culture and politics. Obviously, other factors, such as the nature of work, gender and religious relations, political history and interpersonal relations, are also of importance in this respect (Cooke, 1985).

Locality and local development concepts are important, since it is claimed that recently successful countries are the ones that adapted internationally current forms of production to their local characteristics, including labor, class and relevant social regulations.

The aim of this chapter is to examine the change in production technology in Turkish manufacturing industry by spatial units, and organization of production and labor in the Bursa textile industry, against a background of discussions on flexible production systems and their impact on industrial activities.

THE MEANING OF FLEXIBLE PRODUCTION FOR LDCs

As there is increased competition in international markets and market cross-penetration in the 1990s (Storper, 1990), individual countries find it hard not to be affected by changes in industrial production systems. While specialized products have to search for external markets, increasing productivity, utilizing new technologies and new organizations of labor, and improving the price-performance curve become essential. In short, countries need to adapt to new conditions defined by production and to new marketing, finance and social organization condtions by the use of different regulation mechanisms.

However, even when these conditions are satisfied, the role of developing countries within flexible production systems is not certain. There are two options: they can develop flexible production, or become segmented from the world industrial production system.

Studies (Holmes, 1986; Lyberaki, 1990) indicate that flexible production takes place in networks composed of firms of different size. Flexible relations among them lead to the dissemination of knowledge and sometimes to innovations (Garofoli, 1990), while subcontracting and cooperative work form the basis of a local business culture (Malecki, 1991).

In areas of flexible production systems, there is a need for coordination of local institutions and social practices, and for establishing informal relations of trust (Storper, 1990: 435), to supplement the existing production culture and social relations among the individual producers. Existing small and medium-sized firms that have experience in coping with uncertainties can be a part of the new networks formed by firms of different sizes. On the other hand, strong competition implies a greater turnover of market openings in the capitalist world and the possibility of access to new market niches.

The availability of skilled labor and familiarity of skilled manpower with the new work organization are important in flexible production system. Internal work flexibility requires more polyvalent skills than mass production did (Schmitz, 1989).

The above characteristics of post-Fordist production are both an obstacle and an opportunity for developing countries. In the last decade, a close cooperation can be seen between the modern and traditional small-scale industry segments in some peripheral countries facing the pressures of restructuring. While flexibility became the major characteristic of this new process, new networks of relationships can be identified, and there are clues indicating the transformation of industrial agglomerations into local productive systems. There is evidence from different countries such as Brazil (Storper, 1990), Ghana and India (Schmitz, 1989) about the formation of new production relations and new networks. Obviously, these new industrial districts can have different characteristics from those in developed countries, due to their production culture and other characteristics of the localities.

Obviously, the above hypothesis on transformation of former industrial agglomerations into nodes of production networks is very important and needs to be tested against the experience of other countries. If verified by empirical evidence, it can bring a new approach to industrial policies and planning.

CHANGE OF INDUSTRIAL SPACE IN TURKEY DURING THE PROCESS OF RESTRUCTURING

The theoretical discussions on the change in industrial production systems and transformation to flexible forms of production imply that the changing character of industrial activity creates different pressures on space. In this section, the tendency toward change in spatial distribution of industrial activity in Turkey is presented. The levels of technological change in industrial activity and growth performance by spatial units are then used to identify the future growth nodes. One of these nodes, Bursa, is then presented as a case study of changing forms of organization of work and industrial relations.

The Change in the Spatial Distribution of Industrial Activity

As in many other countries, industrial activities in Turkey are relatively more concentrated in certain nodes of the developed regions. It is not surprising to observe that the regional distribution of industrial employment is parallel to the level of development by regions.

Industrial activity is concentrated in four metropolitan regions, which are characterized by a metropolitan center and a number of provinces around these centers: the Istanbul metropolitan area and the Kocaeli, Sakarya, Tekirdağ and

Bursa provinces around Istanbul: the İzmir metropolitan area and the Manisa, Aydın and Denizli provinces located around İzmir: the Ankara metropolitan area with its extension as Kırıkkale; and finally the Adana, İçel and Hatay provinces, constituting the Adana (Çukurova) region.

In 1988, 52.4 percent of the industrial firms and about 45 percent of employment originated from the Istanbul region alone. The four regions identified above together accounted for 70 percent of total industrial employment. There are also regional centers, such as Eskişehir, Gaziantep, Samsun, Konya and Kayseri, where industrial activity is relatively important. The share of these regional centers is about 10 percent of employment and 7 percent of firms, and the group formed by the 50 remaining provinces have only a 20 percent share of industrial employment and even less (17.5 percent) in terms of industrial firms (Table 10.1).

The growth and distribution of industry in the last two decades exhibit different tendencies. During the 1971-82 period, the general tendency in the growth of industry was toward concentration in the relatively more developed regions of the country. The rate of growth of manufacturing employment was below the Turkish average in the provinces of Eastern and Southeastern Anatolia, constituting the least developed regions. In the three provinces of the eastern part of the country (Sivas, Bitlis and Rize), employment actually declined in absolute terms.

However, there are different tendencies during this period, as influenced by the magnitude and character of economic problems. During the 1971–74 period, when the average annual rate of growth of total manufacturing employment was 8.2 percent, Thrace and the Middle Anatolia regions became the main points of attraction. During the 1974–79 period, total employment declined by an annual rate of 3.7 percent, but, interestingly, growth was higher in the less developed provinces. During the 1980–82 period, when industrial employment increased at a low rate (1.9 percent)[2], the important issue was the decline in industrial employment in many provinces.

Metropolitan decentralization was the dominant facet of change in the 1970s, as settlements around the major metropolitan centers became the new areas of attraction. We can identify three groups in this process.

The first group was the peripheral ring of the Istanbul metropolitan region, namely Tekirdağ, Sakarya and Bursa, with Bursa having its own basis of growth. The high rate of growth of industrial activity in this area can be attributed to the decentralization of manufacturing activity in the Istanbul metropolitan area. In this trend, in addition to newly founded large industrial estates, increasing local capital played an important role.

In the early 1970s, the provinces located at the eastern part of the Istanbul metropolitan area[3] became attractive for the new, large-scale industrial firms, unable to find suitable locations in the Istanbul metropolitan area and adjacent areas in the Kocaeli province. This was followed by a further extension to the Thrace section, which attracted industrial activities trying to be close to the

Table 10.1
Distribution of Employment in Industry by Provinces in Turkey, 1971–88
(Selected Years, Percent)

Provinces	1971	%	1982	%	1983	%	1988	%
Total	*525,796*	*100.00*	*829,878*	*100.00*	*797,587*	*100.00*	*955,217*	*100.00*
İstanbul	199,996	38.04	275,038	33.14	230,888	28.95	284,124	31.09
Kocaeli	24,969	4.34	51,245	6.18	51,973	6.52	56,554	6.19
Bursa	19,035	3.31	40,049	4.83	41,031	5.14	60,091	6.58
Sakarya	7,553	1.31	10,013	1.21	10,696	1.34	10,387	1.14
Tekirdağ	5,313	0.92	10,538	1.27	12,282	1.54	19,158	2.10
İst.Region	*256,866*	*44.61*	*386,883*	*46.62*	*346,870*	*43.49*	*430,314*	*45.05*
İzmir	51,721	8.98	58,288	7.02	73,020	9.16	87,072	9.12
Manisa	5,175	0.90	10,858	1.31	10,362	1.30	19,203	2.01
Aydın	5,466	0.95	7,353	0.89	7,238	0.91	7,415	0.78
Denizli	3,412	0.59	8,204	0.99	7,863	0.99	11,941	1.25
İzmir Region	*65,774*	*11.42*	*84,703*	*10.21*	*98,483*	*12.35*	*125,631*	*13.75*
Adana	22,228	3.86	40,143	4.84	39,760	4.99	43,463	4.76
İçel	6,755	1.17	13,522	1.63	13,169	1.65	14,779	1.62
Hatay	2,617	0.45	19,461	2.35	18,727	2.35	18,098	1.98
Adana Region	*31,600*	*5.49*	*73,126*	*8.81*	*71,656*	*8.98*	*76,340*	*8.35*
Ankara	31,717	5.51	46,203	5.57	43,598	5.47	52,297	5.72
Kayseri	7,892	1.37	14,561	1.75	13,869	1.74	16,337	1.79
Samsun	7,553	1.31	16,195	1.95	15,719	1.97	13,735	1.50
Konya	6,411	1.11	18,797	2.27	20,644	2.59	29,610	3.24
Eskişehir	11,446	1.99	14,311	1.72	14,378	1.80	16,529	1.81
Gaziantep	4,261	0.74	9,133	1.10	7,482	0.94	11,911	1.30
Reg.Centers	*37,563*	*6.52*	*72,997*	*8.80*	*72,092*	*9.04*	*88,122*	*9.64*
Adıyaman	778	0.14	1,227	0.15	1,462	0.18	1,712	0.19
Afyon	1,651	0.29	5,150	0.62	5,183	0.65	5,769	0.63
Ağrı		0.00	312	0.04	304	0.04	934	0.10
Amasya	1,416	0.25	2,117	0.26	2,143	0.27	1,998	0.22
Antalya	4,290	0.75	6,493	0.78	5,657	0.71	5,981	0.65
Artvin		0.00	3,068	0.37	2,870	0.36	4,236	0.46
Balıkesir	5,540	0.96	8,517	1.03	8,343	1.05	8,580	0.94
Bilecik	850	0.15	4,054	0.49	4,700	0.59	6,309	0.69
Bingöl		0.00		0.00		0.00	72	0.01
Bitlis	418	0.07	528	0.06	652	0.08	620	0.07
Bolu	2,146	0.37	5,514	0.66	5,490	0.69	8,398	0.92
Burdur	971	0.17	2,400	0.29	2,284	0.29	2,062	0.23
Çanakkale	544	0.09	4,049	0.49	4,801	0.60	5,722	0.63
Çankırı	208	0.04	350	0.04	251	0.03	509	0.06
Çorum	1,030	0.18	2,114	0.25	1,837	0.23	2,650	0.29
Diyarbakır	1,138	0.20	1,537	0.19	2,107	0.26	2,590	0.28

Table 10.1 Continued

Edirne	606	0.11	5,757	0.69	7,356	0.92	4,643	0.51
Elazığ	4,136	0.72	4,674	0.56	4,582	0.57	4,473	0.49
Erzincan	1,590	0.28	2,485	0.30	2,620	0.33	2,813	0.31
Erzurum	2,230	0.39	2,606	0.31	2,414	0.30	2,387	0.26
Giresun	1,599	0.28	3,391	0.41	2,873	0.36	3,057	0.33
Gümüşhane		0.00	28	0.00	26	0.00	26	0.00
Hakkari		0.00	29	0.00	22	0.00	45	0.00
Isparta	1,197	0.21	4,057	0.49	3,406	0.43	4,109	0.45
Kars	135	0.02	736	0.09	908	0.11	1,311	0.14
Kastamonu	1,509	0.26	1,682	0.20	1,743	0.22	2,953	0.32
Kırklareli	1,736	0.30	4,429	0.53	4,614	0.58	5,187	0.57
Kırşehir		0.00	248	0.03	417	0.05	652	0.07
Kütahya	4,388	0.76	5,492	0.66	5,363	0.67	5,898	0.65
Malatya	4,677	0.81	6,974	0.84	6,897	0.86	6,622	0.72
Kahramanmaraş	1,002	0.17	1,947	0.23	1,884	0.24	2,675	0.29
Mardin		0.00	32	0.00	38	0.00	106	0.01
Muğla	164	0.03	3,102	0.37	2,895	0.36	2,477	0.27
Muş		0.00		0.00	580	0.07	920	0.10
Nevşehir	844	0.15	1,659	0.20	1,483	0.19	1,997	0.22
Niğde	167	0.03	2,190	0.26	2,305	0.29	3,536	0.39
Ordu	2,555	0.44	3,138	0.38	2,744	0.34	2,471	0.27
Rize	14,402	2.50	14,285	1.72	14,037	1.76	15,626	1.71
Siirt	3,244	0.56	3,525	0.42	3,614	0.45	867	0.09
Sinop		0.00	2,475	0.30	2,616	0.33	2,571	0.28
Sivas	5,313	0.92	4,608	0.56	4,575	0.57	4,968	0.54
Tokat	1,879	0.33	3,675	0.44	3,732	0.47	4,243	0.46
Trabzon	4,450	0.77	5,797	0.70	5,424	0.68	6,381	0.70
Tunceli		0.00	18	0.00	33	0.00	67	0.01
Urfa		0.00	764	0.09	427	0.05	658	0.07
Uşak	1,957	0.34	2,819	0.34	2,408	0.30	2,672	0.29
Van	453	0.08	780	0.09	628	0.08	937	0.10
Yozgat	103	0.02	1,011	0.12	922	0.12	1,091	0.12
Zonguldak	20,960	3.64	24,123	2.91	23,218	2.91	23,894	2.61
Other Provinces	102,276	17.76	165,966	20.00	164,888	20.67	180,475	19.75

Source: State Institute of Statistics

industrial core. Bursa, being a manufacturing center, became increasingly integrated with the Istanbul metropolitan area in functional terms, and registered a high rate of growth in industrial employment in this period.

In the second region, with the İzmir metropolitan area at its center, some provinces (Manisa,Denizli, Afyon, Isparta, Burdur and Muğla) attracted industrial activities and attained a high rate of growth of industrial employment in the 1970s[4].

The third region that showed a high rate of growth of industrial employment consisted of some provinces (Yozgat, Çankırı, Çorum, Niğde, Nevşehir and Kırşehir) in the Middle Anatolia region around the Ankara metropolitan area. As these provinces had either a limited or no industrial employment in the beginning of the 1970s, even small additions to industrial activity in later years meant high rates of growth.

During the 1983–87 period, the annual average rate of growth of industrial employment was 2.8 percent, as opposed to 6.8 percent for industrial output. The revitalization of metropolitan cores, especially the Istanbul metropolitan area, was the dominant character of the 1980s, as the development of trade and other service activities as a result of growing foreign trade relations increased the importance of major centers of trade. This process is also confirmed by the direction of migratory movements, with the metropolitan regions having an increasing weight in total migration after 1985 (Eraydın, 1991).

As a result of decentralization in the 1970s and reconcentration in the 1980s, the weight of the Istanbul region did not change in the distribution of industry since the beginning of 1970s. This region accounted for almost one half of both the total number of firms and industrial employment. A similar pattern can be observed in Ankara, İzmir and other provinces, except Samsun, where the regional centers are located. However, both the Adana metropolitan center and the other nodes around Adana exhibit a different tendency. The high rate of growth in the 1970s in this region did not continue, since the industries were not able to cope with the changing circumstances in the past few years.

Although there are important variations among the group (Table 10.1), in general the provinces that are not located in the metropolitan regions and serve as regional centers have a relatively poor performance.

CHANGING INDUSTRIAL TECHNOLOGY IN THE DIFFERENT SPATIAL UNITS

Technological change may in some ways be regarded as a response to economic problems faced in crisis periods, in order to initiate a new period of growth. That is why, after the economic crisis of the 1970s in the world economy, the 1980s became a period of search for different forms of technological change.

Total factor productivity growth, which is used as an indicator of technological change in spatial analysis, is defined as the difference between the growth of total output and the rate of growth of weighted inputs, namely material inputs, labor and capital (Kendrick & Sato, 1963; Freeman, 1981).

Comparing the TFPG rates in 1970s and 1980s by provinces provides important evidence about the spatial aspects and diffusion patterns of technological change in various industrial activities. The TFPG rates for different provinces are calculated by using annual data for purchased inputs, wages and value of total output for the 1971–87 period. The share of capital is estimated as a residual, as unfortunately no data were available on the tax payments and share of auxiliary services for adjusting this factor, which is one of the drawbacks experienced also in other countries (Tyler & Rhodes, 1986).

During the 1971–82 period, TFPG rates were negative in more than half of the provinces that are defined as important industrial centers[5] (Table 10.2). Among them, there are provinces, such as Istanbul, İçel and Adana, that were highly affected by the economic problems faced during this period. Among this group, TFPG rates increased in four provinces, namely İzmir, Ankara, Eskişehir and Bursa. In İzmir and Ankara, structural change in industrial activity was realized in the face of slow growth of employment and wages and a relatively high rate of growth of fixed capital investment. On the other hand, in Bursa, industrial employment, wages and capital investment grew at a rate higher than the national average, and by using the new techniques in industrial sectors, a considerable level of productivity was reached. The same process is replicated in Eskişehir, but the increase in labor demand was relatively slower.

Some provinces with a relatively small share in total manufacturing employment managed to change their industrial structure. During the 1971–82 period, TFPG rates in manufacturing were positive in Afyon, Ağrı, Antalya, Çanakkale, Bitlis, Kastamonu, Edirne, Manisa, Ordu, Van and Yozgat.

At this stage, for manufacturing industry in the core area (Istanbul metropolitan region) there is no clear evidence of technological change. The indicators related to this region for the 1971–82 period show low rates of increase of industrial employment and wages and a decrease in value added per worker and average firm size (Eraydın, 1989), to some extent reflecting the effects of the economic crisis in the late 1970s. It is only after 1979 that the manufacturing industry in this region gives positive signals of productivity increases. Even then, TFPG rates in this region were modest compared to some other provinces. At this point, it should be remembered that indicators for Istanbul are the average of almost 30 percent of the total industrial activity in Turkey, reflecting different tendencies in various industrial activities.

The experience of the regional centers (Konya, Kayseri, Gaziantep, Samsun, Adana) during the economic crisis reveals relatively high growth rates in manufacturing employment, but no significant structural difference over the previous period. However, due to scarcity of capital in the industrial sectors in a large group of provinces, the firms seem to have learned to use capital more efficiently.

During the 1983–87 period, higher TFPG rates can be observed in many provinces. They include the provinces in the category of less developed areas

Table 10.2

Rate of Growth of Employment and TFPG in Turkish Manufacturing Industry by Provinces, 1971–87 (Selected Years, Percent Annual Increase)

	Employment		TFPG	
	1971–82	1983–87	1971–82	1983–87
Adana	5.52	1.78	–2.08	0.99
Adıyaman	4.22	3.16	0.77	6.38
Afyon	10.90	2.14	1.28	1.69
Ağrı		22.45	18.16	–4.75
Amasya	3.72	–1.40	–0.80	3.05
Ankara	3.48	3.64	0.09	2.61
Antalya	3.89	1.11	1.36	1.52
Artvin	4.66	7.79	–6.83	8.63
Aydın	2.73	0.39	0.21	1.98
Balıkesir	3.99	0.56	0.41	0.43
Bilecik	15.26	5.89	–2.05	11.99
Bingöl				0.00
Bitlis	–0.69	–1.01	3.83	1.00
Bolu	8.96	8.50	1.57	3.37
Burdur	8.57	–2.05	–1.87	0.41
Bursa	7.00	5.84	10.29	1.14
Çanakkale	20.02	3.51	3.70	6.10
Çankırı	4.84	14.14	–1.40	6.09
Çorum	6.75	7.33	1.32	0.18
Denizli	8.30	4.88	0.98	1.82
Diyarbakır	2.77	4.13	–3.81	6.37
Edirne	22.51	–9.20	2.94	–3.48
Elazığ	1.12	–0.48	–3.13	7.99
Erzincan	4.14	1.42	–0.87	–0.69
Erzurum	1.48	–0.22	0.26	0.80
Eskişehir	2.05	2.79	0.94	2.28
Gaziantep	7.18	9.30	–0.33	5.68
Giresun	7.07	1.24	0.94	1.37
Gümüşhane		0.00		–8.50
Hakkari		14.31		14.04
Hatay	20.01	–0.68	–5.59	6.41
Isparta	11.74	3.75	1.00	3.54
İçel	6.51	2.31	–1.34	–11.57

Table 10.2 Continued

İstanbul	2.94	2.96	−0.75	1.69
İzmir	1.09	2.88	2.29	−1.09
Kars		7.35	0.99	5.80
Kastamonu	0.99	10.54	2.74	1.66
Kayseri	5.73	3.28	0.76	−0.61
Kırklareli	8.89	2.34	0.20	3.41
Kırşehir	14.54	8.94	−1.01	2.60
Kocaeli	6.75	−1.62	−3.39	−1.08
Konya	10.27	7.21	−2.22	−0.14
Kütahya	2.06	1.90	0.07	1.12
Malatya	3.70	−0.81	−1.35	−0.53
Manisa	6.97	8.91	2.63	5.88
Kahramanmaraş	6.23	7.01	−0.44	4.10
Mardin		20.52		−6.60
Muğla	30.64	−3.12	−5.81	−3.22
Muş		9.23	−2.01	−1.09
Nevşehir	6.34	5.95	−0.51	0.23
Niğde	11.91	8.56	0.57	3.22
Ordu	1.89	−2.10	2.53	−1.79
Rize	−0.07	2.14	−2.56	2.91
Sakarya	7.13	11.85	−2.56	−0.50
Samsun	7.18	−2.70	−1.45	3.41
Siirt	0.76	−28.55	−0.56	−1.00
Sinop	8.64	−0.35	−17.40	6.13
Sivas	−1.29	1.65	−0.93	6.76
Tekirdağ	25.69	7.45	−0.36	2.92
Tokat	6.29	2.57	0.32	14.60
Trabzon	2.42	3.25	0.88	15.20
Tunceli		14.16	1.63	−0.64
Urfa	9.51	8.65	−0.39	10.27
Uşak	3.37	2.08	0.02	1.76
Van	5.06	8.00	3.49	6.75
Yozgat	23.07	3.37	4.03	−3.83
Zonguldak	1.28	0.57	−4.77	−0.98
Turkey	4.4	2.78	1.30	1.02

Source: SIS

Figure 10.1
The Different Patterns of Change in TFPG Rates Between the 1971–82 and 1983–87 Periods

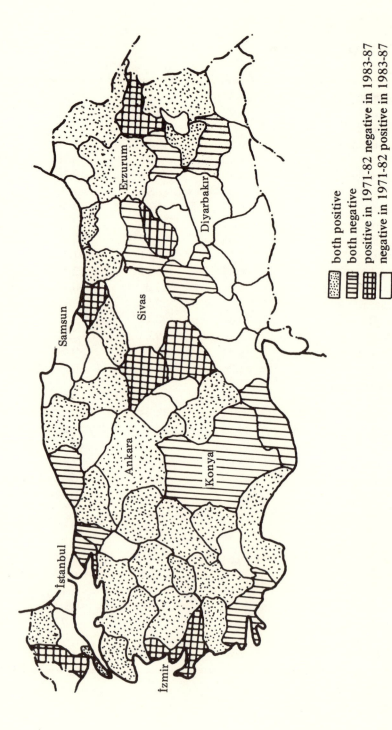

both positive
both negative
positive in 1971-82 negative in 1983-87
negative in 1971-82 positive in 1983-87

Figure 10.2
The Growth and Technological Transformation Areas of Industry, 1983–87

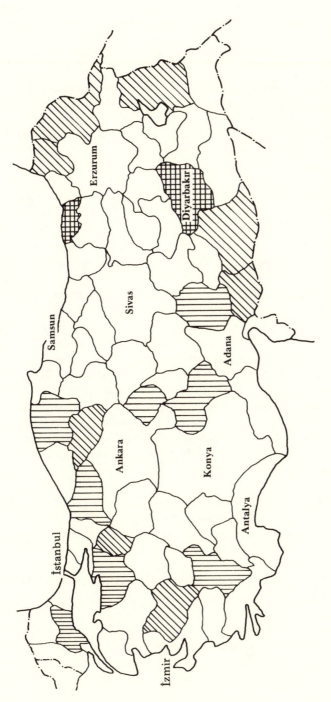

TFPG rate > %5 employment inc. rate > %5
TFPG rate > %TA employment inc. rate > %5
TFPG rate > %5 employment inc.rate > %TA
TA : Turkish average

registering positive TFPG rates. The increase in the output of manufacturing in less developed areas can be linked to the improvement in their labor productivity performance.

The comparison of the TFPG rates between the 1971–82 and 1983–87 periods shows that, among the provinces with positive rates in the first period, there are only three provinces that experienced negative rates in the second period (Figure 10.1). The largest group consists of provinces that changed from negative to positive TFPG rates. Some of them experienced radical change, and most of them are in the group of less developed regions. The analysis indicates that TFPG was not confined to certain parts of the country.

NEW NODES OF GROWTH

The analysis of manufacturing activity by spatial units (provinces) enables us to identify the areas that have undergone an important transformation from their previous structures. Sforzi (1988) and Garofoli (1990) use two indicators, namely the rate of employment and productivity growth, to identify these areas. However, according to their initial base of industrial development, the degree of transformation in various areas may have different meanings.

The results indicate that there are a large number of provinces that experienced high rates of TFPG and whose rate of growth of manufacturing employment exceeded the national average, such as Manisa, Bilecik, Gaziantep, Urfa, Çankırı, Van, Kars and Artvin. In two provinces, namely Trabzon and Diyarbakır, TFPG rates were higher than the national average, but the rate of growth in employment was relatively lower. Also, in some of the provinces, more than 5 percent annual employment increases were realized, with productivity rates higher than the national averages. Although the growth and change may have different meanings in different provinces, the data show that there were some significant attempts to change the industrial base in different parts of the country
(Figure 10.2).

At this point, the question, related to our initial theoretical discussion in this chapter, pertains to how these changes were realized. The rest of the chapter is devoted to this question, with reference to analytical studies on the subject.

HOW TECHNOLOGICAL CHANGE HAS TAKEN PLACE: IS IT FLEXIBILITY?

To examine the character of growth and transformation and identify the changes in the forms of organization of production activities and their interrelations, the textile industry in Bursa is taken as the basis of analytical study. The research on Bursa industry (Eraydın, 1992) was conducted in 1990. The interviews on the different types of industrial firms were determined according to the number of processes they handle and the size of firms, and samples were chosen for interviews in the different types of firms.

Bursa is a large urban area with a population of 612,510 (1985 census), but the area that defines the labor market reaches up to a population level of around 900,000, with a high rate of population growth (6.6 percent per annum in the 1980–85 period). Five and one-half percent of the large industrial firms[6] (in 1984) and 4.5 percent of the total number of firms (in 1980) in the country were located in this area.

Eraydın (1992) indicates that important changes have been taking place in the textile industry in Bursa since the early 1980s. These changes are not confined to additions of new units, increase in production or the introduction of new technologies by existing firms, but also involve the emergence of a new pattern of interrelationship among production units, new labor relations and new technological processes.

The distribution of textile firms by number of employees and their main characteristics are given in Table 10.3.

THE IMPORTANCE OF THE EXTERNAL WORLD FOR RESTRUCTURING

The study shows that foreign dynamics have been very important, and in some production sectors have forced restructuring and agglomerations. However, according to the characteristics of the industrial base and localities, these took different forms. It is obvious that firms with different characteristics, such as large production units exercising mainly Fordist techniques of production and small enterprises mainly engaged in artisanal production, were affected in different ways in this process. More importantly, this process brought about a new set of relations in production and distribution activities.

The change in textile production technology and material equipment in several European countries (mainly Italy and then Switzerland) proved to be an important factor in the restructuring attempts of the textile industry in Bursa. The change of the technological base in these countries led them to sell off their machinery long before the end of their economic life (sometimes equipment only two to threee years old). The firms that began exporting in the early 1980s faced stiff international competition and felt the need to adopt new technologies. As in other regions, capital was the most scarce factor for all types of firms, but especially for medium- to small-size firms. When this low-cost equipment became available in international markets, the large enterprises were able to renovate their technological base.

Two different approaches can be discerned from the experience of the relatively large and technologically advanced firms. The first group of firms

Table 10.3
Selected Indicators of Textile Industry in Bursa, 1989

No of Employees	No of Firms	Average				
		labor	built area[a]	built area/labor	capital[b]	capital/labor
1-10	162	6	450	71.6	43.5	6.62
11-25	117	17	853	51.5	135.2	7.93
26-50	70	37	1954	54.6	350.5	9.60
51-100	38	70	2960	42.2	762.1	10.70
101-250	37	152	5700	38.5	2268.0	14.37
251-500	8	366	19595	53.5	4688.5	12.83
501-1000	6	733	17733	24.3	7842.5	11.43
1000+	8	1650	47617	74.1	37765.7	9.79

Source: The files of The Union of Chambers of Trade and Industry.
[a] meter square
[b] billion TL

emphasized technology transfer to create a technological base that can be competitive in international markets. The second group, on the other hand, preferred to renovate their technology by importing this machinery from Italy, and formed new work organizations based on reduction of labor and other costs in order to increase their international competitiveness.

This change has fostered a second wave, as the old machinery and equipment of the first group of firms became available at relatively low prices in this locality, stimulating the entry of new firms into the industry, and at the same time improving the technological base of the small enterprises.

In order to reduce the risks of starting up a new business, enterprises preferred to begin as subcontractors and only after becoming familiar with the market they emerged as independent producers. The previous workers of some enterprises were able to start up their own production units, and an important portion of this group acted as subcontractors of the large enterprises.

CHANGE IN PRODUCTION TECHNOLOGY AND PRODUCTION ORGANIZATION

The interviews conducted at various firms clearly indicated that in the restructuring of production technology, the major driving force was access to international markets.

However, the outward-oriented marketing policies brought out another issue, namely, fluctuations in demand. When firms were producing basically for the domestic market during the pre-1980 period, demand was relatively stable and the amount of production could be determined on the basis of domestic market conditions. Following increased reliance on foreign markets in the 1980s, flexibility in production and production relations became a necessity to cope with the uncertainties in external demand.

Flexibility here mainly refers to an ability to survive and to respond to new conditions and changing market signals. It also refers to self-exploitation and use of family labor, the evasion of tax and social security contributions and the use of low-wage and young workers, especially for unskilled work.

These conditions are also typical of a vast number of small firms and artisans working in the traditional industries in many developing countries. They provide poor publicity for the ideal Marshallian model, but they do have a real and steadfast existence in Italy. (Amin & Robins, 1990: 19).

Subcontracting is one of the core elements in the flexibility that was created. In some sectors, subcontracting has now proved to be the "most profitable way of restructuring" (Hadjimichalis & Vaiou, 1987: 326). Different types of subcontracting have developed, related to different forms of production organization (Holmes, 1986).

Capital shortage has also emerged as an important factor within the subcontracting relationships in the Bursa textile industry. Some of the firms indicated that, although integration of the different processes was feasible, they use subcontracting firms because they are not able to afford the cost of new equipment in all the processes.

The knowledge base accumulated in the Bursa area is a crucial factor contributing to the textile specialization of this locality. As textile manufacturing (formerly silk weaving) has been the traditional activity of this region, there is a wide skill and knowledge accumulation in printing and dyeing of textile products. When silk yarn production was severely affected by foreign competition (mainly from South Asian countries), firms in this line of activity shifted to dyeing and printing processes, causing a boom in the number of firms in these activities in recent years. Due to increasing demand for dyeing processing from other textile firms, these firms renewed their technologies, increased their capacities and expanded their markets to include both large domestic and foreign firms.

Another form of subcontracting is home-based production. The putting-out system is widely used for embroidery work, ready-made clothing and in the other finishing processes of textile production[7].

In the Bursa textile industry, subcontracting activities were also used to increase the quality of production. The firms that were unable to renovate their production technology in all stages resorted to subcontracting firms that utilized recent technology for certain processes, especially in the production of export goods. The same firms can use another subcontractor for production for the domestic market in order to obtain certain cost advantages.

THE CHARACTERISTICS OF THE LOCALITY AS A DETERMINANT FACTOR OF PRODUCTION

In the formation of new work organizations and interlinkage mechanisms, the characteristics of the locality play a major role.

Bursa is a large urban center with a rapidly increasing population. In the last two decades this center became one of the points of population attraction (Eraydın, 1991). The labor market is turbulent, and newcomers are mainly unskilled. Not only the urban center but also the villages around the urban settlement are growing rapidly. Residents of these rural settlements are also a part of the labor market and form an important source of seasonal labor. During periods of stagnation these people engage in family enterprises.

The high rate of increase of migrant workers identifies the labor market as dynamic, with unformalized working conditions and low wages. However, there are different segments in the labor market. The workers who are members of labor unions have higher status and they want to protect those privileges. The small firms are usually family enterprises that, similar to the small agricultural units, survive through the use of family labor.

The study shows that the gender distribution of the workers did not change during the process of the introduction of new production technologies and disintegration of some activities. In fact, there was limited or no change in the composition of employment. This is very much related to the flow of new entrants to the labor market. In times of severe competition, male workers were forced to accept lower wages. In some jobs female workers are preferred, but the interview results did not explain the reasons for preferring female workers.

On the other hand, the family life-style and traditional production taking place at home contributed to the continuation of the putting-out system. Female workers prefer to work at home if any possibility of work arises. Thus, they do not form an alternative to skilled male labor.

CONCLUSIONS

The new production systems create new priorities on space. However, it is not easy to define the new forms of production organizations, since restructuring is taking place in various ways in different segments of industry, based on the characteristics and production culture of different localities. The new production organizations emphasize local characteristics as the determining factor, indicating the possibility of various modes of development based on different previous trajectories of different spatial units.

Although the limited decentralization of industry experienced in the 1970s was followed by a tendency toward reconcentration in the 1980s, there were several nodes where industrial growth and productivity increases reached important levels. This situation necessitates a detailed analysis at the locality level.

The case study on the Bursa textile industry provides evidence about the changes in different types of industrial production and their interaction with each other, as well as with external forces and local dynamics. As technological change in other countries and requirements for international competition forced the change in production organization, producers tried to exploit the advantages available in the production environment and the labor market. Increased competition also initiated the formation of new mechanisms in this locality. There is evidence of a transition from an agglomeration to a more dynamic industrial entity, and also from individual producers to a network of production. Now, the question is whether the production network of this locality will become one of the nodes of international production in the future.

NOTES

1. Center and periphery concepts are used to describe spatial units both at the universal level and as regions of national economies.

2. All growth rates, unless otherwise stated, are average annual rates.

3. The Istanbul metropolitan area constitutes a part of Istanbul province. The Istanbul metropolitan region consists of Istanbul, Kocaeli, Bursa, Sakarya and Tekirdağ provinces, in addition to the above provinces. The Istanbul region includes these provinces as well as Edirne, Zonguldak, Çanakkale, Kırklareli, Kastamonu and Bolu provinces.

4. After 1983, Manisa became a part of the İzmir metropolitan area and most of the firms that originated from İzmir have settled in the industrial estate established in Manisa.

5. These industrial centers include provinces accounting for at least 1 percent of the total manufacturing employment in 1982. These provinces were Istanbul, Kocaeli, Bursa, Sakarya, Tekirdağ, İzmir, Manisa, Denizli, Adana, Hatay, İçel, Ankara, Kayseri, Samsun, Konya, Eskişehir, Gaziantep, Rize and Zonguldak.

6. Large industrial enterprises include firms employing more than 10 workers until 1982, and with 25 or more workers, thereafter.

7. Home-based production is also important in the South European experience. Studies in Italy and Greece argue that home-based, informal activities and petty commodity

production are not components of a dualistic classification but rather form parts of a continuum of integrated forms of production (Hadjimichalis & Vaiou, 1987; Lyberaki, 1990), which is also valid in the new organization of textile production.

11

International Competitiveness and Industrial Policy: The Turkish Experience in the Textile and Truck Manufacturing Industries

Hacer K. Ansal

INTRODUCTION

The most remarkable rates of economic growth achieved by the newly industrialized countries had a demonstration effect on many developing countries and persuaded them to follow the same path to export-led growth and industrial development. Gaining international competitiveness became the most crucial task for the industrial sector of developing countries after their switch to export-oriented industrialization, while the factors behind the NICs' success became a major issue in the development economics literature.

Neoclassical economists argue that these countries adopted the right policies to establish an economic environment in which market forces could realize the efficient allocation of resources. According to these economists, such an environment was created mainly by liberalizing imports, adopting realistic exchange rates and providing incentives for exports, so that the industrial sector could expand in line with their comparative advantage (e.g., Balassa, 1981a; Krueger, 1978; Bhagwati, 1978). In fact, successful industrial development of the NICs has been heralded by these economists as a case in support of their prescription of a neutral policy regime that does not selectively discriminate among industries. They insist on the importance of uniform infant-industry incentives that are given automatically without administrative discretion.

The recent research conducted on the industrial development of the NICs demonstrates, on the other hand, that market forces alone can not account for the purported market successes of the NICs. In addition to the set of favorable international circumstances (Bienefeld, 1982), selective state intervention has played a major role in this success (e.g., Pack & Westphal, 1985). It also appears that trade considerations are secondary to technological ones in achieving international competitiveness. In fact, there is little disagreement among economists about the importance of technical change for industrial development and for achieving international competitiveness. Virtually all accept that productivity growth and international competitiveness depend heavily on the introduction and efficient diffusion of new and improved products and processes into production systems.

The aim of this chapter is to contribute to this debate by exploring the experiences of the Turkish textile and truck manufacturing industries on the basis of nine (three integrated textile, three clothing and three truck manufacturing) case study firms, with emphasis on their technological efforts to gain international competitiveness.

The industries were chosen for their importance in the Turkish industrialization process as well as the significant divergence in their export performance in the 1980s and hence in the level of international competitiveness that they achieved. The six case study firms in the textile and clothing industry were chosen on the basis of their export performance, so that lessons can be drawn from their experience in international markets. They were all located in Istanbul. The three truck manufacturing firms that were chosen were located in different cities, and together accounted for 70–75 percent of total truck production. Field work involved visits to each truck plant in 1985 and to each textile and clothing firm in 1989, accompanied by interviews with company managers and engineers on the firms' characteristics, performance, technological history and efforts to gain international competitiveness. Additional data were obtained from company records and annual reports, whenever they were made available.

The first section discusses briefly developments in each of the selected sectors against the background of industrialization policies. The second and third sections provide background information and emphasize the most important and common elements of our firm-level investigation for the textile and clothing and truck manufacturing sectors, respectively. Finally, the experience of the two industries is assessed in the light of the experience of some countries that have successfully promoted technological development to gain international competitiveness.

THE TURKISH TEXTILE AND CLOTHING INDUSTRY

The establishment of the Turkish textile industry dates back to the 1920s. The infant industry (with about 82,000 spindles in the spinning sector and 800 looms in the weaving sector), was far from meeting even the local demand, with textiles and clothing together accounting for 41.5 percent of total imports in 1927. Because private capital was lacking, state enterprises were established around 1930 in an effort to promote both textile industry and cotton cultivation. As a result of the import barriers that were imposed to protect the industry, the number of spindles and looms in 1949 reached 270,000 and 5,500, respectively (Alptekin, 1985: 51).

The change of government in 1950 opened a new era that emphasized the role of private sector, accompanied by a short-lived process of import liberalization during 1950–53. As a result, there was an increase in the number and the share of privately owned spindles and looms, with much investment directed to the dyeing, printing and finishing phases of the production process.

Following the adoption of an import-substituting industrialization strategy in the early 1960s within a central planning framework, incentive schemes prepared by the government created an attractive economic climate for private investments for production in the heavily protected local market. As a response to the incentive measures introduced in 1967, there was rapid progress in the industry. The largest increases in spindle capacity were registered between 1972 and 1976, in accordance with rising local demand. The number of spindles installed by the end of 1970s reached around 3 million from 1.3 million spindles in 1972, and the number remained the same until 1982, due to the economic crisis.

After the adoption of an export-oriented industrialization strategy in 1980, the local demand greatly contracted through austerity measures put into effect, especially during 1980–82, and the success on the export front became crucial for economic recovery and growth. The textile and clothing industry has played an important role in the rapid growth in exports in the 1980s, as it occupies the first position among manufactured exports. In 1987, for example, textile and clothing exports, expressed in terms of the Standard International Trade Classification (SITC), accounted for 28.5 percent of total exports and 35.3 percent of the total exports of manufactured goods. SITC 65—textile yarn, fabrics, made-up articles, etc., and SITC 84—clothing, were the most important subcategories (Table 11.1). Moreover, exports of these product categories to developed countries constitute a high percentage of the total, varying between 71 and 96 percent of the total values during this decade. Hence, the industry's export success can be taken as an indication of its international competitiveness.

Various factors have been influential on the industry's export performance. First, Turkey's long tradition of textile production, as boosted by the ISI period, was instrumental in the accumulation of apprenticeship and technological capabilities. Second, being a major cotton producer—the largest in Europe and seventh in the world in the 1980s—provides the industry with a significant advantage. Another important factor is that Turkey enjoys a comparative advantage based on the availability of a large pool of cheap labor. However, it is widely accepted in the sector that this advantage can be eroded by recent technological changes. Producers in developed countries embarked on a massive wave of investments in new technology in the late 1970s, coupled with structural change and market-driven industrial strategy. These developments have significantly improved their future prospects while, at the same time, raising considerable obstacles to the success of developing countries as textile exporters. Technological factors, therefore, have gained increased importance for developing countries in achieving or maintaining international competitiveness. In an effort

Table 11.1
Turkey's Exports of Textiles and Clothing, 1975–87 (Selected Years, Millions of US$)

	1975	1980	1985	1986	1987
SITC 65 - Textile Yarn, Fabrics,					
Made-up Articles,etc	109.5	342.5	1,045.0	934.8	1,190.0
SITC 651 - Textile					
Yarn and Tread	61.3	201.3	449.7	507.4	628.2
SITC 6513- Cotton Yarn					
and Tread, grey	55.2	179.3	248.0	276.7	338.4
SITC 652 - Cotton Fabrics,					
woven	16.9	21.7	128.3	126.1	129.7
SITC 84 -					
Clothing	82.1	131.0	1,208.3	1,245.7	2,213.5
SITC 8411- Clothing of Text.					
Fabric, not knitted	16.8	66.3	464.0	512.1	763.2
SITC 8414- Clothing and					
Accessories, knitted	1.0	15.3	256.7	398.7	749.5

Source: UNCTAD Statistics.

to explore the industry's export prospects regarding these changes in the developed countries, let us now briefly focus on the structure of the Turkish textile industry.

The minimum efficient scale in Turkey has been calculated as 25,000 spindles in the spinning and 100 looms in the weaving sector (Boston Consulting Group, 1985). The average scale prevailing in the industry shows that most of the spinning and weaving plants in the formal sector—excluding thousands of small-scale workshops with fewer than 10 employees—meet the minimum efficient scale criteria. Hence, there is no structural constraint for the industry in achieving international competitiveness in terms of economies of scale.

After a reduction in spinning and weaving capacity and capacity utilization rates during the economic crisis of the late 1970s, there was a notable increase in both of these indicators after the mid-1980s (Table 11.2). Since the capacity utilized for net domestic consumption— excluding indirect exports—decreased in both sub sectors during the period (IDBT, 1989), this increase can be attributed to growing demand in export markets.

Among the variety of process innovations being diffused in the global textile industry, open-end spinning technology and shuttleless looms represent the most striking innovations, since they are considered to have a crucial role in increasing

Table 11.2
Capacities and Capacity Utilization in the Turkish Cotton Spinning and Weaving Sectors, 1977–88 (Selected Years)

	1977	1980	1985	1986	1987	1988
Spinning						
Capacity (000 tons)	413	410	450	503	547	567
Capacity Utilization (%)	75	62	91	86	91	91
Weaving						
Capacity (000 tons)	222	215	272	289	299	311
Capacity Utilization (%)	94	75	93	90	94	93

Sources: Industrial Development Bank of Turkey, 1987, 1988, 1989.

productivity and achieving or maintaining international competitiveness. The data available reveal that significant investments have been made in the new technology in the Turkish textile industry after the mid-1980s (Table 11.3). It can be argued that this has been a very important element in the industry's export success in the second half of the 1980s.

EMPIRICAL STUDY OF TEXTILE AND CLOTHING FIRMS

Initially, managers of three integrated (spinning and weaving) textile firms that were known to have the best export performance in the Istanbul area were interviewed to examine the firms' technological developments throughout their history and to explore factors that have been influential in their efforts to achieve international competitiveness. Although the sample size is small to draw general conclusions for the entire sector, we believe that these three frontier firms' efforts in gaining international competitiveness should provide valuable insights. According to our findings, in the 1960s and 1970s, production was commonly carried out for the heavily protected domestic market. During this period, the firms' main concern was to meet the growing local demand by increasing their production capacities. The highly competitive climate in the local textile market, however, pressured firms to improve their productivity, to increase cost competitiveness and to introduce new and better-quality fabrics. Since more productive machines were adopted in the production processes, the managers believe that the technological level of plants in the formal sector in the 1970s was

Table 11.3
Installed "New Technology" in the Turkish Textile Industry, 1980–88
(Selected Years)

	Open-end Rotors	Shuttleless Looms
1980	16,000	1,431
1982	17,000	1,860
1984	35,000	3,530
1985	55,300	4,400
1986	78,332	4,500
1987	90,000	5,160
1988	94,976	5,930

Source: ITMF, 1989.

not significantly lower than those in developed economies.

After the adoption of EOI, the firms' efforts were directed mostly toward export markets. During the early 1980s, the integrated textile firms tried to penetrate into export markets with their existing facilities and products through the support of government export incentives. Toward the mid-1980s, after having gained experience in exporting and learned the requirements for increased competitiveness in world markets, they started to launch investment programs. New investment by these firms was aimed not only toward increasing their production capacity, but also toward increased productivity, improved product quality and diversification of their product mix. In order to be able to produce increasingly more sophisticated and design- intensive fabrics that were in demand in export markets, it became crucial to adopt recent technological changes that had been rapidly diffused in developed countries in the late 1970s. Mainly as a result of this investment activity, the total value of exports by these firms increased sharply, with the rate of increase during 1983–87 ranging from 260 to 370 percent. Consequently, the share of production for the domestic market in their total production gradually decreased from 70–75 percent in 1982 to 25–30 percent in the late 1980s.

What lay at the center of their export success, however, was the existence of sufficiently developed technological capabilities that enabled them to efficiently operate the new technologies and hence improve their international competitiveness. Moreover, they have been able to design machinery for different phases of the production process and have them manufactured locally.

In the face of growing demand from export markets in Europe, the integrated textile firms have recently adopted additional investment plans to further increase their competitiveness by utilizing computerized systems and completely renewing the remaining part of their machine park by replacing machines that have been in use for five years or more.

In the second half of the 1980s, the firms also started to establish clothing departments to export garments utilizing their own fabrics, thereby increasing the value added of their export products. According to the managers of the two case study firms, exports of their clothing departments account for 70–75 percent of their total exports in recent years.

The growing importance of garment exports for the textile industry and for our case study firms led us to expand the firm-level investigation to include three clothing firms with successful export performance. In analyzing the factors affecting the competitiveness of clothing firms, we have observed a pattern of development that was similar to the integrated textile firms. They were established to serve the domestic market in the early 1960s and expanded in response to growing domestic demand in the 1970s. They became almost totally export oriented in the 1980s. During the 1980–85 period, exporting was based on the firms' existing products and was stimulated by government's export incentives, which served as a process of learning their export potential and how to attain international competitiveness in the absence of these incentives.

In the 1985–87 period, the garment manufacturers carried out significant investments not only to increase their production capacities, but also to improve product quality and diversify their product mix as a response to the quota limitations imposed on the industry by EEC countries in 1985. Additionally, there was a significant effort to increase the value added produced in each product category. Although the next step in increasing value added of export products in the clothing sector is to create design collections, most firms produce garments according to the orders of their foreign customers who bring their own designs, for which domestically produced fabrics are used. This, on the other hand, creates a heavy dependence on the customers at both ends of the production process: design and marketing. The clothing firms that have acquired design capabilities seem to have been successful in marketing their own designs in export markets. However, there is a generally agreed weakness in the clothing sector in terms of design capabilities that negatively affects its international competitiveness.

The export growth of textiles and clothing were partly the result of government policies, as mentioned in the interviews. The main policy instruments that stimulated export growth by these firms during the 1980–84 period included continuous devaluation of the exchange rate (often in excess of the inflation differential between Turkey and its major trading partners), payment of export tax rebates (to compensate for indirect taxes), access to subsidized export credits and duty-free imports of inputs required for export production. Export promotion policy played an important role in changing the mentality of the industrialists many of whom for the first time seriously looked at foreign markets as possible outlets for their products. It also rendered exports more profitable—especially in conditions of depressed domestic demand. The system of export incentives, however, was changed in early 1985, significantly lowering export tax rebate rates, with a view toward gradually phasing them out and abolishing preferential export credits. It can be said that moving away from direct encouragement of exports and the significant pressure on firms to produce better quality products and increase their cost competitiveness induced firms to invest in new technology.

Another nontechnological factor that influenced the firms' export performance against the increasing competitive power of Far Eastern countries was Turkey's geographical proximity to export markets and its associate membership in the EEC, to which the bulk of their exports were directed. Apart from the low transport costs that this entails, the requirement of quick response to changes in market demand and increasingly shorter delivery time (which is now six to eight weeks in clothing), favor Turkish firms. Turkey's exemption from customs duties in the European Community (ranging from 7 to 14 percent) because of its associate membership contributed to the firms' cost competitiveness. The appreciation of the lira in recent years, on the other hand, is mentioned by the firms as a factor adversely affecting their cost competitiveness.

Although there is a growing demand for Turkish products in export markets, the volume of exports in many lines of textile production is limited by quotas. Therefore, firms are forced to produce products with a higher domestic value added, for which they are required to adopt recent technological changes to comply with the demand conditions for more sophisticated goods in export markets. Uncertainties created by the imposition of quotas in major export markets, on the other hand, greatly discourage firms to undertake big investments. Thus, our interviews have indicated that quotas erect a major barrier for the growth of the Turkish textile and clothing industry.

THE TURKISH TRUCK MANUFACTURING INDUSTRY

In the early 1960s, the automotive industry was chosen as one of the prime candidates to speed up the process of ISI in Turkey, since it had a great potential as a lead sector in stimulating the growth of other industries, requiring a variety of inputs from different industries, such as iron, steel, glass, plastics, textiles, rubber and chemicals. The economic climate created by the system of industrial incentives became very attractive for domestic and foreign investments in assembly activities in the industry. High profitability was almost guaranteed for entrepreneurs, since they were protected against foreign competition by high tariff barriers and encouraged by tax exemption and preferential exchange rates for the imported technology.

The Regulations of Assembly Industry (RAI) were passed in 1964, with the objective of transforming the initial stage of assembly operations into full–scale local manufacture and establishing the rules of foreign exchange allocation among the four companies that existed in the sector at the time. The RAI established import restrictions on parts and components once they started to be produced locally. Local content requirements for different motor vehicles each year were also determined. For trucks, for example, it was 20 percent in 1964 and gradually went up to 55 percent in 1970.

Despite all these measures to regulate and control the industry, there were three major deficiencies in the policy framework as a whole, which affected the structure of the automotive industry. First, no concrete measure was taken for the development of the ancillary sector in coordination with the main assembly sector. Second, there was no concern about exploiting economies of scale; therefore, there were no restrictions on the number of assemblers in spite of the limited domestic market. Finally, there was no concern about the development of technological capabilities, neither to ensure the quality of domestically produced parts and components nor to ensure postinvestment technological development of the main assembly sector. As a result, existing vehicle importers and multinational corporations (MNCs), anxious not to lose their existing markets and wanting also to exploit this attractive climate, became interested in establishing assembly plants. The government, not wanting to discriminate against any MNC, issued assembly permits for the major international trade names.

Although it is not possible to make universally valid statements about minimum efficient scales of production because the cost curves are derived assuming certain factor prices (Jenkins, 1977: 197), the annual production volumes in the 1960s ranged between 13,000 and 150,000 among world's leading 42 medium-size truck and bus manufacturers (Baranson, 1969: 10). In Turkey, on the other hand, having all these new plants resulted in such a fragmented market structure that none of these firms was close to operating within this range. Even the record high production level of 19,774 units reached by the industry in 1977 meant that one truck plant alone, operating close to the minimum efficient scale, would be sufficient for the domestic market. The capacity utilization rate of around 35 percent in the late 1960s and the record high of 64.5 percent reached in 1976 shows the severe diseconomies of scale with which the Turkish automotive industry was operating.

Given the low production volumes, the equipment that could be afforded was general-purpose machines in order to minimize capital costs per unit of output. This, together with low production volumes and excess capacity, resulted in Turkish firms having much higher unit costs for capital equipment than their counterparts in other countries employing mass production techniques.

Despite these deficiencies, investments in the sector had a very high rate of return, although in varying degrees depending on the overhead costs of the firms (Gürsoy, 1973: 67). Since the nominal rate of protection enjoyed by the sector was one of the highest within the manufacturing industry (280.2%), high costs could easily be passed on to prices under the prevailing oligopolistic market conditions (Alpar, 1974: 80). However, there were no new entrants into commercial vehicle

Table 11.4
Capacity Utilization in the Truck Industry in the 1980s (Selected Years)

	1980	1982	1984	1986	1988
Capacity Utilization (%)	27	37	44	30	26

Sources: AMA, 1984, 1986, 1989.

manufacturing after 1968, when the more strict control of local content requirements began to force firms that could not meet these requirements to face cuts in foreign exchange allocation.

As the economy enjoyed its longest period of sustained high rates of growth (at an average rate of 6.9% during 1963–77), there was a steady increase in commercial vehicle production. Although local content ratios achieved in the mid-1970s were around 60 percent, increasing production levels created a high demand for foreign exchange to import the remaining 40 percent. The limited foreign exchange allocations to the manufacturers restricted their production programs. In spite of the buoyant domestic demand for transport vehicles in the period, the rate of capacity utilization reached only 68 percent for the entire sector and 64.5 percent for commercial vehicles (CV).

A major shortage of foreign exchange during the economic crisis in late 1970s further restricted imports of necessary parts and components in the sector. As a result, there was a drastic fall in production levels, with capacity utilization in CV production dropping to 27 percent in 1980.

Following the adoption of EOI in 1980, there was a gradual liberalization of the importation of vehicles. Although firms were encouraged to export through a variety of export incentives, domestic demand restraints through restrictive monetary and credit policies in the face of high rates of inflation were causing major financial problems for the industry. Although the difficulties in importing the necessary inputs for production were greatly alleviated by the process of import liberalization, the rate of capacity utilization in the truck industry remained at very low levels (Table 11.4).

The slight increase in production levels after 1980, on the other hand, was mainly due to the recovery of the internal market. Two main developments in particular affected the truck sector. First, government investments in infrastructure and housing subsidies created a demand for trucks in the construction sector. Second, there was an increase in the share of the Turkish transportation sector in international long-distance haulage to the oil-rich Arab countries.

In spite of the government incentives and subsidies, exports in the automotive sector did not show a steady growth (Figure 11.1), reflecting the structural problems confronting the industry.

The comparison of average ex-factory prices for different categories of vehicles in 1984 (excluding consumption tax) with average export prices has shown that, except for buses, exporting resulted in losses in the sector (Table 11.5).

In their report on the problems faced by the industry in gaining international competitiveness, the Automotive Manufacturers Association (AMA) identifies high costs and low quality as well as the lack of a distribution and service network in importing countries as the main obstacles to penetrating export markets (AMA, 1982). A major factor behind the high costs and low quality of production was the high local content of parts and components (reaching 70–75% for trucks), which were produced in relatively small (by world standards) quantities and small-scale production units. The necessary investments for improving quality are considered very costly and risky given the high borrowing rates of interest.

The liberalization of imports of all categories of transport vehicles at the end of 1983 created additional problems for the industry. The sector's reaction to this was to request from the government to be more sensitive toward their problems by committing itself to protection through higher subsidies and incentives to make exporting profitable, a very careful and slow reduction of tariffs, more convenient credit terms to meet their financial problems, and drawing a long-term restructuring program for the industry to make it internationally competitive (AMA, 1984).

EMPIRICAL STUDY OF THE TRUCK MANUFACTURING FIRMS

The examination of the technological histories of our three truck manufacturing firms has indicated that their technological efforts have been very much influenced by external pressures generated by industrialization policies (see Ansal, 1988, for details). During the ISI period, there was a growing demand for automotive products. As expected, firms could sell as much as they could produce without much pressure to minimize production costs or increase the quality of their products in a highly protected market. There were two main government-imposed constraints that determined the firms' technological efforts. These were the RAI local content requirements and the limited foreign exchange allocations restricting their production programs. To increase production levels, it was crucial for the firms to increase local content levels, so that they could import more parts with their limited foreign exchange allocations. Although technological collaboration with ancillary firms was established for successful localization, their limited capacity forced the firms to produce many parts and components in-house, in economically subefficient volumes. Major investment projects such as foundry,

Figure 11.1
Exports in the Turkish Automotive Industry, 1980–88

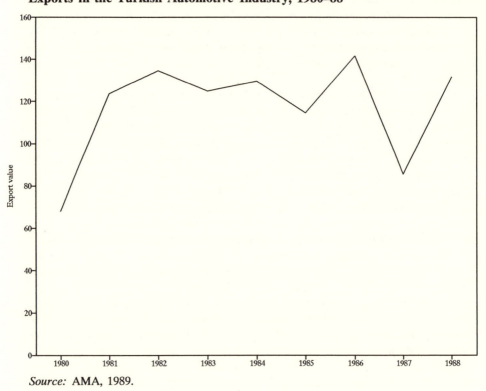

Source: AMA, 1989.

plant expansions and engine plants were also carried out during this period with very little foreign assistance. But it was the quantity, not the quality, of production that the firms had to deal with.

During the economic crisis in Turkey, the pressure to increase local content of production grew even stronger. In the face of low rates of capacity utilization, concern with productivity and production methods came onto the firms' agenda for the first time. Technical changes were implemented to modernize production techniques, and general-purpose machines were replaced by special purpose machines to increase productivity.

Under conditions of EOI during the 1980s, the firms' technological efforts were greatly intensified and directed toward developing new models, increasing the quality of products and improving their production techniques to reduce costs and hence become more competitive in export markets. Quality control methods and equipment were also greatly improved. In their attempts to gain access to international markets, they were compelled to increase their foreign collaborations,

Table 11.5
Export Price/Ex-Factory   Price   Comparison   in   the   Turkish   Automotive Industry, 1984

	Average ex-factory price (TL)	Average export price ($) (1$=243 TL)	Average export price (TL)	Export price/ex-factory price (%)
Car	1,170,575	3,596	873,828	74.6
Bus	10,426,128	65,503	15,917,229	152.7
Midibus	3,262,730	11,088	2,694,384	82.6
Minibus	1,992,000	5,450	1,324,350	66.5
Truck	3,749,318	8,105	1,969,515	52.5
Van	2,335,305	7,682	1,939,626	83.1

Source: Industrial Development Bank of Turkey (1984: 53).

through new foreign partnerships and new licensing agreements for producing more modern and up-to-date   products. In spite of these efforts, none of our case study firms seems to have succeeded in improving its export performance and achieving international competitiveness because they were severely restricted by the industry's structural deficiencies such as a fragmented market, subefficient scales—by world standards—and hence technological backwardness in comparison to their international counterparts, and an insufficiently developed ancillary sector.

In our field work we observed, on the other hand, that technological capabilities in the firms were significantly developed. It seems that a great wealth of experience and technological mastery was accumulated during the ISI period, through carrying out major investment projects to add numerous production lines for in-house production of various parts and components and to expand production capacities. However, as the firms had to deal only with the pressures of the internal market, their technological development was on a limited scale. As firms in the industry did not have prior knowledge about how long the protection would last, catching up with the technological frontier never appeared on the firms' technological agenda. Although they seem to have achieved sufficient technological self-reliance and mastery to be able to cope with domestic economic changes, they had to seek new foreign collaborations to cope with the pressures of EOI in the 1980s.

CONCLUSION

The experiences of the Turkish textile and truck manufacturing industries clearly indicate that the economic environment created by different industrialization policies has strongly influenced their technological evolution and the success of their efforts in gaining international competitiveness.

Unlike the truck industry, the textile industry, which had accumulated apprenticeship and technological capabilities during the ISI period and had reached a high level of development with no structural constraints in terms of economies of scale, had little difficulty in responding to the new set of incentives created by EOI.

The well-known critique of ISI (see, for example, Little, Scitovsky & Scott, 1970) seems to be very much in line with the problems of the Turkish economy under ISI and the development of the Turkish truck industry. Contrary to the policy implications of this analysis of having excessive government intervention under ISI, however, our study of the truck industry and the case studies suggest that there was insufficient government intervention. Measures taken in the ISI period were not concerned with the structure of the industry in terms of exploiting economies of scale and capacity utilization in both the ancillary and main assembly sectors. Neither was there any explicit technology policy to ensure the development of the industry to achieve international competitiveness. As a result, the industry faced major difficulties in adjusting itself to the conditions of EOI. The neoclassical prescription of neutral policy and outward orientation of the economy under market-based policies in the 1980s, which are supposed to solve these problems of restructuring, have not yet been successful in transforming the weak and fragmented truck industry into one that can compete in world markets.

It is pertinent at this stage to discuss the contrasting export performance of the two industries in Turkey in light of the experience of other countries. There is a vast and growing literature showing that market forces alone cannot account for the technological successes of Japan and more recently the NICs. For example, it was pointed out that the Korean government has not practiced neutrality in its treatment of established, internationally competitive industries on the one hand, and new, infant industries that were deemed worthy of promotion on the other (Pack & Westphal, 1985). Government's industrial policy was heavily biased in favor of the selected industries. For the automotive sector, the main emphasis was on the promotion of large-scale investments and the encouragement of specialization among firms. Additionally, Luedde-Neurath (1988) emphasizes the Korean government's heavy influence in negotiations with foreign firms so as to ensure that technology is transferred in accordance with national objectives.

Fransman's (1986) study of the machine tool industry in Taiwan and Japan, for example, identifies the role played by the government as one of the chief factors behind their success in attaining international competitiveness. The major forms of government intervention in Japan included the imposition of protective measures, intervention in the negotiation of technology agreements, attempts to minimize the degree of foreign control over domestic industry, provision of subsidized credit, and planned intervention to increase economies of specialization and scale. Moreover, the government made numerous attempts to shape and direct the evolutionary process of the machine tool industry by encouraging technological improvements.

In his study of Japan's synthetic fiber industry, Ozawa (1980) highlights a unique control system, called a staggered-entry formula, to regulate the structure of an industry. By state control of firms' entry into a sector, in order to promote plants of efficient scale and avoid creating excess capacity, international competitiveness is assured. Although a monopolistic position is accorded to the first entrant, it is insured that its profits will be invested in improving its technology to achieve international competitiveness.

The experience in Turkey, as well as in Japan and Korea, demonstrates that adopting a neutral policy regime and relying on free market forces are not adequate to solve the problems of restructuring in the industrial sector. Different characteristics and different weaknesses and strengths in each industry's structure and different factors affecting their technological evolution direct us to the essentiality of selective government intervention.

12

CONCLUSION AND PROSPECTS

Fikret Şenses

The set of policies implemented in Turkey since 1980 under the stabilization and structural adjustment program has represented a radical change in the environment for the manufacturing sector. The transition from import-substituting industrialization under strong state direction to export-oriented industrialization with emphasis on market-based policies was facilitated by a number of important factors. The severity of the economic crisis in the late 1970s, which was in part due to short-term macroeconomic mismanagement, was successfully presented to the public at large as the crisis of ISI. The fact that the way out of the crisis required external funds led to the acceptance of IMF-World Bank conditionality in support of SSAP. The ensuing inflow of sizable external funds that went a long way toward alleviating the immediate crisis served as a further justification for SSAP. Likewise, the military regime, by silencing all possible sources of opposition, reinforced SSAP at its crucial early stages. Finally, severe domestic demand restraint during the first two years of the program forced large holding companies producing predominantly for the domestic markets to seek outlets in world markets. This was instrumental in cushioning the possible conflicts between ISI firms and EOI firms witnessed in some other countries experiencing a similar transition. The initial boost given by these factors was instrumental in the emergence of a sizable constituency in Turkey in favor of SSAP.

The interaction of industrialization with SSAP can be observed from the impact of the new set of policies on the manufacturing sector as well as the medium- and long-term prospects for industrial development in Turkey. Although the sixth five year plan (1990–94) identified it as one of the primary components of development, industrialization was severely neglected under SSAP. The most favorable impact of SSAP for the manufacturing sector was the sharp increase in exports, accompanied by a dramatic rise in the share of manufactured exports in total exports from 28.8 percent in 1980 to 72.1 percent in 1990. This performance took place against a background of generally unfavorable trends in the global economy and with only a minimal contribution from State Economic Enterprises and foreign investors. Contrary to expectations, the manufacturing sector's record in employment and productivity growth was rather poor, with hardly any improvement in the 1980s. By far the poorest result was in the sphere of manufacturing investment, as the private sector failed to fill in the gap when the state deliberately withdrew from manufacturing activity. Instead, transport, communications and energy have emerged as the preferred activities for public investment, with housing being the preferred area in the private sector. It seems that the overall tendency for positive real rates of interest and real currency depreciation as key components of SSAP, apart from fueling domestic inflation, had a strong adverse effect on private investment. In the face of growing macroeconomic instability and uncertainty associated with it, investment decisions were probably guided by "earning quick trading profits rather than by long term strategic considerations" (OECD, 1993: 68).

The shortfalls in new investment were reflected by the absence of structural change within the manufacturing sector toward capital- and skill-intensive activities. The evidence on the debate over whether public sector investment crowds-in or crowds-out private investment is also blurred in the Turkish case.

There is a dearth of micro-level studies on the response of different sectors and firms to the new set of policies since 1980. The findings of available studies clearly indicate the variety of experience and point to the dangers of generalizing in this respect. Clearly, sectors like textiles and clothing that had experienced a long period of production for the domestic market under ISI until 1980 and acquired technological capabilities in the process had a positive response to export-oriented policies. This was evident from the sharp increase in exports as well as from the intensification of technological efforts to maintain international competitiveness, especially after the mid-1980s.

Even in industries like truck manufacturing characterized by failure to penetrate export markets as a result of their structural constraints, there was a positive response to the new set of policies in the form of increased quality and cost-consciousness, as well as the development of new models and improved schemes for quality control. As expected, the variety of experience in the response to the new set of policies would be even greater if the response of individual firms were considered. It seems, however, from the few studies available on the subject, that there was also an increase in quality–consciousness, as evidenced by falling rejection rates. While some firms have increased their technological efforts to attain international competitiveness, survival through various forms of flexibility, such as resorting to family labor and low-wage young workers has emerged as the chief adjustment mechanism for others.

Although subcontracting has not reached significant proportions across the manufacturing sector, it is possible to identify certain sectors such as textiles and certain regions such as the Bursa industrial area where it is practiced on a wider scale, and certain sectors, such as metal-working, where it had a stronger developmental impact. Whether the fact that exporting sectors had a higher proportion of subcontract-offering firms is indicative of future trends is a matter of conjecture. We can argue with confidence, however, that new forms of production adopting flexible specialization were not visible in the Turkish manufacturing sector on a significant scale, with the possible exception of certain localities such as Bursa.

Given the weight of state economic enterprises in the manufacturing sector, it is important to assess their performance under EOI. Apart from statistical difficulties, such a task is surrounded by a number of conceptual difficulties. The failure of existing performance criteria to incorporate the multiplicity of objectives with deep historical roots that these enterprises have had presents the main difficulty. Likewise, the fact that the policy environment for these enterprises has not been altogether uniform and consistent during the 1980s renders the linking of their performance with EOI especially difficult. The deregulation of their prices in the early 1980s has not precluded governments from delaying price adjustments, especially before elections for purely political reasons. This would throw considerable doubt on the value of studies attempting to measure performance solely on the basis of financial indicators.

The process of industrialization in Turkey in the years ahead is likely to be constrained by a number of factors. As capacity utilization rates have reached very high levels in most activities, there is an urgent need to increase investment in the manufacturing sector. Similarly, manufactured exports are heavily concentrated in the textiles and clothing sectors, which are likely to be threatened by the twin pressures of increased competition from low-wage developing countries and increased protectionism in industrial countries. Manufacturing production was also characterized by small average firm size and heavy spatial concentration. The aging capital stock in a large number of activities is another cause for concern, and calls for a major restructuring in the manufacturing sector as a whole. There is a severe shortage of empirical studies examining the power of domestic industry to withstand external competition. As a result, policy makers are deprived of the necessary information on the optimal level of trade liberalization in various activities (Senses, 1990b). On top of these factors, growing macroeconomic instability after the mid-1980s, as characterized by sizable public sector deficits and high rates of inflation, has led to a further deterioration of the investment climate and relegation of the industrialization objective to the background. In fact, one can argue with some confidence that although SSAP was initially introduced as a short-term stabilization program, successive governments showed little willingness to come to grips with stabilization issues by getting public deficits and inflation under control. This indifference, which can be explained by the return to populist policies under political liberalization and the reduction in the direct influence of the Bretton Woods institutions in domestic policy making, was responsible for the preoccupation with short-term issues and provided the basic excuse for the neglect of industrialization. Despite the lip-service paid by planners and policy makers alike to increasing the pace of industrialization, the policy framework comprising SSAP was not compatible with the diversification and upgrading of the industrial structure.

Given the severe neglect of industrialization under SSAP, there is an urgent need for an active industrialization strategy. The first task of such a strategy would be to accelerate investment in export activities as well as for efficient import substitution. The state is expected to play a dual role under this strategy (Senses, 1990a). As one commentator has rightly argued[1], "without efforts to *enable* producers to respond, getting the price and trade policies right may have no more effect than pushing on a piece of string." Second, the state as a direct initiator of new enterprises in capital- and skill-intensive lines of activity should resume its role as the main vehicle of structural change within the manufacturing sector. The experience of the recent successful cases (most notably South Korea) demonstrates that it is possible to follow different paths along an export-oriented strategy and provides an effective challenge to the market-based strategies as propagated by the Bretton Woods institutions. Among the lessons that can be drawn from this experience, learning how to invest in upgrading and diversifying the industrial structure by concentrating on priority sectors under state guidance and the emphasis on the development of technological capabilities through investment in education and research and development activities are of special relevance for the Turkish case. Among other relevant lessons, one can cite the emphasis of governments on macroeconomic stability, flexibility of the industrial structure in view of changes in the global economy, the importance of increasing productivity to attain international competitiveness and the strict conditionality the state imposes in return for the incentives it provides for big business for predetermined objectives.

It is essential, also, that policy makers in Turkey and other LDCs should learn from Turkey's valuable experiences under two alternative industrial trade strategies. While ISI was instrumental in the creation of substantial learning effects and, in the process, a sizable industrial base, the EOI episode has gone a long way in removing import premiums and provided substantial learning effects vis-a-vis the penetration of new markets. There is, therefore, a strong need to be less ideological and more flexible in the choice of a new industrial trade strategy. Not overlooking also the fact that Turkish export growth in the 1980s originated basically from industries established under ISI, one should attach much credence to the view that the two strategies can be complementary (Senses, 1990a). In deepening as well as restructuring the industrial base through active state participation, however, it is necessary to recognize the fact that state industrial activity and rentseeking have gone hand in hand under both ISI and EOI. As Öniş and Riedel (1993: 92) have rightly argued,

Governments in Turkey have possessed substantial decision-making autonomy, but they have traditionally lacked the power to extract the economic resources required to implement their vision of the national interest.

The reactivation of the industrialization drive in the years ahead therefore requires a strong will not only to put the industrialization objective back on the development agenda, but also to improve the quality and efficiency of the state's administrative capacity.

NOTE

1. R. Wade as quoted in Kirkpatrick (1987a: 83).

BIBLIOGRAPHY

Adhikari, R. 1988. Expost Economic Efficiency of Public Enterprises: A Case of Manufacturing in Nepal. *Public Enterprise Quarterly Journal* 8 (4).

Agarwala, R. 1983. Price Distortions and Growth in Developing Countries. World Bank Staff Working Paper No. 575, Washington, DC.

Aktan, O. 1991. GATT ve AT Mevzuatı Karşısında Türkiye'nin İhracatı Teşvik Politikası: Geçmişi ve Geleceği. *Proceedings of the Third Izmir Economics Congress.*

Albertsen, N. 1988. Postmodernism, Post-Fordism, and critical social theory. *Environment and Planning D: Society and Space* 6: 339-365.

Alpar, C. 1974. Türkiye'nin AET Üyeliği ve Katma Protokol Karşısında Dış Ticaret Politikamızın Değişen Koruyucu Niteliği ve Sanayileşme Sorunu. In *Cumhuriyetin 50. Yılında Türkiye'de Sanayileşme ve Sorunları Semineri,* 799-834. Ankara: Siyasal Bilgiler Fakültesi.

Alptekin, A. T. 1985. Textiles in Turkey. In Adapting to Changing Market Conditions: Textiles in Turkey. *International Textile Manufacturing* 8.

AMA (Automotive Manufacturers Association). 1982. *Otomotiv Sanayii Ürünlerinin İhracatı, İhracat Sorunları.* Istanbul:AMA.

―――. 1984, 1986 and 1989. *General and Statistical Information about the Turkish Automotive Industry.* Publication No.13, 15 and 19, İstanbul: AMA.

Amin, A. and K. Robins. 1990. The Reemergence of Regional Economies? The Mythical Geography of Flexible Accumulation. *Environment and Planning A: Society and Space* 8: 7-34.

Amsden, A. H. 1989. *Asia's Next Giant: South Korea and Late Industrialization.* New York and Oxford: Oxford University Press.

―――. 1991. Big Business and Urban Congestion in Taiwan: The Origins of Small Enterprise and Regionally Decentralized Industry (Respectively). *World Development* 19 (2): 1121-35.

Amsden, A. H. and Y-D. Euh. 1990. South Korea's Financial Reform: What Are the Lessons? Paper prepared for the UNCTAD Secretariat, Geneva, Switzerland.

Ansal, H. 1988. *Technical Change in the Turkish Truck Manufacturing Industry*. D.Phil Thesis, University of Sussex, UK.

Arıcanlı, T. and D. Rodrik (eds.). 1990. *The Political Economy of Turkey: Debt, Adjustment and Sustainability*. London: MacMillan.

Aşıkoğlu, Y. 1992. Strategic Issues in Exchange Rate Liberalization: A Critical Evaluation of the Turkish Experience. In *Economics and Politics of Turkish Liberalization*, edited by T. F. Nas and M. Odekon, 101–23. Bethlehem, PA: Lehigh University Press.

Aysan, M. and S. Özmen. 1981. *Türkiye'de ve Dünyada Kamu İktisadi Teşebbüsleri*. İstanbul: Kardeşler Basımevi.

Ayub, M. A. and S. O. Hegstad. 1987. Management of Public Industrial Enterprises. *World Bank Research Observer* 2 (1): 79–101.

Bademli, R. R. 1977. Distorted and Lower Forms of Capitalist Industrial Production in Underdeveloped Countries: Contemporary Artisan Shops and Workshops in Eskişehir and Gaziantep, Turkey. Unpublished Ph.D. dissertation, Massachusetts Institute of Technology.

Balassa, B. 1981a. A Stages Approach to Comparative Advantage. In *Newly Industrializing Countries in the World Economy*, edited by B. Balassa. New York: Pergamon.

———. 1981b. *A Stages Approach to Comparative Advantage. In Newly Industrializing Countries in the World Economy*, edited by B. Balassa. New York: Pergamon.

Balassa, B. and J. Williamson. 1987. *Adjusting To Success: Balance of Payments Policy in the East Asian NICs*. Policy Analyses in International Economics 17, Institute for International Economics, Washington, D.C.

Ballance, R. H. 1987. *International Industry and Business: Structural Change, Industrial Policy and Industry Strategies*. London: Allen and Unwin.

Baranson, J. 1969. *Automotive Industries in Developing Countries*. Baltimore, MD: John Hopkins Press.

Barkey, H. J. 1990. *The State and the Industrialization Crisis in Turkey*. Boulder, CO.: Westview.

Barlow, R. and F. Şenses. 1992. The Turkish Export Boom: Just Reward or Just Lucky. Mimeo. Department of Economics, Middle East Technical University, Ankara.

Başbakanlık Yüksek Denetleme Kurulu. 1989. *Kamu İktisadi Teşebbüsleri Genel Raporu 1987*. Ankara: Başbakanlık Yüksek Denetleme Kurulu.

Baysan, T. and C. Blitzer. 1991. *Turkey*. Volume 6 in *Liberalizing Foreign Trade*, edited by D. Papageorgiou, M. Michaely and A. M. Choksi. Cambridge: Basil Blackwell.

Bernstein, H. 1982. Industrialization, Development and Dependence. In *Introduction to the Sociology of Developing Societies*, edited by H. Alavi and T. Shanin, 218–35. London: Macmillan.

Bhagwati, J. N. 1978. *Foreign Trade Regimes and Economic Development: Anatomy and Consequences of Exchange Control Regimes*. Cambridge, MA: Ballinger.

————. 1990. Export-Promoting Trade Strategy: Issues and Evidence. In *Export Promotion Strategies: Theory and Evidence from Developing Countries*, edited by C. Milner, 11–39. New York: New York University Press.

Bienefeld, M. A. 1982. The International Context for National Development Strategies: Constraints and Opportunities in a Changing World. In *The Struggle for Development: National Strategies in an International Context*, edited by M. A. Bienefeld and M. Godfrey, 25-64. Chichester: John Wiley.

Biggs, T. S. 1988. Financing the Emergence of Small and Medium Enterprise in Taiwan: Financial Mobilization and the Flow of Domestic Credit to the Private Sector. Employment and Enterprise Policy Analysis Discussion Papers No. 15, Employment and Enterprise Development Division, Office of Rural and Institutional Development, Bureau of Science and Technology, U. S. Agency for International Development, Washington, DC.

Blejer, M., and M. S. Khan. 1984. Government Policy and Private Investment in Developing Countries. *IMF Staff Papers* 31: 379–403.

Boratav, K. 1990. Inter-Class and Intra-Class Relations of Distribution Under "Structural Adjustment": Turkey During the 1980s. In *The Political Economy of Turkey: Debt, Adjustment and Sustainability*, edited by T. Arıcanlı and D. Rodrik, 199–229. London: Macmillan.

Boratav, K. and O. Türel. 1988. Notes on the Current Development Problems and Growth Prospects of the Turkish Economy. *New Perspectives on Turkey* 2 (1): 37–50.

Boston Consulting Group. 1985. *Turkish Textile Sector Restructuring Study*. Vol. 8. London: Textile Consulting Services Inc.

Bowles, S., D. Gordon and T. Weisskopf. 1986. Power and Profits: The Social Structure of Accumulation and the Profitability of the Postwar U.S. Economy. *Review of Radical Political Economics* 18 (1–2): 132–67.

Broad, R. and J. Cavanagh. 1988. No More NICs. *Foreign Policy* 72: 81–103.

Cable, V. and B. Persaud, eds. 1987. *Developing with Foreign Investment*. London: Croom Helm.

Celasun, M. 1989. Income Distribution and Employment Aspects of Turkey's Post-1980 Adjustment. *METU Studies in Development* 16 (3–4): 1–32.

————. 1991. *Trade and Industrialization in Turkey: Initial Conditions, Policy and Performance in the 1980s*. Ankara: Department of Economics, Middle East Technical University.

Celasun, M. and D. Rodrik. 1989. Debt, Adjustment, and Growth: Turkey. In *Developing Country Debt and Economic Performance, Country*

Studies—Indonesia, Korea, Philippines, Turkey, edited by J. Sachs and S. M. Collins, Book 4, 615–808. Chicago and London: University of Chicago Press.

Chandler, A. D., Jr. 1990. *Scale and Scope*. Cambridge, MA.: Harvard University Press.

Chenery, H. B., S. Robinson and M. Syrquin. 1986. *Industrialization and Growth: A Comparative Study*. New York: Oxford University Press for the World Bank.

Cheng, H-S. 1986. Financial Policy and Reform in Taiwan, China. In *Financial Policy and Reform in Pacific Basin Countries*, edited by H-S. Cheng. Lexington, MA.: Lexington Books.

Chou, T-C. 1988. The Evolution of Market Structure in Taiwan. *Rivista Internazionale di Scienze Economiche e Commerciali* 35 (2): 171–94.

Çınar, E. M., G. Evcimen and M. Kaytaz. 1988. The Present Day Status of Small-Scale Industries (Sanatkar) in Bursa, Turkey. *International Journal of Middle East Studies* 20: 287–301.

Cizre–Sakallıoğlu, Ü. 1991. Labor: The Battered Community. In *Strong State and Economic Interest Groups: The Post-1980 Turkish Experience*, edited by M. Heper, 57–69. Berlin and New York: de Gruyter.

Cline, W. R. 1982. Can the East Asian Model of Development be Generalised?. *World Development* 10 (2): 81–90.

Cody, J., R. Kitchen and J. Weiss. 1990. *Policy Design and Price Reform in Developing Countries*. London: Wheatsheaf.

Colman, D. and F. Nixson. 1986. *Economics of Change in Less Developed Countries*. 2nd ed. Oxford: Philip Allan.

Conway, P. 1992. Economic Stabilization and Structural Adjustment in Turkey: Evidence from Macroeconomic Accounts. In *Economics and Politics of Turkish Liberalization*, edited by T. F. Nas and M. Odekon, 124–42. Bethlehem, PA: Lehigh University Press.

Cook, P. and C. Kirkpatrick. 1988. Privatization in Less Developed Countries: An Overview. In *Privatization in Less Developed Countries*, edited by P. Cook and C. Kirkpatrick, 3–44. London: Wheatsheaf.

Cooke, P. 1985. The Changing Urban and Regional System in the United Kingdom. *Regional Studies* 20: 243–51.

———. 1988. Flexible Integration, Space Economies and Strategic Alliances: Social and Spatial Mediations. *Environment and Planning D: Society and Space* 6: 281–300.

Corden, W. M. 1974. *Trade Policy and Economic Welfare*. Oxford: Clarendon.

Council for Economic Planning and Development. 1988. *Taiwan Statistical Data Book*. Taiwan: Council for Economic Planning and Development.

———. 1989. *Taiwan Statistical Data Book*. Taiwan: Council for Economic Planning and Development.

Cowing, T. and R. Stevenson, eds. 1981. *Productivity Measurement in Regulated Industries*. New York: Academic Press.

Dahlman, C. 1984. Foreign Technology and Indigenous Technological Capability in Brazil. In *Technological Capability in the Third World*, edited by M. Fransman and K. King, 317–34. New York: St.Martin's Press.

————. 1990. Technology Strategy and Policy for International Competitiveness: A Case Study of Thailand. Mimeo, World Bank, Industry Development Division.

de Janvry, A. and E. Sadoulet. 1983. Social Articulation as a Condition for Equitable Growth. *Journal of Development Economics* 13: 275–303.

Dinç, G. 1989. The Turkish Experience with the Built-Own-Transfer Model. Paper presented to the International Conference on New Forms of Financing Infrastructural Projects, Rabat, Morocco.

Doğramacı, A., ed. 1981. *Productivity Analysis: A Range of Perspectives*. Boston: Kluwer Nijhoff.

Doğramacı, A. and N. R. Adam, eds. 1981. *Aggregate and Industry-Level Productivity Analysis*. Boston: Kluwer Nijhoff.

Dollar, D. and K. Sokaloff. In Press. A Comparison of Productivity in South Korea and Taiwan. In *Korean Economic Development*, edited by J. Kwon. Westport, CT: Greenwood Press.

Dore, R. 1986. *Flexible Rigidities*. Stanford, CA: Stanford University Press.

Dornbusch, R. 1980. *Open Economy Macro Economics*. New York: Basic Books.

DPT (Devlet Planlama Teşkilatı). 1971. *Esnaf ve Sanatkarların Sosyal ve Ekonomik Sorunları Araştırması*. Ankara: DPT.

————. 1987. *Yabancı Sermaye Raporu, 1983–86*. Ankara: DPT.

————. 1989. *Küçük Sanayi*. Ankara: DPT.

————. 1990. *Yabancı Sermaye Raporu, 1987–89*. Ankara: DPT.

————. 1991. *Temel Ekonomik Göstergeler*. Ankara: DPT

Economic and Social Studies Conference Board (ESSCB), 1968. *State Economic Enterprises*. Istanbul: Celtut Matbaacılık.

Economic Planning Board. 1984. *Major Statistics of Korean Economy*. Seoul: Economic Planning Board.

————. 1989. *Major Statistics of Korean Economy*. Seoul: Economic Planning Board.

Englander, A. S. and A. Mittelstadt. 1988. Total Factor Productivity: Macroeconomic and Structural Aspects of the Slowdown. *OECD Economic Studies* (10): 7–56.

Eraydın, A. 1989. Regional Differentiation of Changing Industrial Structure and Labor Demand. Paper presented to the Conference on Industrial Change, August 1989, Rabka, Poland.

————. 1991. Migratory Movements in Turkey: Regional Dimensions. Paper presented at the Japan-German and Turkish Joint Seminar on Migration and Development, 12–15 April 1991, Ankara.

————. 1992. *Post-Fordism ve Değişen Mekansal Öncelikler*. Ankara: ODTÜ Mimarlık Fakültesi.

Erdilek, A. 1982. *Direct Foreign Investment in Turkish Manufacturing: An Analysis of Conflicting Objectives and Frustrated Expectations of a Host Country*. Tubingen: J. C. B. Mohr (Paul Siebeck).

————. 1988. The Role of Foreign Investment in the Liberalization of the Turkish Economy. In *Liberalization and the Turkish Economy*, edited by T. F. Nas and M. Odekon, 141–59. Westport, CT: Greenwood Press.

Ersel, H. 1991. Structural Adjustment: Turkey (1980–1990). Paper presented in the IMF-Pakistan Administrative Staff College joint seminar on Structural Adjustment and Macroeconomic Issues Lahore, October, 26–28.

Fitzgerald, E. 1988. State Accumulation and Market Equilibria: An Application of Kalecki-Kornai Analysis to Planned Economies in the Third World. *Journal of Development Studies* 24 (4): 50-74.

Fransman, M. 1986. International Competitiveness, Technical Change and the State: The Machine Tool Industry in Taiwan and Japan. *World Development* 14 (12): 1375–96.

Freeman, C. 1981. Technology and Development: Long Waves in Technical Change and Economic Development. In United Nations, *Methods for Development Planning*. Paris: UN.

Froutan, F. 1990. *Foreign Trade and Its Relation to Competition and Productivity in Turkish Industry*. Mimeo. Washington, DC: World Bank.

Garofoli, G. 1990. Local Development: Patterns and Policy Implications. In *Local Development*, edited by N. Konsolas, 87–98. Athens: Athens Regional Development Institute.

Gerni, C. 1991. Türkiye'de 1980–1990 Döneminde Uygulanan İstikrar Politikaları Üzerine Bir Değerlendirme. *Proceedings of the Third Izmir Economics Congress*.

Gupta, S. C. 1981. Subcontracting Between Factories and Workshops: A Case Study of Automotive Industry in Bursa, Turkey. MCP Dissertation, Middle East Technical University.

Gürsoy, C. T. 1973. *Türkiye'de Otomotiv Sanayii ve Otomotiv Yan Sanayii*. Istanbul: Iktisadi Araştırmalar Vakfı.

Güvemli, O. 1992. Türkiye'de Yatırımların Özendirilmesindeki Gelişmeler. *Proceedings of the Third Izmir Economics Congress*.

Hadjimichalis, C. and Vaiou, D. 1987. Changing Patterns of Uneven Regional Development and Forms of Reproduction in Greece. *Environment and Planning D: Society and Space* 5: 319-333.

Hale, W. 1980. Ideology and Economic Development in Turkey, 1930–1945. *British Society for the Middle Eastern Studies Bulletin* 7 (2): 100–17.

Hall, R. E. 1988. The Relation Between Price and Marginal Cost in U.S. Industry. *Journal of Political Economy* 98 (5): 921–47.

Harvey, D. 1989. *The Condition of Post-Modernity*. London: Basil Blackwell.

Helleiner, G. 1973. Manufactured Exports from Less Developed Countries and Multinational Firms. *Economic Journal* 83 (329): 21–47.

Helleiner, G. K. 1988. Direct Foreign Investment and Manufacturing for Export in Developing Countries: A Review of the Issues. In *Policies for Development: Essays in Honour of Gamani Corea*, edited by S. Dell, 125–53. London: Macmillan.

Heper, M., ed. 1991. *Strong State and Economic Interest Groups: The Post-1980 Turkish Experience*. Berlin and New York: de Gruyter.

Hill, H. 1985. Subcontracting, Technological Diffusion, and the Development of Small Enterprise in Philippine Manufacturing. *Journal of Developing Areas* 19: 245–62.

Hirschman, A. O. 1958. *The Strategy of Economic Development*. New Haven, CT: Yale University Press.

Holmes, J. 1986. The Organization and Locational Structure of Production Subcontracting. In *Production Work and Territory*, edited by A. J. Scott and M. Storper, 80–103. London: M. Allen & Unwin.

Hulten, C. R. 1979. On the Importance of Productivity Change. *American Economic Review* 69 (1): 126–36.

IDBT (Industrial Development Bank of Turkey). 1984. *Report on the Automotive Industry*. Publication No. 5, İstanbul: IDBT.

———. 1987 and 1988, *Textile Sector Reports*. İstanbul: IDBT.

———. 1989. *İmalat Sanayii'nin Seçilmiş Sektörlerinde 1988 Sonuçları ve 1989 Beklentileri*. İstanbul: IDBT.

İlkin, S. and İ. Tekeli. 1987. *Dünyada ve Türkiye'de Serbest Üretim Bölgelerinin Doğuş ve Dönüsümü*. Ankara: Yurt Yayınları.

ILO (International Labor Organization). 1987. *Yearbook of Labor Statistics*. Geneva: ILO.

ISO (Istanbul Sanayi Odası). 1989. *Türkiye'nin 500 Büyük Sanayi Kuruluşu*. Istanbul: Istanbul Sanayi Odası Yayını.

———. Beşyüz Büyük Firma Anket Sonuçları. *İstanbul Sanayi Odası Dergisi* (various years).

ITMF (International Textile Manufacturers Federation). 1989. *International Cotton Industry Statistics*. Zurich: ITMF.

Jenkins, R. 1977. *Dependent Industrialization in Latin America*. New York: Praeger.

———. 1987. *Transnational Corporations and Uneven Development*. London: Methuen.

Jones, L. 1975. *Public Enterprise and Economic Development: The Korean Case*. Seoul: Korean Development Institute.

Kalecki, M. 1976. Observations on Social and Economic Aspects of Intermediate Regimes. In *Essays in Developing Economies*, edited by M. Kalecki. Brighton: Harvester Press.

Kashyap, S. P. 1988. Growth of Small-Size Enterprises in India: Its Nature and Content. *World Development* 16: 667–82.

Kaytaz, M., G. Evcimen and E. M. Çınar. 1989. A Case Study of Some Economic Characteristics of Small-Scale Manufacturing Enterprises. *Boğaziçi University Journal of Economic and Administrative Studies* 3: 1–20.

Kendrick, J. W and R. Sato. 1963. Factor Prices, Productivity and Economic Growth. *American Economic Review* 53: 987–88.

Kepenek, Y. 1990. *100 Soruda Gelişimi, Sorunları ve Özelleştirilmeleriyle Türkiye'de Kamu İktisadi Teşebbüsleri (KİT)*. Istanbul: Gerçek Yayınevi.

Killick, T. and S. Commander. 1988. State Divestiture as a Policy Instrument in Developing Countries. *World Development* 16 (12): 1465–80.

Kıraç, C. 1973. Türk Otomotiv Sanayiinde Yan Sanayiin Yeri ve Önemi. In *Türkiye'de Otomotiv Sanayii ve Otomotiv Yan Sanayii*. Istanbul: İktisadi Araştırmalar Vakfı.

Kırım, A. 1990a. *Türkiye İmalat Sanayiinde Teknolojik Değişim*. Ankara: Türkiye Odalar ve Borsalar Birliği.

———. 1990b. *Türkiye'nin Hazır Giyim Sektörünün Yeniden Yapılanma Gerekleri*. İstanbul: Friedrich Ebert Vakfi.

Kirkpatrick, C. 1987a. Trade Policy and Industrialization in LDCs. In *Surveys in Development Economics,* edited by N.Gemmell, 56–89. Oxford: Basil Blackwell.

———. 1987b. The UK Privatization Experience: Is It Transferable to LDCs? *Oxford Center for Management Studies* (7).

Kirkpatrick, C. and P. Cook. 1988. Privatization in Less-Developed Countries: An Overview. In *Privatization in Less Developed Countries*, edited by C. Kirkpatrick and P. Cook, 3–44. London: Wheatsheaf.

Kirkpatrick, P. and Z. Öniş. 1991. Turkey. In *Aid and Power World Bank and Policy Based Lending*, edited by Paul Mosley et al., Vol. 8, 9–38. London: Routledge.

Kitchen, R. and J. Weiss. 1987. Prices and Government Intervention in Developing Countries. *Industry and Development* (20): 51-99.

Korea Industrial Research Institute. 1989. *Major Industrial Technology*. Seoul: KIRI.

Krueger, A. O. 1974. *Foreign Trade Regimes and Economic Development: Turkey*. New York: Columbia University Press for NBER.

———. 1978. *Foreign Trade Regimes and Economic Development: Liberalization Attempts and Consequences*. Cambridge, MA.: Ballinger.

Krueger, A. O. and O.H. Aktan. 1992. *Swimming Against the Tide: Turkish Trade Reform in the 1980s*. San Francisco: Institute for Contemporary Studies.

Krueger, A. O. and B. Tuncer. 1982. Growth of Factor Productivity in Turkish Manufacturing Industries. *Journal of Development Economics* 11 (3): 307–25.

Kwon, J.K. 1986. Capital Utilization, Economies of Scale and Technical Change in the Growth of Total Factor Productivity. *Journal of Development Economics* 15: 75–89.

Landau, D. 1986. Government and Economic Growth in Less Developed Countries: An Empirical Study for 1960–80. *Economic Development and Cultural Change* 35 (1): 35–75.

Leborgne, D. and A. Lipietz. 1988. New Technologies, New Modes of Regulation: Some Spatial Implications. *Environment and Planning D: Society and Space* 6: 263–80.

Leeson, P. F. and F. I. Nixson. 1988. Development Economics and the State. In *Perspectives on Development*, edited by P. F. Leeson and M. Minogue, 56–88. Manchester: Manchester University Press.

Lipietz, A. 1986. New Tendencies in the International Division of Labor: Regimes of Accumulation and Modes of Regulation. In *Production, Work and Territory*, edited by A. J. Scott and M. Storper, 6–40. London: Allen & Unwin.

Little, I. M. D. 1982. *Economic Development: Theory, Policy and International Relations*. New York: Basic Books.

Little, I. M. D., D. Mazumdar and J. M. Page. 1987. *Small Manufacturing Enterprises*. Oxford: Oxford University Press.

Little, I. M. D. and J. A. Mirrlees. 1974. *Project Appraisal and Planning for Developing Countries*. London: Heinemann.

Little, I. M. D., T. Scitovsky, and M. Scott. 1970. *Industry and Trade in Some Developing Countries— A Comparative Study*. London, New York, Toronto: Oxford University Press for OECD.

Luedde-Neurath, R. 1988. State Intervention and Export-Oriented Development in South Korea. In *Developmental States in East Asia*, edited by G. White, 68–112. London: Macmillan.

Lyberaki, A. 1990. Crisis and Restructuring in the Greek Clothing Industry: Implications Related to Size and Space. Paper presented at the Thirtieth European Congress of Regional Science Association, August 28–30, 1990, Istanbul.

Malecki, E. 1991. Culture's Influence on Technological Development and Economic Growth. IGU Commission on Industrial Change, August 1991, Penang.

Mehmet, Ö. 1990. *Islamic Identity and Development Studies of the Islamic Periphery*. Kuala Lumpur: Forum.

Milanovic, B. 1986. Export Incentives and Turkish Manufactured Exports, 1980–84. World Bank Staff Working Paper No. 602.

Millward, R. 1986. The Comparative Performance of Public and Private Ownership. In *Privatization and Regulation— The UK Experience*, edited by J. Kay, C. Mayer and D. Thompson, 119–44. Oxford: Clarendon Press.

————. 1988. Measured Sources of Inefficiency in the Performance of Private and Public Enterprises in LDCs. In *Privatization in Less Developed Countries*, edited by P. Cook and C. Kirkpatrick, 143–61. London: Macmillan.

Milner, C., ed. 1990. *Export Promotion Strategies: Theory and Evidence from Developing Countries*. New York: New York University Press.

Moran, T. H. 1988. Multinational Corporations and North-South Relations: Old Threats and New Opportunities in the Coming Decade. In *Rekindling Development: Multinational Firms and World Debt*, edited by L. A. Tavis, 267–83. Notre Dame, IN Notre Dame University Press.

Mutlu, S. 1990. Price Scissors in Turkish Agriculture. *METU Studies in Development* 17 (1–2): 163–212.

Nadiri, M.I. 1970. Some Approaches to the Theory and Measurement of Total Factor Productivity: A Survey. *Journal of Economic Literature* 8: 1137–77.

Nas, T. and M. Odekon, eds. 1988. *Liberalization and the Turkish Economy*. Westport, CT: Greenwood Press.

National Science Council Taiwan. 1989. *Science and Technology Data Book*. Taiwan: National Science Council.

Nelson, R. R. 1981. Research on Productivity Differences. *Journal of Economic Literature* 19: 1029–64.

Nishimizu, M. and S. Robinson. 1984. Trade Policies and Productivity Change in Semi-Industrialized Countries. *Journal of Development Economics* 13: 177–206.

Nixson, F. 1984. Economic Development: Utopian Ideal or Historical Process? *METU Studies in Development* 11 (1–2): 81–92.

―――. 1987. Economic Development: A Suitable Case for Treatment?. In *The Historical Dimensions of Economic Development*, edited by B. Ingham and C. Simmons. London: Frank Cass.

―――. 1990. Industrialization and Structural Change in Developing Countries. *Journal of International Development* 2 (3).

―――. 1991. Industrialization and Development. *Journal of International Development* 3 (1): 79-85.

OECD (Organization for Economic Co-operation and Development). 1988. *The Newly Industrializing Countries: Challenge and Opportunity for OECD Industries*. Paris: OECD.

―――. 1990. *Turkey: Annual Country Survey, 1989–1990*. Paris:OECD.

―――. 1991. *Economic Surveys: Turkey 1990/1991*. Paris:OECD.

―――. 1992. *Economic Surveys: Turkey*. Paris: OECD.

―――. 1993. *Economic Surveys Turkey*. Paris: OECD.

Okyar, O. 1965. The Concept of Etatism. *Economic Journal* 75 (297): 98-111.

Olgun, H., S. Togan, and H. Akder. 1988. *External Economic Relations of Turkey*. Ankara: Turktrade.

Oman, C. 1984. *New Forms of International Investment in Developing Countries*. Paris : OECD Development Center.

Öniş, Z. 1989. *Türkiye'de Dış Ticaret Politikaları ve Dış Borç Sorunu, 1980–1988*. Istanbul: Istanbul Ticaret Odası Yayını.

―――. 1991. Political Economy of Turkey in the 1980s: Anatomy of Unorthodox Liberalism. In *Strong State and Economic Interest Groups*: The Post-1980

Turkish Experience, edited by Metin Heper, 27–39. Berlin and New York: de Gruyter.

———. 1992. Organization of Export-Oriented Industrialization: The Turkish Foreign Trade Companies in Comparative Perspective. In *The Economics and Politics of Turkish Liberalization*, edited by T. Nas and M. Odekon, 73–100. London: Associated Universities Press.

Öniş, Z. and S. Özmucur. 1988a. Supply Side Origins of Macroeconomic Crises in Turkey. Boğaziçi University Research Papers, ISS/Ec 89-15, İstanbul.

———. 1988b. The Role of the Financial System in the Creation and Resolution of Macroeconomic Crises in Turkey. Boğaziçi University Research Papers. ISS/Ec 89-16, Istanbul.

———. 1991. Capital Flows and the External Financing of Turkey's Imports. OECD Development Center Technical Papers, No 36, Paris: OECD.

Öniş, Z. and J. Riedel. 1993. *Economic Crises and Long-Term Growth in Turkey*. Washington, DC: World Bank Comparative Macroeconomic Studies.

Ottoway, M. 1988. Mozambique: From Symbolic Socialism to Symbolic Reform. *Journal of Modern African Studies* 26 (2): 211-26.

Ozawa, T. 1980. Government Control over Technology Acquisition and Firms' Entry into New Sectors: The Experience of Japan's Synthetic-Fibre Industry. *Cambridge Journal of Economics* 4: 133–46.

Özmucur, S. 1987. *Sanayide Mali ve Ekonomik Göstergeler (1983–1984)*. Istanbul: Istanbul Sanayi Odası.

———. 1988. Productivity and Growth in Turkish Manufacturing and Implications for Macroeconomic Instability. Boğaziçi University Research Papers, ISS/Ec 89-07, Istanbul.

———. 1989. Financial and Economic Indicators of Five Hundred Largest Firms in Turkey, 1980–1988. Boğaziçi University Research Papers, ISS/Ec 89-17, Istanbul.

———. 1991a. Gelirin Fonksiyonel Dağılımı. Boğaziçi University Research Papers, No. ISS/Ec 91-16, Istanbul.

———. 1991b. Prices and Income Distribution. Boğaziçi University Research Papers, No. ISS/Ec 91-17, Istanbul.

Özmucur, S. and Y. Esmer. 1988. Total Factor Productivity in Turkey: A Longitudinal and Comparative Analysis of Total Factor Productivity Growth in Turkish Manufacturing Industries, 1970–1985. Boğaziçi University Research Papers, No. ISS/Ec 89-06, Istanbul.

Özmucur, S. and C. Karataş. 1990. The Public Enterprise Sector in Turkey: Performance and Productivity Growth, 1973–1988. Boğaziçi University Research Papers, No.ISS/EC 90-11, Istanbul.

Pack, H. and L. E. Westphal. 1985. *Industrial Strategy and Technological Change: Theory Versus Reality*. Mimeo, Swarthmore College, Swarthmore, PA.

Page, S. 1987. Developing Country Attitudes Towards Foreign Investment. In *Developing with Foreign Investment*, edited by V. Cable and B. Persaud, 28–43. London: Croom Helm.

Peet, R. 1991. *Global Capitalism: Theories of Societal Development*. London: Routledge.

Petrol–İş. 1990. *Almanac of the Petroleum Workers Union of Turkey*. Istanbul: Petrol–İş.

Piore, M. and C. Sabel. 1984. *The Second Industrial Divide: Possibilities for Prosperity*. New York: Basic Books.

Reynolds, L. G. 1983. The Spread of Economic Growth to the Third World: 1850–1980. *Journal of Economic Literature* 21 (3): 941–80.

Rittenberg, L. 1991. Investment Spending and Interest Rate Policy: The Case of Financial Liberalization in Turkey. *Journal of Development Studies* 27 (2): 151–67.

Roberts, M. J. 1988. *The Structure of Production in Columbian Manufacturing Industries 1977-1985*. Mimeo, World Bank.

Rodrik, D. 1988. External Debt and Economic Performance in Turkey. In *Liberalization and the Turkish Economy*, edited by T. Nas and M. Odekon, 161-84. Westport, CT: Greenwood Press.

Sachs, I. 1964. *Patterns of Public Sector in Underdeveloped Countries*. New Delhi: Asia Publishing House.

Sağlam, D. 1967. *Türkiye'de Kamu İktisadi Teşebbüsleri*. Ankara: Ankara Üniversite Basımevi.

Sandbrook, R. 1988. Patrimonialism and the Failing of Parastatals: Africa in Comparative Perspective. In *Privatization in Less Developed Countries*, edited by P. Cook and C. Kirkpatrick, 162–79. London: Macmillan.

Sato, Y. 1988. Small Business in Japan: A Historical Perspective. *Small Business Economics* 1: 121–28.

Sayer, A. 1989. Postfordism in Question. *International Journal of Urban and Regional Research* 13: 666–95.

———. 1991. Behind the Locality Debate: Deconstructing Geography's Dualism. *Environment and Planning A* 23: 283–303.

Schive, C. 1978. Direct Foreign Investment, Technology Transfer, and Linkage Effects: A Case Study of Taiwan. Unpublished doctoral dissertation. Cleveland: Case Western Reserve University.

Schmitz, H. 1982 Growth Constraints on Small-Scale Manufacturing in Developing Countries: A Critical Review. *World Development* 10: 429–50.

Schmitz, H. 1989. Flexible Specialization—A New Paradigm of Small-Scale Industrialization? IDS Discussion Paper, No.265, University of Sussex, Brighton.

Schoenberger, E. 1988. From Fordism to Flexible Accumulation: Technology, Competitive Strategies, and International Location. *Environment and Planning D: Society and Space* 6, 252–62.

Scott, A. J. 1988. Flexible Production Systems and Regional Development : The Rise of Industrial Spaces in North America and Western Europe. *International Journal of Urban and Regional Research* 12: 171–86.

Şenses, F. 1983. An Assessment of Turkey's Liberalization Attempts Since 1980 Against the Background of Her Stabilization Program. *METU Studies in Development* 10 (3): 271–322.

―――. 1989a. The Nature and Main Characteristics of Recent Turkish Growth in Export of Manufactures. *Developing Economies* 27 (1): 19–33.

―――. 1989b. *1980 Sonrası Ekonomi Politikaları Işığında Türkiye'de Sanayileşme Bugün ve Yarın.* Ankara: V Yayınları.

―――. 1990a. Alternative Trade and Industrialization Strategies and Employment in the Turkish Manufacturing Sector. Middle East Technical University, Economic Research Center, Working Paper No. ERC/1990-1.

―――. 1990b. Foreign Trade Liberalization in an Arch-Type Import Substituting Economy: The Case of Turkey. In *Trade Liberalization in the 1990s*, edited by H. W Singer et al. 387–406. New World Series, Vol. 8. New Delhi: Indus.

―――. 1990c. An Assessment of the Pattern of Turkish Manufactured Export Growth in the 1980s and Its Prospects. In *The Political Economy of Turkey Debt, Adjustment and Sustainability*, edited by T. Arıcanlı and D. Rodrik, 60–77. London: MacMillan.

―――. 1991. Turkey's Stabilization and Structural Adjustment Program in Retrospect and Prospect. *Developing Economies* 29 (3): 210–34.

―――. 1992. Labor Market Response to Structural Adjustment and Institutional Pressures, Middle East Technical University, Economic Research Center, Working Paper No. ERC/1992-1.

Sforzi, F. 1988. The Geography of Industrial Districts in Italy. Unpublished manuscript, Department of Economic Sciences, University of Florence.

Shea, J. D. and P. S. Kuo. 1984. An Analysis of the Allocative Efficiency of Bank Funds in Taiwan. Proceedings of a Conference on Financial Development in Taiwan, Taipei Institute of Economics, *Academia Sinica*, December (in Chinese).

Shinohara, M. 1968. A Survey of the Japanese Literature on Small Industry. In *The Role of Small Industry in the Process of Economic Growth*, edited by B. F. Hoselitz. The Hague: Mouton.

Short, R. P. 1984. The Role of Public Enterprises: An International Statistical Comparison. In *Public Enterprise in Mixed Economies*, edited by R. Floyd, C. Gray and R. Short. Washington, DC,: IMF.

Silin, R. H. 1976. *Leadership and Values: The Organization of Large-Scale Taiwanese Enterprises*. East Asian Research Center, Harvard University. Cambridge, MA: Harvard University Press.

Singer, H. W. and P. Alizadeh. 1988. Import Substitution Revisited in a Darkening External Environment. In *Policies for Development: Essays in Honour of Gamani Corea*, edited by S. Dell, 60–86. London: Macmillan.

Singh, A. 1984. The Interrupted Industrial Revolution of the Third World: Prospects and Policies for Resumption. *Industry and Development* (12): 43–68.

State Institute of Statistics. (a). *Census of Manufacturing* (various years). Ankara: SIS.

————. (b). *Annual Manufacturing Industry Statistics* (various years).

————. (c). *Statistical Yearbook of Turkey* (various years). Ankara: SIS.

————. (d). *Monthly Bulletin of Statistics* (various issues). Ankara: SIS.

————. 1988a. *1985 Census of Industry and Busine Establishmentsts: Second Stage Results, Large Scale Industries.* Ankara: SIS.

————. 1988b. *1988 Statistical Pocket-Book of Turkey.* Ankara: SIS.

————. 1991. *Manufacturing Industry Survey, 1988.* Ankara: Prime Ministry.

————. 1992. *Annual Manufacturing Industry Statistics, 1989.* Ankara: SIS.

State Planning Organization (SPO). *Annual Program* (various years). Ankara: Prime Ministry.

Statistical, Economic, and Social Research and Training Center for Islamic Countries. 1987. Small and Medium Sized Manufacturing Enterprises in Turkey. *Journal of Economic Cooperation Among Islamic Countries* 8: 55–114.

Storper, M. 1990. Industrialization and the Regional Question in the Third World: Lessons of Post-Imperialism; Prospects of Post-Fordism. *International Journal of Urban and Regional Research* 14: 423–44.

Storper, M. and A. J. Scott. 1988. The Geographical Foundations and Social Regulation of Flexible Production Complexes. In *The power of geography*, edited by J. Wolch and M. Dear, 24–59. Boston: Allen & Unwin.

T.C. Başbakanlık Yüksek Denetleme Kurulu. *Kamu İktisadi Teşebbüsleri Genel Raporu.* Ankara (various years).

Takao, T. 1989. Management in Taiwan: The Case of the Formosa Plastics Group. *East Asian Cultural Studies* XXVIII (1-4).

Teitel, S. and F. E. Thoumi. 1986. From Import Substitution to Exports: The Manufacturing Exports Experience of Argentina and Brazil. *Economic Development and Cultural Change* 34 (3): 455–90.

Tekeli, I., S. İlkin, A. Aksoy. and Y. Kepenek. 1983. *Türkiye'de Sanayi Kesiminde Yoğunlaşma.* Ankara: Maya Matbaası.

Togan, S. 1992. 1980'li Yıllarda Dış Ticaretin Liberalizasyonu. *İşletme ve Finans* 7 (78): 17–30.

Trebat, T. 1983. *Brazil's State-Owned Enterprises: A Case-Study of the State as Entrepreneur.* Cambridge: Cambridge University Press.

Türel, O. 1993. The Development of Turkish Manufacturing Industry During 1976–87: An Overview. In *The Political and Socioeconomic Transformation of Turkey* , edited by A. Eralp et al, 69–95. Westport, CT: Praeger.

TÜSIAD.(Türk Sanayicileri ve İşadamları Derneği). 1982. *KİT Raporu.* TÜSİAD Yayın No T/82.5.74. İstanbul.

————. 1989. *İstikrarlı Kalkınma ve Yeniden Sanayileşme için Ekonomik Çözümler*. Istanbul: TÜSİAD.

————. *The Turkish Economy*. Istanbul (various issues).

Tyler, P. and J. Rhodes. 1986. The Census Production as an Indicator of Regional Differences in Productivity and Profitability in the UK. *Regional Studies* 20: 331–39.

Türkiye Bankalar Birliği. *Bankalarımız*, various issues. Ankara: Türkiye Bankalar Birliği.

Undersecretariat of Treasury and Foreign Trade. *Treasury Monthly Indicators* (various issues).

————. Kamu Iktisadi Tesebbusleri. Ankara (various years).

UNCTAD (United Nations Conference on Trade and Development). 1987. *Trade and Development Report*. Geneva: UN.

————. 1990a. *Trade and Development Report, 1990*. New York: UN, UNCTAD/TDR/10.

————. 1990b. *Transfer and Development of Technology in Developing Countries: A Compendium of Policy Issues*. Geneva: UN, UNCTAD/ITP/TEC/4.

UNIDO (United Nations Industrial Development Organization). 1979. *Industry 2000: New Perspectives*. New York: UN, ID/237.

————. 1983. *Industry in a Changing World*. New York: UN, ID/304 (ID/CONF. 5/2).

————. 1984. *Handbook of Industrial Statistics*. New York: UN.

————. 1988a. *Handbook of Industrial Statistics, 1988*. Vienna: UN, ID/359.

————. 1988b. *Industry and Development: Global Report 1988–89*. Vienna: UN, ID/360.

United Nations Center on Transnational Corporations.1988. *Transnational Corporations in World Development, Trends and Prospects*. New York: UN, ST/CTC/89.

United Nations. 1990. *Global Outlook 2000: An Economic, Social, and Environmental Perspective*. New York: UN, ST/ESA/215/Rev. 1.

Uras, G. 1979. *Türkiye'de Yabancı Sermaye Yatırımları*. Istanbul: Formül Matbaası.

Uygur, E. 1990. *Policy, Productivity, Growth and Employment in Turkey, 1960–89*. Geneva: International Labor Office, MIES 90/4.

Wade, R. 1988. State Intervention in Outward-Looking Development: Neoclassical Theory and Taiwanese Practice. In *Developmental States in East Asia*, edited by G. White, 30–67. London: Macmillan.

Walstedt, B. 1980. *State Manufacturing Enterprise in a Mixed Economy: The Turkish Case*. Baltimore, MD: Johns Hopkins University Press (World Bank publication).

Warde, A. 1988. Industrial Restructuring, Local Politics and the Reproduction of Labor Power: Some Theoretical Considerations. *Environment and Planning D: Society and Space* 6: 75–95.

Warren, W. 1973. Imperialism and Capitalist Industrialization. *New Left Review* (81): 3–44.

Watanabe, S. 1971. Subcontracting, Industrialization and Employment Creation. *International Labor Review* 104: 51–76.

———. 1974. Reflections on Current Policies for Promoting Small Enterprise and Subcontracting. *International Labor Review* 110: 405–22.

Waterbury, J. 1992. Export-Led Growth and the Center-Right Coalition in Turkey. In *Economics and Politics of Turkish Liberalization*, edited by T. F. Nas and M. Odekon, 44–72. Bethlehem,PA: Lehigh University Press.

Weiss, J. 1986. Japan's Post-War Protection Policy: Some Implications for Less Developed Countries. *Journal of Development Studies* 22 (2): 385–406.

———. 1988. *Industry in Developing Countries: Theory, Policy and Evidence*. London and New York: Routledge.

White, G. and R. Wade. 1988. Developmental States and Markets in East Asia: An Introduction. In *Developmental States in East Asia*, edited by G. White, 1–29. London: Macmillan.

World Bank. 1980. *Turkey, Prospects for Small-Medium Scale Industry Development and Employment Generation*. 3 vols. Washington,DC: World Bank.

———. 1983. *World Development Report*. Washington, DC: World Bank.

———. 1987. *World Development Report, 1987*. Washington, DC: World Bank.

———. 1989. *World Development Report, 1989*. Washington, DC: World Bank.

———. 1991. *World Development Report, 1991*. Washington, DC: World Bank.

———. 1992. *World Development Report, 1992*. Washington, DC: World Bank.

YASED (Yabancı Sermaye Derneği). 1986. *Foreign Capital Legislation in Turkey*. Istanbul: YASED Publications.

Yaser, B., N. Weed and R. Marchesini. 1988. *A Comparison of Selected Financial Ratios for the Private Manufacturing Industries in Turkey and the United States, 1983–1984*. Istanbul: Istanbul Chamber of Industry Publication.

Yasuoka, S. 1984. Introduction. In *Family Business in the Era of Industrial Growth: Its Ownership and Management*, edited by S. Yasuoka. Tokyo: University of Tokyo Press.

Yeldan, A. E. 1989. Structural Adjustment and Trade in Turkey: Investigating the Alternatives Beyond Export-Led Growth. *Journal of Policy Modeling* 11 (2): 273–97.

———. 1990. İhracata Yönelik Sanayileşme ve Bölüşüm-Uyumsuz Büyüme: Türkiye 1980–1989. *Boğaziçi University Journal of Economics and Administrative Studies* 4 (2): 323–33.

————. 1991. Conflicting Interests and Structural Inflation: Turkey, 1980–1990. Bilkent University Department of Economics Discussion Paper No. 91-9, September.

Yeldan, A. E. and T. L. Roe. 1991. Political Economy of Rent-Seeking Under Alternative Trade Regimes. *Weltwirtschaftliches Archiv* 127 (3): 563–83.

Yıldırım, E. 1989. Total Factor Productivity Growth in Turkish Manufacturing Industry Between 1963-1983: An Analysis. *METU Studies in Development* 16 (3-4): 65-83.

INDEX

Aktan, O., 72 n.5, 83
Alizadeh, P., 19, 20, 24 n.4
Amsden, A., 2, 3, 20, 38 n.1
Ansal, H., 6, 73, 175, 185
Automotive Manufacturers
    Association (AMA), 184, 185,
    186

Bademli, R. R., 154 n.2
Balassa, B., 26, 35, 175
Barlow, R., 73 n.9
Baysan, T., 88 n.1
Bernstein, H., 22
Biggs, T. S., 30
Boratav, K., 81, 87
Boston Consulting Group, 178
Bowles, S. D., 79
Bretton Woods institutions, 3, 193
build-operate-transfer (BOT), 97
Bursa, 5, 157, 158, 169–73, 192

Celasun, M., 73 n.11, 79, 88 n.1
Chandler, A. D. Jr., 31
Cheng, H-S., 29
Cizre-Sakallıoğlu, Ü., 76
Cline, W. R., 19

Cook, P., 43, 112
Cooke, P., 155–57
Çınar, E. M., 154 n.2

deindustrialization, 107
deregulation, 3, 27, 36, 37, 38
diversified business group, 27, 29
Dore, R., 37
dynamic comparative advantage,
    25–26, 31, 36

Economic and Social Studies
    Conference Board (ESCB), 113
economies of scale, 6
employment, 4, 67, 159, 162
Export-oriented industrialization
    (EOI), 8, 19–20, 22, 92, 177,
    180, 184, 187, 191, 193–94
Eraydın, A., 5, 169
Erdilek, A., 62, 64, 94–96, 98, 106
Ersel, H., 78
European Community, 101, 103,
    181–82
exchange rate, 3, 65, 76, 78, 82
export incentives (*see also* export
    subsidies), 81, 96

export subsidies, 82
exports, 4, 6, 63–64, 78

flexible accumulation, 156
flexible production, 155, 157-58
flexible specialization, 3, 31
Fordist production system, 5, 155
Foreign Direct Investment (FDI), 4, 21, 62, 64, 91
foreign trade companies, 58, 82
Fransman, M., 188
free trade zones, 96
Freeman, C., 162

Garofoli, G., 157, 168
General Agreement on Trade and Tariffs (GATT), 58
Gerni, C., 81
Gordon, S., 79
government intervention, 6, 30, 47, 48, 49 (*see also* state intervention)
Güvemli, O., 58, 89 n.6

Hadjimichalis, C., 171, 174 n.7
Helleiner, G.K., 18, 22
Hill, H., 149, 154 n.7
Hirschman, A. O., 26, 27, 38
Holmes, J., 157, 171

Import-substituting industrilaization (ISI), 8, 9, 18–20, 22, 44, 52, 177, 182, 185, 187–88, 191, 192, 194
import substitution, 1, 2
income distribution, 4, 75, 79
Industrial Development Bank of Turkey (IDBT), 142, 178–79, 186
industries, textiles and clothing, 5, 176–77; metal-working, 5; truck manufacturing, 6, 182
industry, spatial distribution, 2, 5, 158–62

interest rate, 3, 57, 65
intermediate regimes, 49
international competitiveness, 5, 6, 175, 177
International Labour Office (ILO), 102
International Monetary Fund (IMF), 1, 27, 36, 41, 54–55
International Textile Manufacturers Federation (ITMF), 18
investment, 4, 5, 64–65
investment certificates, 58
Istanbul Sanayi Odası (ISO), 104, 121, 123

Kalecki, M., 49
Karataş, C., 4, 5
Kaytaz, M., 5
Kirkpatrick, C., 43, 55, 112, 113, 195 n.1
Korea Industrial Research Institute, 35, 36
Krueger, A. O., 72 n.5, 94, 112, 175
Kuo, P. S., 30

Landau, D., 43
late industrialization, 27, 29, 30, 37
late-industrializing countries, 25–26, 32, 35–37
Leeson, P. F., 9, 23 n.1
liberalization, 3, 27; financial, 1, 36, 37, 38, 64–65; trade, 1, 57
Little, I.M.D., 39, 41, 46, 188
Luedde-Neurath, R., 188
Lyberaki, A., 157, 174 n.7

Millward, R., 43, 112
Mirrlees, J. A., 41

Nas, T., 6 n.1, 96
Newly-industrilalizing Countries (NIC), 4, 7, 14, 16–19, 23 n.3, 94
Nixson, F., 2, 13, 22, 23 n.1

Odekon, M., 6, 96
Organization for Economic Co-operation and Development (OECD), 58, 61-62, 83, 107
outward orientation, 2, 75, 82
Ozawa, T., 189
Öniş, Z., 4, 89 n.5, 194
Özmucur, S., 4, 5, 112, 121, 123

Peet, R., 22
Persaud, B., 92, 93
Piore, M., 31
planning, 3, 37, 47
post-Fordist production system, 5, 155, 158
price support policy, 81
privatization, 36, 38, 43, 112; Turkey, 1, 3, 59, 61–62
product quality, 6
productivity, in public sector, 43, 112; in manufacturing, 4, 6, 25, 66, 78
profits, real, 76, 78
public sector borrowing requirement (PSBR), 60
public enterprises, 3, 4; Brazil, 44
public investment, 59, 116; Brazil, 44; Taiwan, 44

R&D, 26, 28, 35, 36, 156; Japan, 37; Korea, 35; Taiwan, 35
restructuring, 36, 37
Reynolds, L.G., 23 n.2
Riedel, J., 194

Sabel, C., 31
Sachs, I., 39, 40, 49
Sadoulet, E., 79
Schmitz, H., 93, 154 n.6, 158
Short, R. P., 41, 42
Silin, R.H., 29
Singer, H.W., 19, 20, 24 n.4
Singh, A., 11

Small and Medium Industry Development Organization (SMIDO), 152–53
South Korea, 12, 17, 19–20, 23–24, 27–28, 30–31, 33, 35, 37, 47, 49, 53, 100, 102, 188–89
Stabilization and Structural Adjustment Program (SSAP), 1, 3, 4, 51, 191, 192, 193; policy environment for industrialization, 54–56, 191, 193–94; neglect of industrialization, 59–62, 194; impact on the manufacturing sector, 62–70, 191
state economic enterprises, 52, 59, 64, 113–14, 116, 191; deficits, 60; employment, 60–61, 117; productivity and efficiency, 61
State Institute of Statistics (SIS), 123, 154 n.3
state intervention, 3, 24
State Planning Organization (SPO), 52, 62, 95, 96, 141, 154 n.3
State-owned enterprises, 40 (see also state economic enterprises)
structural adjustment loans, 82
structure of production, 67–70
subcontracting, 5, 142; Taiwan, 31
surplus transfer, 4
Şenses, F., 3, 4

Taiwan, 2, 12, 23, 27, 28, 29, 31, 33, 37, 47, 49; direct foreign investment, 35; interest rates in, 29, 30; public enterprises, 44; small-scale firms, 26–28, 34–35, 37
Takao, T., 32
Teitel, S., 19
Tekeli, İ., 96, 131
terms of trade, agriculture, 81
Third World Industrialization, statistical overview, 9–16

Thoumi, F.E., 19
Total Factor Productivity (TFP), 5,
    112, 123
Total Factor Productivity Growth
    (TFPG), 66, 112–13, 125, 129,
    132, 137–38, 162–68
Trans National Corporations (TNC),
    21, 92, 109
Trebat, T., 44
Tuncer, B., 112
Türel, O., 25, 87

United Nations (UN), 9, 14
United Nations Center on
    Transnational Corporations
    (UNCTC), 21, 92
United Nations Conference on Trade
    and Development (UNCTAD), 24
    n.6
United Nations Industrial
    Development Organisation
    (UNIDO), 7, 9, 13, 16, 42

Vaiou, D., 171, 174 n.7

wages, real, 3, 57, 76, 78, 81
Watanabe, S., 141, 142, 147
Weiss, J., 3, 8, 18, 39, 47
World Bank, 1, 18, 27, 36, 41, 51,
    54, 55, 59, 191

Yabancı Sermaye Dernegi (YASED),
    96
Yasuoka, S., 27
Yeldan, A. E., 4, 84, 88 nn.1, 2, 3, 5

About the Contributors

ALICE H. AMSDEN is Professor in the Department of Economics at the New School for Social Research, New York, U.S.A.

HACER K. ANSAL is Associate Professor of Economics in the Economics Department at Istanbul Technical University, Istanbul, Turkey.

AYDA ERAYDIN is Associate Professor in the Department of City and Regional Planning at the Middle East Technical University, Ankara, Turkey.

CEVAT KARATAŞ is Associate Professor of Economics at Boğaziçi University, Istanbul, Turkey.

MEHMET KAYTAZ is Professor of Economics in the Department of Economics at Boğaziçi University, Istanbul, Turkey.

FREDERICK I. NIXSON is Reader in Economics in the Department of Economics at the University of Manchester, England.

ZIYA ÖNIŞ is Associate Professor of Economics in the Department of Economics at Boğaziçi University, Istanbul, Turkey.

SÜLEYMAN ÖZMUCUR is Professor of Economics in the Department of Economics at Boğaziçi University, Istanbul, Turkey.

FIKRET ŞENSES is Professor of Economics in the Department of Economics at the Middle East Technical University, Ankara, Turkey.

JOHN WEISS is Professor of Economics in the Department of Economics at the University of Bradford, Bradford, England.

A. ERINÇ YELDAN is Associate Professor of Economics in the Department of Economics at Bilkent University, Ankara, Turkey.